# *Brisbane: Moreton Bay Matters*

*Edited by Murray Johnson*

*Brisbane History Group*
*Papers No.19*
*2002*

First published by Brisbane History Group (Incorporated)



National Library of Australia
Cataloguing-in-Publication data:

Moreton Bay Matters

Bibliography
Includes index

ISBN 0 9586255 6 5 ISSN 1035-4050

1.Moreton Bay (Qld.) - History – 19th century. 2.Moreton Bay – History – 20th century. 1. Johnson,
Murray (Murray David), 1956- (Series: Papers (Brisbane History Group); no.19).

994.31

Edited by Murray Johnson

Designed & produced by Church Archivists Press, Brisbane

Printed by Toowoomba Education Centre

Published by Brisbane History Group (Incorporated)
PO Box 12, Kelvin Grove DC
Qld 4059 Australia

# *Contents*

# *Contributors*

**Rosemary Ahearn** researched the history of Moreton Island for her Postgraduate Diploma in Arts at UQ, and is currently a property consultant in Brisbane.

**Thom Blake**, a doctoral graduate in history at UQ and professional historian, researched Peel Island history for a conservation report by Robert Riddel Architect.

**Rod Fisher**, honorary research consultant of UQ Applied History Centre and editorial adviser for BHG, promotes Brisbane's past in particular and history for the community generally.

**Joe Goodall** researched the history of Dunwich Benevolent Asylum for his PhD at UQ, while furthering his teaching career.

**Murray Johnson** is currently completing his PhD in History at UQ on soldier settlement in Queensland following the First World War.

**David Jones** completed a short history of the Tangalooma whaling station for the Nautical Association of Australia in 1980.

**John Mackenzie-Smith,** a doctoral graduate in history at UQ and former guidance officer, has published extensively on early settlement at Moreton Bay.

**Nonie Malone** graduated from UQ in politics and history, and is currently a policy officer with Education Queensland

**Yvonne Reynolds** was a field archaeologist on St Helena Island, before migrating to South Australia and completing her PhD.

**Shirleene Robinson** is currently completing her PhD at UQ on Aboriginal child labour in the nineteenth and twentieth centuries until 1945.

# *Illustrations*

# *Preface*

This volume of Brisbane History Group papers is an amalgam of subjects on Moreton Bay. While several papers were written some years ago, the earliest being 1980, others date from 2001. Those by John Mackenzie-Smith, Joe Goodall and Nonie Malone derive from Straddie Day in 1996, one of several Bay events organised by the BHG since 1989. The papers by Yvonne Reynolds and Thom Blake are based on archaeological and heritage studies. Most contributors are past and present postgraduate students of the University of Queensland.

With the exception of David Jones' discussion on the Tangalooma whalers, none of this material has previously been published. In view of the recent publications on Moreton Bay's fascinating past, the present compilation can also be seen as an 'infill' volume, plugging some of the gaps which remain in our understanding of the region's history. As such, the articles canvas a range of topics including Aboriginal, maritime, social, medical and environmental issues.

As a former professional fisherman pursuing crustaceans in Moreton Bay waters, I was privileged to experience the fluctuating moods of Moreton Bay. There were times when placid turquoise waters led to an almost overwhelming feeling of peace and tranquility. Occasionally, they gave way to violent storms when lives can be, and at times are lost. They continue still. Nature's unpredictable patterns are therefore reflected in the history of Moreton Bay, particularly as it relates to the original inhabitants. As a number of these studies show, they were alternately subjected to benevolence and violence. The clash of two cultures resulted in profound loss for the indigenous people.

This volume was dependent on many people, not the least of whom were the actual contributors, who have shared their intellectual acumen for the benefit of many. A special debt of gratitude is also due to Owen Johnson, without whose computer skills this compilation would probably not have reached completion. The guiding hands of Rod Fisher, Barry Shaw and Bill Oliver may also be recognised by many Brisbane History Group readers; their continuing expertise has ensured that publications remain of a very high quality. Finally, a word must be said for the staff of John Oxley Library, who have made available a number of important images to complement the written text in this volume. Many thanks to all.

Perhaps more than anything else, the contributions in this volume show that Moreton Bay really does matter. Let the story unfold.

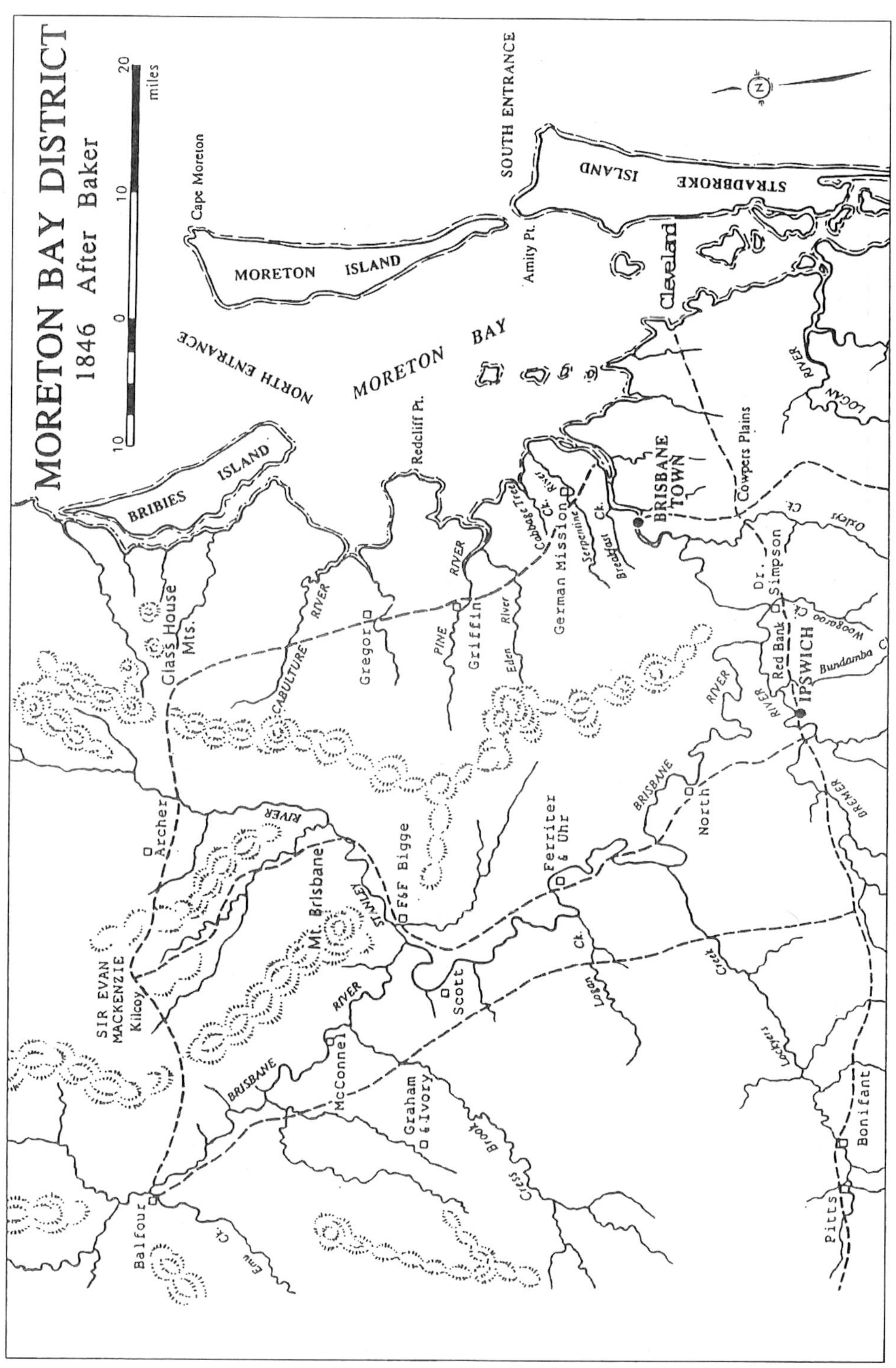


*0.2 Moreton Bay District 1846*

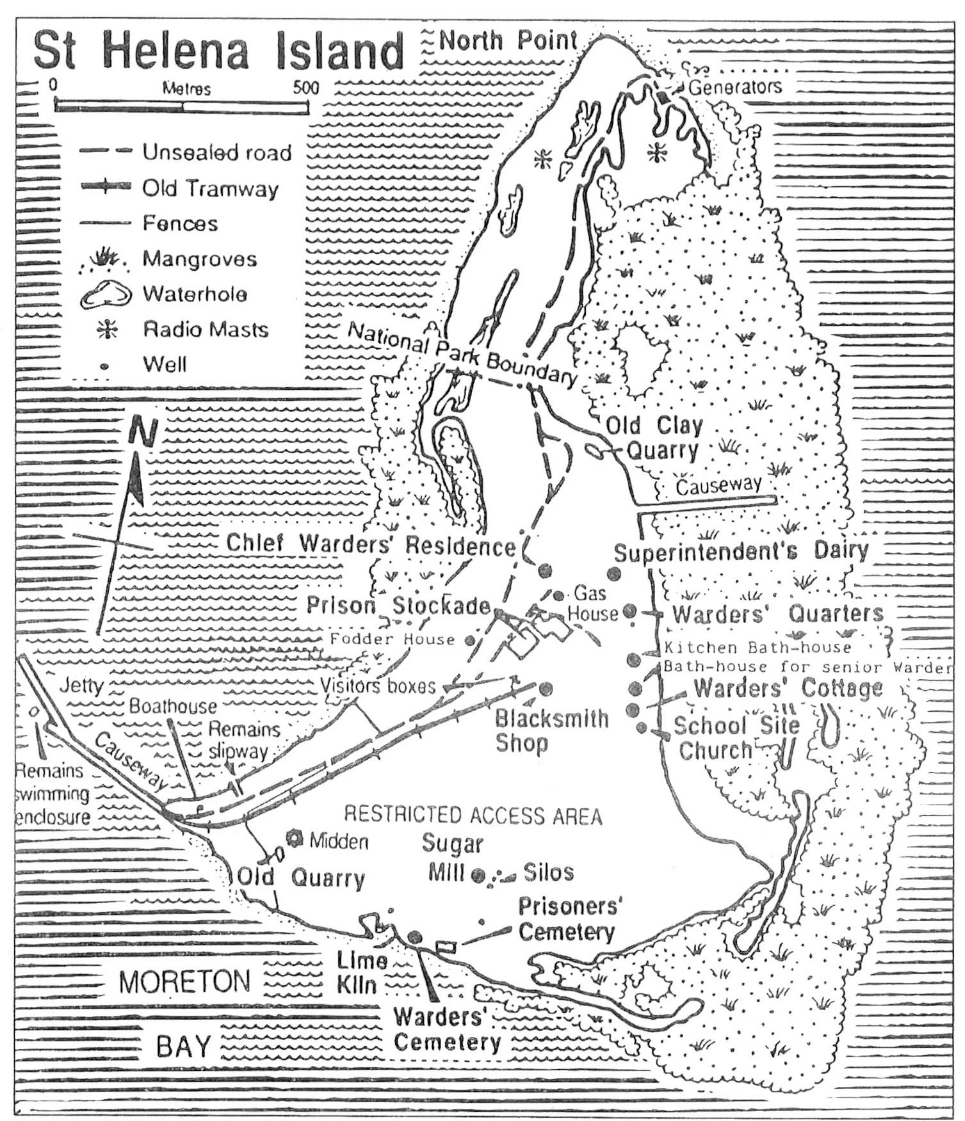


*0.3 St. Helena Island (AHC).*

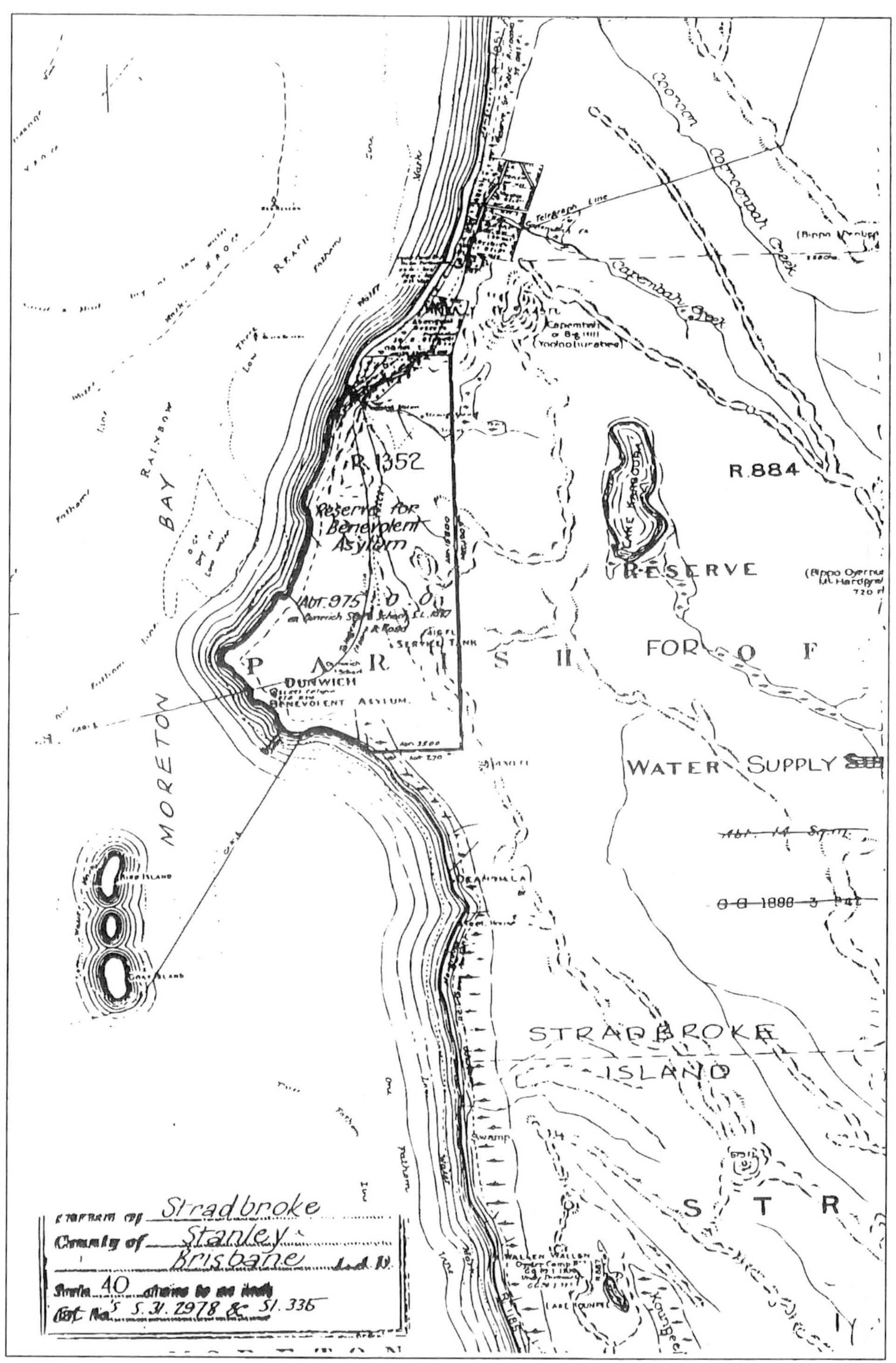


0.4 Dunwich Benevolent Asylum reserve 1913 (QSA).

## *Chapter 1*

# Dunwich: Convicts, Passionists and shattered hopes

## *John Mackenzie-Smith*

In September 1824 when John Oxley was engaged in the task of determining the location of the principal settlement upstream of the Brisbane River, the days of the military post and stores depot at Red Cliff Point were numbered. The buffeting and near loss of Oxley's survey vessel, 'Amity', during a heavy squall in the midst of the unloading process caused fellow traveller, Allan Cunningham, to conclude that the Redcliffe roadstead was virtually unsafe, providing poorly sheltered anchorage. Bitter experience revealed that Moreton Island did not offer the presumed buffer against Pacific Ocean turbulence after all.[1]

Concurrently, Oxley and Cunningham discovered the southern entrance to that large land-locked bay between Moreton and Stradbroke Islands, declaring the proposed southern route better than the current time-consuming practice of skirting the northern tip of Moreton Island. After interviewing Oxley, the *Sydney gazette* reported that the southern entrance 'will doubtless be productive of many advantages to the New Settlement and facilitate the loading of timber that may be procured on the Brisbane River ... and vessels can now proceed with a Northerly wind to sea, which was not the case until this passage was explored; it cuts off, in consequence between 50 and 60 miles'.[2]

The following November, Surveyor-General Oxley in the distinguished company of Sir Thomas Brisbane, governor of New South Wales, and Chief Justice Sir Francis Forbes, sailed north on the 'Amity' to decide upon the site for the principal settlement on the river which was to bear the governor's name. Having entered Moreton Bay by the northern channel, the party departed via the south head extremity which was named Point Amity because of the cordial relations this official group enjoyed with the local Aborigines when they landed at Minjerriba. This unexpected, friendly occasion was probably facilitated by the welcome presence of John Finnegan, a former shipwrecked timber-getter who had been befriended by the Nunukul Aborigines of Stradbroke Island and other bayside clans.[3]

Historian Raymond Evans has reconstructed the adaptive and stable nature of Aboriginal life of the Nunukuls before European encroachment on Minjerriba. Substantial dome-shaped huts built from Melaleuca or ti-tree materials, one of which was fifteen metres across, were grouped together as small villages above the tide line. Clan members reaped the rich sea harvest of mullet, dugong and turtle along the coastlines of the nearby bay islands.[4]

It is estimated that the Redcliffe settlement was relocated on the banks of the Brisbane River in May 1825. As this was further upstream than the vice-regal choice of Breakfast Creek, official displeasure was possibly behind the prompt dismissal of commandant Henry Miller. At the same time, the pilot of Port Jackson was involved in surveying and buoying the bay and southern channel. Thereafter, vessels followed the route which took them up the Brisbane River via Amity Point, the southern side of Peel Island and after beating up St Helena, Mud and Green islands.[5]

*1.1 North Entrance, Moreton Bay (ML Richard Watt collection)*

Evans has estimated that European occupation of Stradbroke Island commenced in September 1824. At that time it was the base for a party of convicts from the Redcliffe penal establishment while Robert Hoddle and Charles Penson sounded the South Passage. John Tosh, living in a large bark hut at Amity Point with a few soldiers from 1825, occupied the position of superintendent and pilot between 1827 and 1830. When the permanent pilot station was established at Amity Point in 1827, the settlement consisted of two soldiers, a crew of five oarsmen, three guards and seven convicts occupying four buildings.[6]

Between 1827 and 1828 Amity Point succeeded Redcliffe as the storage base for those ships whose draughts were too large to negotiate the treacherous bar at the mouth of the Brisbane River. Thus, cargoes were discharged at Amity and transported over a tedious sixty kilometre trip by a leaky boat with a capacity to take two tonnes of cargo to the new settlement. It is surmised that in July 1825 the 'Lalla Rookh' which bore Miller's replacement, Captain Peter Bishop, and the new superintendent of convicts, L.V. Dulhunty, was probably the first ship to unload at Amity Point. Also discharged from its hold were convicts and soldiers from the 40th Regiment.[7]

In June 1827 HMS 'Rainbow', under the command of Captain Henry John Rous RN, earned the singular honour of being the first warship to enter Moreton Bay. Aboard was the governor of NSW, Sir Ralph Darling, who was undertaking an inspection tour of his most northerly outpost. On this voyage, vice-regal approval was apparently granted to Europeanise the Aboriginal place-names. Minjerriba was henceforth known as Stadbroke Island in honour of Rous's father – the first Earl of Stradbroke. The passage between Stradbroke and Moreton islands was named Rous's Channel. However, among Darling's decisions resulting from this excursion was his dissatisfaction with the location of the Brisbane settlement and his positive reaction to a suggestion made by commandant Patrick Logan in a despatch dated 29 July 1827. Logan recommended that the settlement be moved to a place more accessible to shipping, such as Dunwich on Stradbroke Island, which was known to the Aborigines as Goompi.[8]

In relation to the river settlement, Darling noted that 'the tediousness and difficulty of access render it extremely inconvenient'. So convinced was Logan that Dunwich would become the principal settlement that he requested that the treadmill already ordered from Sydney should be delivered there instead of Brisbane. While Darling initially agreed to this suggestion, he quickly had a change of heart. The prospect of Dunwich as a major penal settlement that would also receive supplies and export timber proved illusory. Accordingly the 'steel mill' was re-directed to Brisbane, the future of which seemed momentarily secure.

In a despatch to Viscount Goderich dated 26 September 1827, Darling nevertheless explained his intentions to erect a warehouse to receive stores at either Dunwich or Green Point, to be operated by a few convict labourers under the surveillance of a small military guard. Under this scheme, quick deposits of cargoes at a centre eight sailing hours from Brisbane would discourage the smuggling propensities of ships' crews. Darling outlined his plans:

> I propose, as a means of remedying in some degree this inconvenience, to form a small Settlement at "Dunwich" on the Isle of Stradbroke, being the southern boundary of the Bay, for the purpose of receiving in the first instance the supplies sent from this to the Settlement, and the Timber etc to be forwarded thence to Sydney. According to this arrangement, the Vessels employed in communicating with Moreton Bay will not be detained any longer than necessary to discharge and take in their cargoes at Dunwich, it being intended to station a small Vessel at that place for the purpose of conveying the supplies to the Settlement and bringing down the timber, etc.[9]

Rafts of pine for transportation to Sydney were moored off Green Point as early as July 1827. Intentions for the military outpost, penal establishment and warehouse were realised in September, when Logan received the relevant plans prepared by the civil engineer along with building materials from Sydney. In May 1828 Logan reported to Governor Darling that the military and penal barracks had been occupied and the magazine was nearly completed – well ahead of the erection of the prisoners' barracks at the Brisbane settlement. To the left of the barracks and store the convicts built a rough stone jetty twenty-seven metres long and six metres wide to effect the loading and unloading of stores which had been discharged from anchored craft via smaller vessels. More rapid communication between Dunwich and Brisbane was conducted by a primitive telegraphic device, with a signal station on Campbell's Range (Mount Petrie), or by boat to Emu Point (Cleveland) and thence by road to Brisbane. Exports, in addition to pine, included lime and coal which was shipped downstream from Bremer's Creek.[10]

Presaging the limited life of this island settlement, the ill-fated Moongalba cotton plantation, which had been established early in 1827 and occupied the labours of thirty prisoners, had already fallen into an advanced state of neglect. As the cultivated land at Moongalba encroached upon an Aboriginal camping ground and the area between Amity Point and Dunwich held ritual significance, European occupation made considerable psychological, social and economic incursions into local Aboriginal life. As Evans commented, 'To have the Moongalba area stripped and cleared, and alien flora planted there, must have been a serious affront'.[11]

Logan spent as much time as possible at Dunwich. He often covertly sojourned there for up to five days of rest and recreation when he could be spared from his demanding commitments to Brisbane and Limestone Hills (later Ipswich). Charles Bateson noted that Logan accompanied his despatches to Dunwich on either of the two cutters ('Regent Bird' and 'Glory') to ensure that the official documents were safely deposited on the out bound vessel. On the pretext of interviewing the supervisor, monitoring building progress and checking the state of the cotton plantation, the commandant managed to snatch 'some pleasant relaxation in attractive and refreshing surroundings'.[12]

Logan's first-hand knowledge of transport problems to and from the bay was turned to good effect in the form of an off-shoot industry. Arising from the necessity to provide shallow draught vessels with a reasonable loading capacity and the capability of crossing the treacherous Brisbane River bar, a boat-building enterprise materialised under the surveillance of the enthusiastic commandant. Local dissatisfaction with the two small open boats and the use of the pilot's whaleboat, when not otherwise engaged, provided the stimulus for the embryonic boat-building industry. In the style which typified Logan, he took matters into his own hands to provide the settlement with suitable craft, being heartily tired of Sydney-based indecision and tardiness. As Bateson pointed out, 'knowing that the settlement had need of a vessel to ferry passengers and goods from vessels anchored in the bay, he ignored the regulations and the admonitions of the Sydney officials and went ahead and built one of considerable size'. The newly-launched cutter 'Regent Bird', was captained by John Martin and manned by four free men.[13]

The unstated reasoning in this northern outpost, particularly under Logan, was that Sydney would be unconcerned about matters when it received little or no information. Thus, it is not surprising that little intelligence was received in the well-removed Colonial Secretary's Office concerning inter-racial antagonism. Right from the foundation of Redcliffe, the commandant was required to maintain friendly relations with the Aborigines while making contingency plans for protection from them. Past experience had already shown that European encroachment on traditional land, unwelcome sexual encounters with female indigenes and Aboriginal propensities for pilfering made some form of conflict almost inevitable.

The extent of defence precautions at Dunwich can be ascertained by reference to plans showing a three metre-thick brick wall erected around three sides of the warehouse and barracks complex. The front, a sentry-guarded brick and iron barrier, was built as close as possible to the sea. In the remote possibility that a frontal attack by water was successful, a last-ditch stand could be mounted in either of the main buildings, which were connected by an underground tunnel.[14]

It appears that Aboriginal-European relations did indeed follow the predictable pattern experienced in the south, with deterioration following an initial period of peaceful co-existence. The joy of the Aborigine who spontaneously rolled himself in the sand when re-united with the castaway timber-getter Finnegan, and the daily offering of fish to the guards at Amity Point, gave way to open hostility at Dunwich with the spearing of a soldier in mid-1828. This was around the time when it was decided to abandon the idea of removing the major penal settlement to Stradbroke Island. Sexual affront to Nunukul women and territorial encroachment were reportedly related to the death of a convict, James Wood, who was working in the garden at Dunwich three years later – shortly before the decision was taken in October 1831 to disband this settlement.[15]

Apparently the final show-down in the penal era at Stradbroke occurred at Amity Point in January 1832, following the murder and decapitation of a Nunukul elder who had brandished a spear at a soldier. After the retaliatory death of the alleged murderer, dubbed 'Chooroong' by the Aborigines, the pilot station was attacked on two separate occasions. European casualties amounted to the severe wounding of two soldiers and a convict. According to Commandant Clunie, the second assault resulted in the death of one Aborigine. Ominously, the Europeans had issued warnings that dire consequences would follow any indigenous aggression.

The cycle of revenge and retaliation began in earnest. On the basis of Aboriginal evidence, the later Moreton Bay authority, Thomas Welsby, stated that the military attacked the Nunukul camp at Moonguloa, about five kilometres north of Dunwich. According to Welsby's informant, a pitched battle was fought on the flat ground at the mouth of Cooran-Cooran-Pah Creek, where the boggy terrain gave the Aborigines an advantage. Wounds were suffered on both sides during the encounter that raged throughout the day, but no fatalities occurred. With both sides fatigued and the result inconclusive, Welsby's informant stated that a truce was reached and no further hostility took place on Stradbroke Island.[16]

However, a less romantic version of this conflict was recorded, and dismissed, due to the informant's criminal standing. Despite official omission in the commandant's report to Colonial Secretary Macleay, a former convict later told J.J. Knight that European retaliation was in fact severe. Following the spearing of two men under the command of chief constable McIntosh, 'a detachment of military was sent out to Point Lookout ... with instructions to shoot every black that was met with'.[17] How extensive this reprisal was is not known with any certainty, though the Nunukul people fortuitously escaped the fate meted out to their neighbours on Moreton Island a year after Dunwich was abandoned. Although his account should be tempered with caution due to possible exaggeration, the child immigrant of 1849, James Porter, reported interaction with an Aborigine who claimed to be the sole male survivor of military reprisals on Moreton.[18]

Yet, it must also be noted that it was only after the military expedition to Point Lookout that Stradbroke Island was regarded thereafter as a safe haven for Europeans. It was probably on the basis of the ensuing pacific reputation of Stradbroke's Nunukul Aborigines that the Dunwich penal complex was revitalised some twelve years later as a centre of Roman Catholic evangelism.

Archbishop John Bede Polding, who has been assessed as being a century ahead of his time in understanding the Aborigines, was at the forefront of opposition to European actions accompanying dispossession and settlement which resulted in the corruption, degredation and genocide of the original inhabitants. Accordingly, Polding welcomed Governor Sir George Gipps' decision to permit the temporary establishment of a Catholic mission in and around the abandoned and decaying Dunwich buildings. Flying in the face of failure incurred by the German Mission near Brisbane, and against the advice of Episcopal layman Thomas Mort (supervisor of Cressbrook), to eschew fruitless missionary efforts to Aborigines, Polding was convinced that the conditions for conversion of the indigenes were virtually ideal on Stradbroke.[19]

Commencing with the forty people who comprised the Dunwich clan, the missionaries would be directed to live among the inhabitants, learn their language, manners and customs, gain their confidence and thereafter exploit their supposed facility to 'comprehend the principal truths of the Catholic faith'. Over time these converts would create a radiating, ripple effect to save the souls of the remaining 100 indigenes. Dismissing the opportunity to evangelise the belligerent Wide Bay clans in the vicinity of the remote Bunya Bunya country, and the dangerous Ninghi Ninghi of Bribie Island, Polding estimated that the optimum conditions existed to demonstrate successful missionary endeavour on Stradbroke Island, which then supported a mere seven Europeans operating the pilot station.[20]

Isolation from European settlement, evangelising on Aboriginal home territory and protection for the missionaries were considered to be prerequisites for the success of Aboriginal outreach. On barren, sandy Stradbroke Island, which held little economic attraction for Europeans, the three friendly clans comprising some 140 members were indeed isolated from settler society; but protection for the missionaries was readily available eleven kilometres away at Amity Point and in Brisbane via Cleveland Point or the river.

Having unsuccessfully sought missionaries from the ranks of British Benedictines and the French clergy on his way to Rome to be commissioned as Archbishop of Sydney in 1842, Polding ultimately obtained the services of four enthusiastic, unrealistic and poorly-briefed Italian-based priests belonging to the Passionist order. Father Joseph Snell, an experienced missionary of Swiss birth, was the only linguist. With proficiency in four European languages, he was nevertheless expected to master English with ease and make a good fist of Stradbroke's Aboriginal dialects. Fathers Luigi Pescialori and Maurice Lenconi, both ready volunteers to convert the heathen and speaking only their native Italian, were distinguished by their spirit of piety, cheerfulness and self-sacrifice.[21]

However, the Father General of the Congregation of the Passion, Reverend Anthony Testa, certainly entertained grave doubts about the leadership qualities of the volatile priest who was appointed Superior of the mission and outside the jurisdiction of a surprised, frustrated and eventually thwarted Archbishop Polding. Against his better judgement and in deference to the wishes of an unsuspecting Polding, the Father General approved the appointment of the divisive, over-confident and uncompromising Father Raymond Vaccari as missionary leader. Osmund Thorpe, writing of the Dunwich mission nearly a century after its closure, unearthed correspondence in the Vatican archives in which Vaccari was described variously as 'having an interfering disposition', being 'unsuitable to hold a position of authority over others', and 'a man no one could get on with or ever would'.[22] With the prospects of personality clashes, generally poor linguistic interaction with the target group and the colonists, naive expectations and lack of accountability to Australian religious authorities, the ingredients for an unsuccessful missionary endeavour were certainly sown even before departure from Rome.

Engaged as he was on a desperate search and recruit quest, Polding was nonetheless convinced that he possessed the formula to make the Aborigines 'comprehend the principal truths of the Catholic faith'. He would not be easily obstructed by the predicted temperamental, organisational, fiscal and language barriers. In addition, Thorpe suggested that 'it was very unlikely that Bishop Polding revealed the other side of the picture' to the Passionist priests who, for a start, arrived in a ruthless and conniving society wallowing in the depths of economic depression.[23] Although Governor Gipps granted the buildings and ground for two years from May 1843, he could not, and would not, contribute any funding towards the endeavours of these dedicated priests. For some time Archbishop Polding met the mission's major expenses from his own pocket, to the disadvantage of other bodies such as the Marist Brothers, who received merely a fraction of the initial grant of £300 per annum allocated to Stradbroke Island.

Thorpe has further disclosed that friction probably existed between Polding and Vaccari before the mission 'even got off the ground'. Observing that the archbishop was accompanied only by Father Joseph during the mission's foundation work, Thorpe interpreted this as either a decision to leave the over-bearing Father Raymond in Sydney or an indication of the head missionary's refusal to accompany the party to Goompi. As Snell was rapidly gaining proficiency in the English language, Polding alternatively may have left the Italian priests in Sydney until diplomatic relations with the local Aborigines could be established through the latter's own variety of English.

In addition to providing basic instruction in net fishing, setting down rules relating to the distribution of food and assessing the state and use of the buildings, Polding also required Snell to compile a vocabulary of the Nunukul dialect and thus create a positive impression, while facilitating minimal interaction in everyday affairs. Commencing with communication, the distribution of government issue blankets and the popular colourful Sydney-made calico dresses and coats, the missionaries would demonstrate to the Nunukuls that they came as friends. The archbishop intimated that the desired effect was indeed made upon the 'quiet, inoffensive' Aborigines when he described how they skipped and jumped with joy 'when one got his blue coat, another his red coat and another his black coat'. Those who were non-compliant were denied these coveted symbols of civilisation until they showed sufficient repentance, which included making the sign of the cross.[24]

The missionaries attempted to establish the principle that the distribution of food was contingent upon labour in the garden and fishing with the nets and boat which Polding provided for the settlement. Offended by nakedness, the Passionists also decreed that clothes were to be worn (at least in their presence) by the forty or so Aborigines who formed the nucleus for their conversion of all Stadbroke's indigenous people. Thorpe concluded that the Aborigines believed they were being looked after and became dependent on the European provisions. When the blankets, invariably used for barter, ceased to be distributed, Brisbane supplies of alcohol, tobacco and food also dried up. Perhaps not surprisingly, the Aborigines could not grasp that the scarcity of food and clothing was related to the lack of funds available to Polding, or even from occasional delays of vessels arriving from the south. Inability to assist was therefore interpreted as unwillingness, and it is recorded that failure to provide brought out the fickleness and hostility of an otherwise gentle and accepting people.[25]

Lack of funds for maintenance and sustenance, internal priestly antagonism, mutual dissatisfaction between the missionaries and Polding, and the unstable nomadic life of the Aborigines were to be the major factors causing the demise of the short-lived mission. There were, however, problems from the very beginning. The Aborigines, for example, were not free from the corrupting influences of Europeans. Amity Point was the site of the pilot station where the staff of seven cohabited with Aboriginal women. Sexual contact, willing and unwilling, between Aboriginal women and the lusting crews of ships anchored off Dunwich were regular occurrences. Indeed, in the presence of Archbishop Polding, three teenage girls were abducted for sexual exploitation aboard one of those vessels. Furthermore, Polding's temporary success in removing some of the offspring from mixed-race liaisons to his personal care in Sydney caused considerable animosity among the Nunukul people. After threatening the lives of the priests, the affronted indigenes demanded the return of their children.[26]

John Harris, who examined the Aboriginal encounter with christianity over a period of 200 years, noted that 'the reality of the mission was nothing like the mission of their imagination before leaving Europe'. Some forty years earlier, Thorpe had expressed the sudden sense of reality which confronted the Passionists on seeing their island home: 'The romance associated with an enterprise at the other end of the world evaporated, leaving an uneasy realisation of the magnitude of their task'.[27] The buildings, the material core of their enterprise, were virtually derelict as they could not be maintained during the prolonged seven months of rain during 1843. The bark slabs used to replace the shingles were completely ineffective, often leaving the priests soaked to the skin. A forlorn Vaccari commented that 'though we have mended the roofs as many as seven times we are always in water'.[28] Polding described the ruinous former penal buildings which he hoped would be transformed into a monastery:

> There is a detached building which the blacks call their own; in this they sleep: this I intend for their school and dwelling when they choose. Then there are four rooms consecutive, in another building, enclosed and adjoining a large store, 56 feet by 30 feet; this I propose to be their church.[29]

Evidently the church, 'beautifully ornamented with shells', became a reality with the help of the Aborigines, although it was apparently a wooden structure rather than the brick edifice envisaged by the archbishop. Vaccari supplied the reason for construction of a new chapel: 'In this locality there are six or seven rooms, all one story high, with an underground passage and a place large enough to serve as a church. However, the latter and all the other rooms are in a state of ruin through the weather'.[30]

After a lengthy sea voyage aboard the 'Templar', and sharing residence for three months in Sydney, Polding was not sanguine about the Passionists' prospects for success as missionaries among Stradbroke Island's Aborigines. In his correspondence the archbishop criticised their dedicated but fruitless efforts. The priests may well have been 'models of virtue and of the religious life', but they were too ill-prepared for the difficulties of establishing a mission and its concomitant temporal affairs, such as finance and economy. Having incurred a debt of £500 to meet the needs of the mission in 1844, Polding drew the line at the expectation of his providing food and clothing for all the 'native children'.[31]

Just before leaving Brisbane in June 1843, Polding wrote to his English Benedictine cousin, Father Heptonstall, expressing his pessimism and suspicion that Passionist contact with Rome would be established to deliberately by-pass him. As Denis Martin noted, Polding deeply resented the Passionists' 'claim to an independent jurisdiction'. Anticipating future needs, Polding intimated that he was not above subterfuge himself, for he stated that he would actively seek English Benedictine priests as replacements for the Passionists:

> I fear our Italian friends will be but bunglers. Except Snell none seem to have an aptitude for languages. They cannot express themselves in English even now, for the commonest purpose. However we shall see ... I suspect the Passionists after a time will endeavour to open a communication with the Prop. De la Foi. This I will not permit. They are really more ignorant of the world and more contracted in their notions than I could have supposed possible.[32]

It did not take the Passionists long to re-direct their energies from the adults to the children, which was effected in 1844 with the opening of a school. Although the priests toiled valiantly to learn customs, manners and language by enduring extreme privation – even attempting to accompany the clan on frequent inland treks – it was made very clear by gestures and looks that they were not always welcome. Moreover, the priests found it extremely frustrating that the Aborigines were nearly always on the move, 'never [encamping] for more than eight or ten days in the one valley'. Seven months after arriving, Vaccari informed Polding that 'the natives have not been with us for more than two months and a half'.[33] Thus it was not unexpected that the long-term plan to encourage the clan to live together in a sedentary community was doomed to failure.

As well, negative expectations of the adults arose from a naive assessment of Aboriginal attitudes, behaviour and culture in terms of the alien European work ethic. The head of the mission reported on the three Stradbroke Island clans, citing a number of 'ruthless' behavioural characteristics which, incidentally, they undoubtedly shared with some of the colonists on the mainland:

> These poor Aboriginals have naturally strong passions and depraved inclinations, which require time and patience and prayer to overcome them. Among these evil dispositions of the natives I may mention an extreme sloth and laziness in everything, a habit of fickleness and double-dealing, an uncontrollable vindictiveness, so much so that they will stop at nothing in pursuit of revenge; they are deceitful and cunning and prone to lying; they are insatiable in the extreme in gluttony and if possible will sleep both day and night.[34]

Despite taking every opportunity to acquire the Aboriginal language, the missionaries ultimately possessed only a rudimentary knowledge of the local dialect. The learning process was indeed difficult. The missionaries experienced extreme problems with the speech patterns and the nasal and guttural nature of articulation in the Dunwich dialect. Clearly conversion was impossible without the means of communicating the basic tenets of Roman Catholicism to the target group whom Polding finally assessed as having little notion of religious worship and lacking a stationary, captive audience. By 1845 it was admitted that the Passionists had been unable to do anything for the adults and were limited to baptising only the dying.[35]

Nonetheless the honest and earnest Passionist presence encouraged the Aborigines to regain their confidence in Europeans who had hitherto betrayed, deceived and maltreated them. On the other hand, the Passionists were wary of the Aborigines who, in 1844, were 'still very far from the holy ideas of faith'. Colonists had already warned the priests 'not to trust too much to these appearances, for they are of a treacherous nature even to those who do them good'.[36] It transpired that the peaceful co-existence did in fact turn into hostile animosity when supplies either arrived late – or ran out.

The mission appeared pre-doomed to failure when Vaccari wrote to the Cardinal Prefect of the Sacred Congregation of Propaganda, the font of catholic missionary enterprise in mid-1845. While citing Polding's annoyance at Vaccari's accountability to Rome, the mission superior nevertheless praised the economic and moral support for their endeavours. The single-minded evangelist stated, 'the poor archbishop looks after us as best he can, and wrote to me recently that he is disappointed he cannot do more'. However, the state of the missionaries' shelter and clothing was described in wretched terms; economic depression ensured that the cost of living was prohibitive, even for those living on the edge of society. At the beginning of his missive, a frustrated and angry Vaccari pondered 'it is impossible to know what are his [Polding's] intentions about us, for all that is an English mystery'. He finally concluded that 'we are terribly confused in mind about everything, not knowing how this whole affair is going to turn out'.[37]

A piqued Polding had obviously moved to the state of indifference despite the fact that Vaccari reported continuing good relations between the Aborigines and his missionary group. By the end of 1845, Vaccari was able to convey to the Cardinal Prefect that Polding had belatedly acknowledged the former's position as Prefect Apostolic with an annual accountable grant of £200 for the mission. For all that, relations with the Australian prelate who had 'other ideas about the welfare of our Mission' had slipped to an ominous 'satisfactory' level.[38] The final straw was possibly the result of machinations between Cardinal Franzoni and Vaccari, involving Bishop John Brady of Western Australia, recommending the transfer of the Passionists to Perth – outside Polding's influence and potentially destroying his Stradbroke Island project.

In those last days the government refused to grant a permanent reserve for the mission and Polding once more journeyed to Europe. The personal attention and moral support which he formerly provided to the missionaries and which had helped them to overcome their dire circumstances was thus no longer available. After all, if Vaccari wished to take his directions from distant Rome – so be it. This impaired relationship with the Passionists' Australian shepherd and mentor almost certainly depleted priestly morale. Increased settler contact with the Nunukul Aborigines also ensued, 'with disastrous results'. Finally, it appears that a split occurred between Vaccari and his colleagues, who departed for Western Australia but eventually settled in Adelaide in mid-1846.[39]

An isolated and deranged Vaccari, whose relations with the Aborigines deteriorated markedly, managed to hold out for another year. After enduring insults, taunts, threats and aggression, the helpless priest was finally driven from the island by an Aboriginal known as 'Canary'. This followed a fruitless last-ditch appeal to Brisbane's catholic establishment, Reverend James Hanly and William Duncan, sub-collector of customs. Despite the support of two eyewitnesses, one of whom actively defended Vaccari at Dunwich, the matter was treated as frivolous in Brisbane. It was suggested that Vaccari was exaggerating the situation, and accordingly a letter to the police magistrate begging for protection was suppressed. Denis Martin has indicated that Vaccari was well known to Hanly as they had both travelled to New South Wales aboard the 'Templar'.[40] On the other hand, the dismissive Duncan was a catholic intellectual, champion of Aboriginal rights and estranged confidant of Polding, having laid the groundwork for his accession to the Archbishopric of Sydney. In view of the Polding factor in the rejection of Vaccari's pleas, it is perhaps not too fanciful to suggest a possible conspiracy to terminate the Dunwich mission.

Disappointed, frightened, rejected and mentally disoriented, Vaccari finally abandoned the mission, heading as far away from Brisbane as possible. After travelling by open boat to the Tweed River, he was taken aboard the cedar schooner 'Elizabeth Jane' which berthed in Sydney on 20 July 1847. Surviving a shipwreck, Vaccari reached Lima in Peru where, for more than a decade, he worked as a gardener in a Franciscan friary under an assumed English name. He finally entered the order after being exposed by a former acquaintance.[41]

The ultimate failure of the Dunwich mission was laid squarely at the feet of Archbishop John Bede Polding by the influential *Freeman's journal*, to which the archbishop's former champion, William Augustine Duncan, was a major contributor. Cardinal Moran, citing this vehicle for catholic debate, argued that the Passionists had been driven out by the Benedictine prelate, who had turned upon his idealistic project.[42] Certainly, Polding's expectations for the conversion of the Aborigines, and the experience of the missionaries, were incongruent. Resentful of the Passionists' assertion of independent jurisdiction and their apparent subterfuge with Italian authorities, Polding did indeed withdraw his support. By so doing, he left the missionaries, of whom he had a low opinion, virtually isolated with meagre financial funding. The result was almost a foregone conclusion, particularly with the undiminishing and unrelenting demands made by the Aborigines throughout the life of the mission. After all, in Aboriginal eyes the missionaries' raison d'etre was related to the provision of food and clothing, rather than the saving message they hoped to spread.

In common with those sincere people who toiled at the German Mission at Zion's Hill, the Passionists' exertions over nearly five years of privation and frustration at Dunwich produced a negative result. Cardinal Moran, in his massive history of the Australian Catholic Church, emphasised this failure by recording the observations of Archdeacon Rigby who visited the ruined mission in 1858, accompanied by the Passionists' former servant, Peter Hartley. Eventually, Rigby found a pupil from the Passionist mission school who had also served at mass but, sadly, he noted that 'all traces of religious education had completely vanished from [the young man's] mind'.[43] The reality was thus a far cry from Polding's idealistic claim some fifteen years earlier that it would be easy 'to make them comprehend the principal truths of the Catholic faith'.[44] In the long run Polding, who was arguably the most outspoken church leader on the maltreatment of Aborigines, failed to achieve his dream because of the cumulative effects of those human frailties which he, and his innocent well-meaning recruits, eschewed – money, sins of the flesh, covetousness, jealousy, ambition and power.

*Chapter 2*

# Whose guilt? What reward?: The loss of the 'Sovereign' 1847

## *Murray Johnson*

Amidst the windswept dunes above the beach at Marramerang, near Ulladulla on the far south coast of NSW, children from the Collins family chanced upon some exposed skeletal remains in 1920. Believing the fragments to be Aboriginal, they reinterred them with unusual reverence, though they retained a crescent-shaped breastplate that bore the name 'Woondu of Amity Point'. The finer engraving revealed that Woondu had been instrumental in saving a number of lives after a shipwreck on Moreton Bay's South Passage bar in March 1847 – a disaster which ostensibly claimed forty-six victims.[1] The actual death toll was forty-four, and though much uncertainty surrounds the events which unfolded on that tragic day, it did accelerate safer navigation in Moreton Bay waters. While the sacrifice had therefore not been in vain, the Aboriginal rescuers, and their descendants, did not experience such a beneficial outcome in the greater span of time.

Built at Balmain, Sydney, in 1842, the 'Sovereign' was a timber paddle-steamer of 119 tons register owned by the Hunter River Steam Navigation Company.[2] Into her hull went two salvaged engines from a wrecked predecessor, 'King William IV'.[3] Initially placed on the run between Sydney and Newcastle, the vessel made her first voyage to Brisbane in February 1843 under the command of Captain Henry Cape, and thereafter remained on that northern service. Together with the 'Thistle', skippered by Captain Mulhall, the two steamers opened up a substantial trade,[4] particularly after James Pearce began conveying produce from the 'head of navigation', at Ipswich, to Brisbane aboard his pioneer river steamer 'Experiment' in 1846.[5]

*2.1 Steamer 'Experiment' (AHC)*

In turn, the 'Sovereign' and 'Thistle' were soon joined by competitors. It was perhaps not surprising, as the 'Sovereign' was totally ill-equipped to perform such a demanding service. Her two engines generated a mere thirty-five horsepower each: She was intended for river navigation only, not extended coastal voyages.[6] In August 1844 the explorer, Ludwig Leichhardt, had his party and equipment conveyed from Sydney to Brisbane aboard the

'Sovereign', to prepare for their overland crossing of northern Australia. The Hunter River Steam Navigation Company generously provided a free passage for the expedition, but Leichhardt lamented that the voyage lasted a week, instead of the scheduled three days. His horses, in particular, suffered greatly from lack of fodder and water.[7]

On another occasion the 'Sovereign' underwent an extensive overhaul in Sydney lasting four months, only to have her machinery break down off Newcastle on the first venture north. Repairs took five days to effect. It appears that Captain Cape was resigned to the fact that at least one of his engines could fail at any time. For increased speed or in the event of mechanical failure, the 'Sovereign' also carried an auxiliary sail;[8] but it was only after her founding that serious allegations were raised concerning the state of the vessel's hull:

> From the opinions which have been elicited from the most competent persons who have examined the wreck, and from those who were previously acquainted with her condition, it is apparent that the timbers of the vessel were originally very defective as regards the planking and the fastenings, and greatly weakened subsequently by the number of treenail and bolt holes from repeated repairs; while the inner planking was perfectly rotten.[9]

In view of what transpired, there seems to have been more than a little truth to this claim. Cape had previously been fortunate that only one of his engines had failed at any one time, and that the sail could be raised if necessary. On 11 March 1847, when the machinery connecting both engines collapsed, the wind was of insufficient strength to effect an escape.[10] Perhaps of even greater import to the eventual tragedy was the master's chosen route between Brisbane and Sydney.

All the early navigators in Moreton Bay waters – Flinders, Rous, Stirling, Oxley – had entered by the North Passage.[11] Flinders had actually attempted to enter through the South Passage, but shoal water forced him back. To reduce sailing time between the Moreton Bay penal settlement and Sydney, however, the South Passage was sounded by Robert Hoddle and Charles Penson in 1824, and the following year it was buoyed by the Port Jackson pilot, John

2.2 *Steamer 'Shamrock' (NLA)*

Gray.[12] The latter was sent north specifically for marking a line of navigation from the South Passage to the mouth of the Brisbane River.[13] A pilot station was accordingly established shortly afterwards at Amity Point on Stradbroke Island.[14]

It was a dangerous passage and so narrow that Moreton and Stradbroke Island Aborigines could reputedly converse with each other during periods of calm weather.[15] On his own admission, Cape had never used the northern entrance during his long term of service.[16] Although he was prepared to venture through the South Passage day or night, the last fateful voyage showed that he was clearly aware of the dangers that it presented. While the 'Sovereign' left her Brisbane berth on 3 March 1847, she was still riding at anchor off Amity Point eight days later due to the boisterous weather conditions.[17] In addition to the fifty-four passengers and crew,[18] the vessel also carried 139 bales of wool and a large quantity of timber and sundries.[19] What finally prompted Cape to attempt a passage in unfavourable circumstances is still shrouded in mystery.

Writing many years, later the well-known Moreton Bay fisherman Fred Campbell held that Cape was pressured into his fatal decision. With a number of passengers protesting that the captain was in collusion with the steward to prolong their stay on board, Cape reluctantly gave in – 'whatever be the consequences'.[20] Conversely, another later commentator, Archibald Meston, maintained that the decision rested entirely with the master. According to Meston, the wealthy and influential Darling Downs squatter Robert Gore implored Cape to remain at anchor until the weather improved. He certainly had reason to be concerned: his wife and two young children were among the passengers.[21] Yet this nevertheless conflicts with contemporary accounts, which credit Gore with a cavalier display of exuberance while the 'Sovereign' tackled the first of three large breakers as her bows headed towards the open sea.[22]

There is another possibility why Cape may have acted with undue haste. Steam was only raised on the 'Sovereign' when a rival vessel, the 'Tamar', was observed heading across the bay for the North Passage.[23] Rivalry, then, perhaps played its own part, but with the pilot absent on the 'Tamar', and his assistant aboard the 'William', which had entered from the south three days before,[24] Cape must certainly bear some responsibility for the tragedy which unfolded.

As Gore allegedly cheered on, the 'Sovereign' took the first of three large breakers with her beam ends shivering. Hit by the second, the engineer Sommerville raised the alarm that the machinery had broken and both engines were out of commission. Cape quickly confirmed the report, and let go the starboard anchor in a desperate attempt to keep his vessel's head towards the surging water. On his direction, the crew hoisted sail and the steam was shut down to prevent an explosion. Such was the force of the water, however, that the rudder chains parted and the starboard anchor, 'with about fifty fathoms of chain', disappeared into the swell. It was all to no avail, and the vessel steadily drifted towards the northern spit, approximately six kilometres from the safety of Moreton Island. Striking the shallows, the cargo hurtled across the deck, killing at least three people, and breaking the limbs of several others.[25] Lifeboats were apparently shattered at the same time.

The force of impact also threw a number of passengers and crew into the foaming sea. With water surging aboard, tarpaulins were hastily nailed over exposed hatchways 'but these proved as tissue paper', and failed to stem the flow.[26] Although the crew were later credited with emulating the example of their captain by leaving 'no means untried that could by any possibility have ensured the safety of the passengers and vessel',[27] it was actually three cabin passengers who laboured at the pumps until they became choked. The three men, Dennis, Berkeley and Elliott, then assisted in heaving overboard the remaining deck cargo;[28] none of them survived the ordeal. One survivor, Richard Stubbs, later described the rapid destruction of the 'Sovereign' and the chaos that followed:

> When the first breaker struck the vessel it swept a number of passengers off the deck, and amongst others myself. I saw men raising their arms wildly in the water round me, shrieking for help, and going down never to rise again, and I struggled hard to get up to the steamer; when near her another wave struck her, and she actually crumbled to pieces. I had dived down as the breaker came, but when I came up again there was no ship visible, but around me were scattered dead and drowning people who struggled with each other, and with anything they could get hold of, such as pieces of wreck, bales of wool and all sorts of things. I saw Mrs. Gore's maid floating near me still alive and I swam to her, and helped her on to a bale of wool, but when the wool became saturated it sank, and she was never seen alive again. The tide was coming in at the time, and had drifted me, and a few people who clung to a spar, clear of the breakers, and when on the crest of a wave we could see Moreton Island, but it looked a hopeless distance off. We were fearfully torn about by pieces of wreck, with nails in them, striking against us in the water, so much so that I have thirty-two nail holes in various parts of my body.[29]

Three separate groups of people witnessed the founding of the vessel. At Amity Point William Rollings, the convict servant of the pilot, quickly organised an Aboriginal boat crew who rowed across to the southern tip of Moreton Island. Two European fishermen on Moreton Island, William Clements and William Richards, also raced to assist;[30] so, too, did a number of Moreton Island Aborigines. The latter, led by a remarkable man named Toompani, swam through the surf to rescue four people, including Stubbs and Cape. Six other passengers and crew were saved from watery graves by Rollings' boat crew and the fishermen, bringing the total number of survivors to ten. Stubbs again recalled:

> We must all have perished had not assistance come to hand. A number of blacks had breasted the breakers, and when we were more than half-a-mile from shore they surrounded us, and taking hold of us, three or four to each white, they swam with us to land, took us up to their camp, tended our wounds, wrapped us up in their blankets while they dried our clothes, set food before us, and treated us with every mark of the most heartfelt pity and commiseration. I shall never forget the debt of gratitude we owe to those poor blacks, or the risks they ran in

*2.3 Harbour master's Aboriginal boat crew, Moreton Bay 1848 (ML Owen Stanley collection)*

saving us; for I have no doubt but what a large number of lives lost were owing to sharks, which were to be seen in all directions.[31]

Stubbs was the only survivor to publicly mention the role of the Moreton Islanders, and the issue was further clouded by the fact that Toompani was occasionally employed at the Amity Point pilot station on Stradbroke Island.[32] That there were two separate groups of Aborigines involved in the rescue is nevertheless clear, and Thomas Welsby was certainly correct in coming to that conclusion.[33]

In all, forty-four people perished in the turbulent waters, and the total monetary loss, including the vessel itself, was estimated at £20,000.[34] The salvage rights were put up for auction just five days after the disaster, but such was the unlikelihood of recovery that the highest bid was a mere £14 10s.[35] Remaining on Moreton Island, Clements and Richards managed to open a number of wool bales that washed ashore, spreading their contents above high water to dry. The cost of carriage, however, mitigated against financial gain,[36] and it appears that only two bales of wool were returned to Brisbane.[37] Along with the cargo, human corpses also came ashore on the eastern side of Moreton Island during the ensuing weeks. All were in various stages of decomposition, which often made identification extremely difficult. Recovery and burial once more fell heavily on the Aborigines:

Captain Wickham, accompanied by Mr. Thornton, his boat's crew [i.e. the customs boat], and several of the natives from Stradbroke Island, reached Cape Moreton on Friday last, having walked along the beach a distance of upwards of twenty miles. They found the bodies of nine males and three females, scattered over a space of eight miles, so that they were compelled to make separate graves for each corpse – a most arduous and disgusting task, and one which could not have been accomplished without the assistance of the blacks. The bodies were horribly disfigured, some were without arms and legs, and some with scarcely any flesh upon them. One had been deprived of his head, and all were more or less mutilated. The bodies of Isaac Smith, a man named John Higgins, and Mrs. Bishop were identified, the latter by a ring which she wore on her finger. It was stated in our last number that Mr. Gore's child had been found with the other bodies. This is incorrect. What was alleged to be the corpse of the child turns out to be a dead goat.[38]

The entire Gore family was lost in the catastrophe, and only the bodies of Mary Gore and one of the children were recovered. The following August their remains were disinterred from makeshift graves on the island and taken to Brisbane, where they were laid in 'their final resting place in the Episcopalian burial ground'.[39] With Robert Little acting as honorary secretary, a relief fund was established to assist those rendered destitute by the shipwreck, and to afford 'some mark of public approbation' for the Aborigines involved in the rescue.[40] Among the early subscribers was Henry Stuart Russell, who was fortunate not to have been among the victims.[41] Intending to travel south for a well-earned rest, urgent work on his western Darling Downs run delayed Russell's departure so that he arrived in Brisbane while the 'Sovereign' was anchored off Amity Point. Determined to join the vessel, he tried to secure a boat for conveyance across the bay, and it was while returning to his lodgings after yet another futile search that he was informed of the disaster. Russell relinquished all thoughts of a holiday that year.[42]

Perhaps even more fortunate was John McQuade, who was actually on the vessel. Under sentence for wilful damage to the police cells in Brisbane, McQuade and his escort embarked on the 'Sovereign'. Surrendering himself to the authorities after his rescue, he was formally discharged as an act of compassion.[43] One of the vessel's firemen, John Scard, was also among the survivors, although his injuries were so severe that he was hospitalised on arrival in Brisbane. Recovering, he later left for Sydney, and it was there that he received a 'munificent sum' from the relief fund in July.[44] In all, £66 13s 10d was raised by public subscription,[45] but there is no evidence that the Aboriginal rescuers received any remuneration from that source.

On the contrary, the NSW government 'rewarded' six Aborigines, including Woondu and Toompani, with brass breastplates commemorating their heroic actions. It was also directed that Toompani should receive a small fishing boat for his own conspicuous role in the rescue,[46] but here a dreadful mistake occurred; the boat was inadvertently given to a mainland clan who had played no part in the drama. Moreover, they later received a second boat. It was not until September 1871, with Toompani now an elderly man, that Fred Campbell made a vociferous protest on his behalf in the Brisbane press.[47] Apparently this had the desired effect and the matter was rectified, for Welsby remembered Toompani in possession of a boat that the shipping office kept in regular repair.[48] The master of the ill-fated 'Sovereign', Henry Cape, did not receive another vessel.

John McCallum was the only survivor from the engine-room, and soon after being rescued he informed William Clements that the machinery had broken. This statement was later reiterated in the presence of James Hexton, the Amity Point pilot, and both Clements and Hexton made sworn affidavits to that effect before the Police Magistrate, J.C. Wickham, on 7 June 1847. McCallum, however, later retracted his statements. Thus, when conducting an inquiry into the loss of the 'Sovereign', representatives of the Hunter River Steam Navigation Company accepted McCallum's evidence that the master had been negligent, and the founding was not due to mechanical failure. Cape was dismissed from the company's service.[49]

That he was partly responsible for what occurred is undeniable, but it is also clear that Cape was also offered up as a convenient scapegoat, a manoeuvre 'badly seconded by the public'.[50] Cape was a well-known and highly-respected figure in the small Brisbane community,[51] and from the available evidence there is little doubt that the machinery, which had not been fitted correctly, did in fact fail. This specifically related to the plummer-blocks that held the shafts turning the paddles. When they broke, the shafts dropped out of position and the vessel was therefore devoid of mechanical power. From that point on, Cape did all that was humanly possible to save his vessel, passengers and crew, but his efforts were further frustrated by the deficient state of the hull.[52]

In the final analysis, the company should be seen to bear much of the culpability for the disaster, as they had placed an unseaworthy vessel on a demanding service where the risks were high. The NSW government was also at fault by delaying a thorough survey of the safer North Passage. The South Passage was known to be dangerous and unpredictable for ingress and egress, yet that was the recommended route between Moreton Bay and the south, with the pilot station being located there. It took the deaths of forty-four innocent people to alter the lethargic attitude, and it is relevant that the survey of the North Passage was completed little more than one month after the disaster.[53] The pilot station was transferred to Bulwer, on Moreton Island, shortly afterwards.[54]

The hero of the drama, Toompani, lived until 1886 and was buried near Amity Point. With his wife, Thruppan, the pair experienced personal tragedy when their only child, Jacky, was shot by fellow members of the Native Mounted Police after falling asleep on duty. The dishonour and grief never left them.[55] The fate of Woondu is not known, though it is unlikely that he fled Moreton Island through superstition as suggested by Welsby.[56] His breastplate was probably bartered among the coastal Aboriginal clans until coming to rest at Marramerang in southern NSW. It was returned to Queensland after Welsby made a pecuniary offer to the Collins family.[57]

The wreck of the 'Sovereign' certainly shocked the small settlement of Brisbane, where 'there was not a family … that did not mourn the loss of a friend or a relation'.[58] The published list of those drowned was thus:

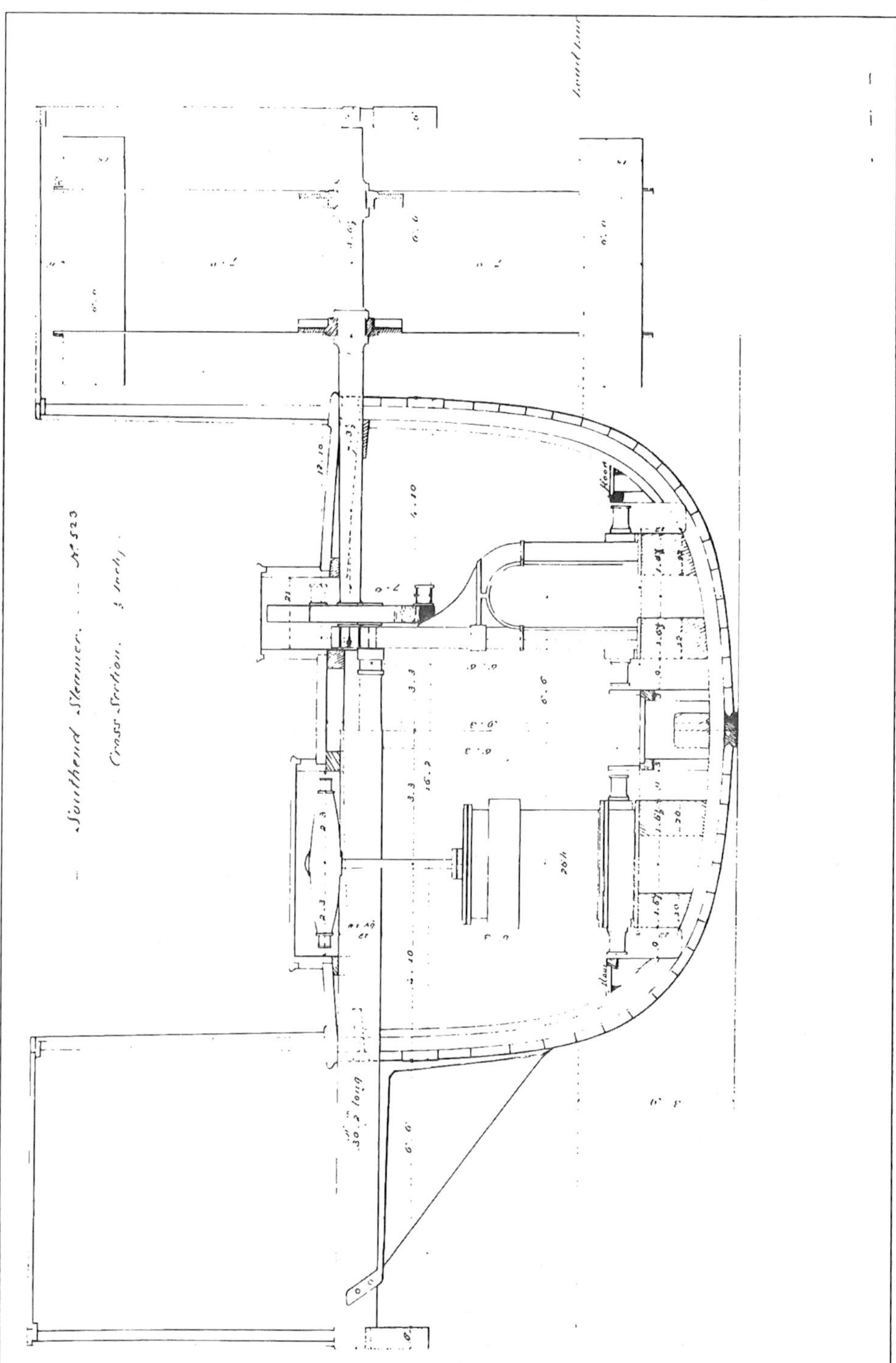


2.4 Internal cross-section of the steamer 'William IV' (AHC)

CABIN PASSENGERS

Mr and Mrs Robert Gore, two children, and servant girl

| | |
|---|---|
| Mr H. Dennis | Darling Downs |
| Mr Berkeley | Brisbane |
| Mr Joyner | Pine River and Sydney |
| Mr Elliott | Clarence River |

STEERAGE

| | |
|---|---|
| Mrs Bishop | South Brisbane |
| Mrs Chettle | North Brisbane |

And sixteen male passengers

[CREW]

| | |
|---|---|
| James Ryan | Steward |
| ________ | Stewardess |
| Michael Mooney | 2nd Steward |
| Harry _____ | 3rd ditto |
| _________ | 4th ditto |
| Mr Gibson | 1st Officer |
| Mr Brown | 2nd Officer |
| Mr Sommerville | 1st Engineer |
| Mr Robertson | 2nd ditto |
| John Smith | Fireman |
| Isaac Smith | Seaman |
| Robert Mackenzie | Ditto |
| Henry Cumberland | Ditto |
| John Miller | Ditto |
| John ____ | Ditto |
| John Blaim | 1st Cook |
| _______ | 2nd ditto.[59] |

It was an unprecedented calamity, and although the disaster did lead to safer navigation in Moreton Bay, the event itself faded slowly from memory. In 1920 it was rekindled by the chance find of the Collins children playing among the sand dunes far to the south. By then, all the Aboriginal rescuers – and many of their descendants – had departed on their own voyages into eternity, swept away by the white tide of colonialism. In 1847 an even greater tragedy was still unfolding for the indigenous people of Moreton Bay, and no amount of courage could halt its remorseless advance.[60]

*Chapter 3*

# 'Sweet surrender': Sugar production at St Helena penal establishment 1867-89

**Yvonne Reynolds**

On 20 May 1867 the first prisoners were officially confined on St Helena Island which had been proclaimed as Her Majesty's Penal Establishment six days before by the governor of Queensland, Sir George Ferguson Bowen. John McDonald, an inspector with the water police in charge of the prison hulk 'Proserpine', was appointed as the first superintendent. From late 1865 McDonald had been supervising the men from the hulk in building a new quarantine station on the island to replace the inadequate facilities at Dunwich. These plans were abandoned later the following year when it was decided St Helena would be better suited as a penal settlement. Prison accommodation in Brisbane was overcrowded and with this as a more urgent problem, the quarantine buildings were modified to become part of the new penitentiary.

McDonald set about establishing a prison where the inmates were fully occupied in productive labour. At first the tasks of land clearance and building construction were the main consideration. Once this was well underway the superintendent planned a system where the men would be taught trade and agricultural skills under the guidance of instructor warders. The notion that a prison might be a self-supporting establishment was an attractive economic proposition. The proposal for sugar cane cultivation on the island was first suggested by William Thornton, the visiting justice, in his November 1867 report to the Colonial Secretary:

> Considerable progress has been made in clearing the scrub which encourages me in the belief that we can have at least 50 acres of the best land under sugar cane before the expiration of 12 months if you should approve of such cultivation – I have already spoken on this subject with Captain Hope who is willing to take the cane from the island and manufacture into Sugar and Rum on the same terms which he has offered to the farmers in his neighbourhood – I took to Sugar growing as the readiest way of making the Establishment self supporting.
>
> With your permission I would purchase sufficient cane cuttings to plant about two acres of land already cleared on the island so as to ensure a sufficient quantity of cuttings for planting larger quantities of ground when cleared. The cultivation of sugar cane would not interfere with production on the Island of corn and vegetables required by the Establishment.
>
> I may mention that St Helena is also adopted for the growth of cotton and that I hesitated for some time whether to recommend the cultivation of sugar cane or cotton but from which I ascertained from others practicably acquainted with these matters I inclined to the belief that the former would be the more beneficial, at the same time before you may arrive at a decision in so important a matter I would suggest that Mr Hill Director of the Gardens be invited to offer an opinion on the subject.

Thornton's suggestion was approved by the authorities with the remark on the margin: 'Suggestions approved. Try 2 acres of land'.[1]

In the early 1860s the colony of Queensland was developing rapidly. Immigration was encouraged, money was available for pastoral expansion and the building of railways opened the land. During this period of optimism, Captain Louis Hope established cane growing at Ormiston in the Cleveland district in 1862. This was the same year that John Buhot manufactured granulated sugar from Tahitian canes grown at the Botanic Gardens in Brisbane. Sugar cane was one of the experimental plants being studied and assessed as early as 1828 for adjustments to climate, soil and rainfall and their potential as commercial crops in the colony.

Walter Hill, curator of the government gardens wrote to the *Brisbane courier* of 26 April 1862, forwarding a sample of sugar and a report on its quality and manufacture by Buhot who had experience in the Barbados sugar industry in the West Indies. Hill stated that it was a hurried experiment using green canes. The equipment was three makeshift iron pots in the open air. He reported that Buhot felt confident that 'with proper appliances, a superior quality of sugar, to what I have seen generally sold in Brisbane, can be produced from similar canes, only riper'.

In a letter to the *Brisbane courier* on 6 June 1862, Buhot himself commented on the experiment, giving further details. From the green canes fifty litres of juice produced two kilograms of sugar which was discoloured because of the length of boiling time using iron pots which were new.

Buhot worked for Hope as a manager until December, then for Captain Claudius Buchanan Whish at Caboolture as superintendent for eleven months before becoming an adviser in various sugar regions.[2] Whish had established a plantation, 'Oaklands', on the south bank of the Caboolture River in February 1863. He had no experience in agriculture, having been an officer in the 14th Light Dragoons in India, but he carefully assessed the possibilities of the young colony and weighed up the scant advice available to decide on sugar rather than cotton cultivation.[3]

*3.1 Ruins of St Helena sugar mill, December 1928 (JOL)*

During the early 1860s the government encouraged the establishment of the sugar industry with bounties and assistance for growers.[4] The August 1864 'Sugar and Coffee Regulations' gave further official sanctions to the development of the industry. In 1866 a decline in the Queensland economy occurred with severe unemployment, a reduction in immigration and financial collapse. Unemployment created problems that increased the crime-rate and caused further overloading of prison facilities.

The opening of the rich Gympie goldfields in 1867 restored prospects in the colony and by the end of the 1860s progress was steady. The development of the rural economy helped this stabilisation.[5] In particular sugar with high production yields per acre [0.4 hectare] became a valuable export which continued until the bounty-supported sugar beet industry of continental Europe lowered world prices after 1884.[6]

Sugar production also stimulated secondary industries for processing the crop. In turn, these led to the building of railways and ports, and stimulated settlement along the tropical coast of Queensland. In his analysis of the Queensland economy between 1860 and 1915, historian John Laverty stated:

> The sugar industry ... besides requiring commercial, banking and the general services, created new demands for timber, shipping, transport and communications, while the mechanization of sugar cultivation and the milling and refining of the sugar fostered the manufacture of agriculture implements and necessitated the installation of expensive plants and machinery, which, in turn, gave an impetus to engineering work and foundries. [7]

Thornton and McDonald, by recommending sugar production on St Helena, were in fact introducing an innovative program which would help support the prison expenses as well as giving the men skills which were in great demand in the fledgling industry. Rehabilitation into society was a decided possibility within the grasp of discharged prisoners from St Helena who had gained experience in cultivation, mill and sugar house.

Sugar production was a labour intensive occupation with a variety of tasks in each step from field to factory. The prison had a ready supply of manpower which eliminated the main problem of those on private plantations who were employing Melanesian labour for cane cutting. The cost of European workers was exorbitant compared to that of indentured Islanders so that farming cane could not be considered without cheap labour until the advent of co-operative mills. Ralph Shlomowitz listed the main labour-intensive activities for the unskilled workers in the farming and milling of sugar:

> The principal occupation in sugar cane farming are plowing, planting, cleaning the crop (that is, keeping the growing plant free of weeds), trashing (that is, pulling off the leaves from the cane before the harvest), cutting, loading, and transporting the cut cane to the mill for crushing ... as quickly as possible because the cut cane deteriorates rapidly in sugar content. [8]

The growth of the sugar industry led to the building of townships on the deltas and level soils of the main rivers and creeks of the tropical river systems. In later years this industry was able to sustain the economy and cushion the full effects of depression such as that experienced in the 1890s.[9] It would certainly be worth the effort if, on St Helena, production could be sustained and government institutions supplied with the finished product. In actual fact McDonald was able to do better than this and in the years which followed regularly sent sugar consignments for sale.

The scheme got under way with the visiting justice submitting his December 1867 'Report to the Colonial Secretary', mentioning that Captain Hope had delivered cuttings to the island and advised that the soil was suitable: 'in consequence of your approval of any suggestion that a sugar plantation should be formed on the Island two acres of land between the Superintendents quarters and the prison thoroughly prepared as a nursery for canes and planted with cuttings'.[10]

The report continued that Hope was prepared to manufacture the cane on the same terms offered to other sugar planters; that is, to receive half the sugar and rum to be produced for manufacturing the cane. Hope calculated that the spot marked off by McDonald for the plantation would produce 'three tons of sugar to the acre'. Thornton expected that before long the 'Establishment would be self-supporting in a great measure'.[11] The superintendent's report gives more detail of Hope's visit to the island on the 30 December when he delivered '3060 sugar cuttings' and examined the soil pronouncing it 'first class sugar land'.[12]

In his February report Thornton stated that he had been 'obliged to get 3000 more sugar plants from Mr Raff's plantation as only 100 of those which we have had from Captain Hope have taken root'.[13] George Raff's property and mill at Morayfield adjoined that of Whish on the Caboolture River. Raff's brother Alexander was a partner in Smellie & Co., the engineering firm manufacturing mills and other equipment for the sugar industry. The officers in charge of St Helena were certainly seeking advice and assistance from those with the best knowledge of the crop and its processing. Thornton reported that there were about 4000 cane plantings which, 'with those previously grown here will be sufficient to furnish plants for fifty acres'.[14]

In August 1868 McDonald reported clearing the ground for sugar, corn and cotton. He planned, if possible, twelve hectares of sugar, twelve of corn and a few hectares of cotton.[15] By September the superintendent could advise the Colonial Secretary that a 'great deal of clearing has been done during the past month, for sugar and corn, on the 25th ult. I received 21,000 sugar plants from hon. L. Hopes plantation. Five acres of sugar has been planted & I have got plants enough to plant ten acres more'.[16] By October all the sugar canes received from Cleveland had been planted, '13 acres have been planted from the Cleveland canes, 2 acres planted from canes grown on the island, which makes altogether fifteen (15) acres of land planted during the last month'.[17] Again there was a setback in the canes taking root. In January 1869 the superintendent's report read:

> About ten acres of land cleared for corn & sugar … a great number of the sugar cane plants received from 'Hopes' plantation did not come up, & had to be planted a second time, which has been done with canes grown on the island.[18]

At last success was fully achieved with the help of good rains at the right time. In February McDonald wrote:

> Five acres planted with sugar canes …. a good deal of work has been done in hilling and keeping the sugar canes clean. The late rains has done a great deal of good to all growing crops, the sugar canes & lately planted corn is looking remarkably well.[19]

Progress was being made and T.H. Barron, the new visiting justice, wrote to the Colonial Secretary on 13 May 1869 indicating the desirability of providing a sugar mill at St Helena. With no less than eight hectares of cane under cultivation, 'which will be ready for crushing in a few months', he calculated a profit of £1000 from sugar and molasses in the following year when more land would be placed under cultivation. He did not recommend the original plan of having the crushing done by a private mill away from the island, with the charge for so doing being 'half of the sugar and molasses yielded'.[20] No mention was made of Hope's original offer, to mill for the charge of half the sugar and rum produced, and he obviously felt this would be an inappropriate activity for the prisoners!

A reporter writing under the pseudonym of 'The Sketcher', for the *Queenslander* on 30 October 1869, came to the same conclusion when he stated: 'It is intended to boil the molasses and extract all the sugar possible, instead of manufacturing rum, which would not be a very judicious course in such a place'. Barron gave some useful advice regarding equipment:

> Being desirous that the Establishment should be made as self-supporting as possible I would respectfully recommend that a Sugar-Mill, now on sale at the foundry of Messr. R.R. Smellie & Co. be purchased for the Island – the necessary buildings could be erected by prisoners without any further expense to the government – in material or otherwise – the price of the above 'plant' would be one hundred and twenty pounds.

With his letter Barron enclosed a 'sample of sugar manufactured by a similar mill'.[21] On 18 May McDonald wrote to Arthur Hodgson, the Colonial Secretary, asking for an early answer to his application for permission for the supply of a sugar mill so he could make preparation for the fittings and 'thereby greatly expedite matters'. He enclosed for Barron an 'Estimate Cost of Machinery for the Erection of a Sugar Mill at St Helena and Estimated Returns for 1869/70'. The outlay amounted to £120 for the mill and boilers; £1 for two saccharometers, and another £1 for two thermometers; and £3 for nails. No estimate was provided for timber and sundries.

McDonald calculated eight hectares fit to be crushed and manufactured during the 1869 season, 'estimated by competent judges who have visited the island to yield not less than 2 ton per acre'. In 1870 the estimate was twenty hectares of sugar cane at four ton per hectare (at £35 per ton) and molasses worth £500 (the same rates as for 1869). He concluded his estimate with a memo stating that 'the appraisement is according to the judgement of those well versed in the culture and manufacture of sugar'.[22]

Barron followed up this request with a recommendation of the expenditure of a sum not exceeding £130 in the purchase of the sugar mill and necessary appliances for crushing the cane, the amount to be charged to the 'Incidentals' of the Penal Establishment.[23] When he forwarded the estimates to the colonial secretary he was instructed personally to purchase the necessary machinery.[24]

The inmates of St Helena were totally involved in the establishment of sugar production on the island. The various work gangs included the No.2 gang of thirteen men who were engaged in clearing and caring for the sugar cane. In 1869 McDonald reported that he had twenty hectares under cultivation. The No.3 gang was employed in quarrying stones for the foundation of the new sugar mill and No.5 gang was excavating the earth for 'the erection of a sugar house and well under the superintendence of Mr Cameron the Sugar manufacturer and overseer'.[25]

Barron and McDonald were able to carry out the establishment of mill and sugar house. 'The Sketcher' reported on 30 October that 'sugar production was progressing well and the venture successful ... much credit is due to the manager of the concern, Mr McDonald and the warder Brown, who, with no previous knowledge of sugar-making, have got over many difficulties, and now produce a household sugar fit for any table in the country'.[26] One of the earlier sugar mills in Queensland had been established on an island prison.

'The Sketcher' continued that three varieties of cane were being grown – green or yellow (New Caledonis), ribbon, and Bourbon, 'probably they are as fine as could be found in Australia'. The green cane was yielding:

> ... very clean liquor, making 11 upon the saccharometer ... The result was a light brown sugar of a good grain, samples of which can be seen at our office ... The mill is by Smellie and Co. of the Queensland Foundry. It is driven by horse power. By sinking the mill into the side of a bank, the horses are made to travel over the heads of the men who feed in the cane, and thus the power is brought close to the rollers, without an elevated shaft. The rollers are held by an iron frame, and there is a solidity and steadiness about the working of the whole concern which might profitably be looked into by parties about to erect horse mills. The liquor runs by gravitation into the clarifiers, of which there are two, where it is tempered at a temperature of 140 degrees, raised to 190, and then run into the evaporators. The battery is set in brickwork; there are four square pans and a circular tache, all of iron, and the very cheapest material, as may be understood by the total cost, exclusive of labour, being £130. The coolers and drainers are of timber; the former have beveled sides; the latter are nearly square. The liquor in the tache is boiled up to 231 degrees, the fire is then drawn, when the contents are ladled into a shoot, and so conveyed to the coolers. This is the only case wherein the liquor is lifted; it is made to gravitate from the mill to the tache. Rockhampton lime is alone used for tempering, and it answers excellently, as the sugar in the drainers testified. The canes are perfectly free from any effects of frost, and yield a very clear and pure liquor .... The yield per acre so far, is about three tons; and from the splendid appearance of the canes, it will be up to all probability

> to that quality throughout .... The crushed cane when dry is used for fuel ... Mr McDonald thinks with a few additional hands he could have in 100 acres of cane by Christmas, and we trust that some of the men now idling away their time in the gaols of the Colony will be placed at his disposal, when they will learn something useful, and will not only aid in making St Helena reproductive, but positively profitable to the country.[27]

In 1870 Angus MacKay wrote of the early sugar mill on St Helena and described how he added lime to balance acidity, and experiments with bisulphite of lime, 'a decided improvement upon lime tempers'. He had previously tried lime made from coral and shells but found stone lime from Rockhampton far superior. MacKay also mentioned that a 'centrifugal machine is being constructed which is indented to work either with a small steam engine or hand labour'.[28]

The engineering firm of R.R. Smellie & Co. was run by three partners, John Sinclair in charge of the engineering side of the business, Robert Russell Smellie the merchant and Alexander Raff in charge of finance. The company made many early mills, including those for Whish and also William Gibson at Hemmant, whose property 'Clydesdale', on Doboy Creek, was in the same area as Hope's at Ormiston from whom he obtained his first canes.

In 1868 Sinclair had designed for Gibson a horse-driven vertical two-roller mill, with a capacity of ten tons of cane per day. The St Helena mill had three vertical rollers each 'eighteen inches in diameter and fifteen inches high'.[29]

In NSW sugar experiments had been conducted in the 1820s at the Port Macquarie convict settlement, and juice had been produced from the cane, but attempts to establish an industry were abandoned in 1831. There was a revival in interest when, in the 1860s sugar was selling at £60 per ton in Sydney. Small farmers set up plots and small primitive mills, often with more enthusiasm for capital gain than a real knowledge of the operation. Most failed in their attempt.[30]

The Colonial Sugar Refining Company (CSR) had emerged in the late 1860s with its large refinery and adequate capital to establish sugar growing as the major primary industry of the Northern Rivers area.[31] The company became interested in the Queensland industry in 1881 when a Queensland director of CSR visited the Johnstone River.

In its heyday Innisfail was capable of an annual production of cane to the value of over £2 million, more than double the gold return of Charters Towers when production was at its peak. The penal establishment at St Helena had certainly been amongst the earliest farms in Queensland, which became the major colony for cane farming, milling and refining. In the first five years expansion of the industry in the colony had been rapid:[32]

| *Year* | *Mills* | *Sugar (tons)* |
|---|---|---|
| 1866 | 3 | 168 |
| 1867 | 6 | 338 |
| 1868 | 10 | 619 |
| 1869 | 28 | 1490 |
| 1870 | 29 | 2854 |

On the island, improvements were consistently being made in the day-to-day running of the mill. A Mr Cameron was employed as a sugar boiler, but not being satisfactory his services were dispensed with, McDonald reporting that 'I find we can make much better sugar without him'.[33] The mill was working well and McDonald added that 'In a short time I will be in a position to forward for sale a considerable quantity of good sugar, which will greatly reduce the heavy expenditure laid out on St Helena ... by the end of 1870, St Helena would return a large revenue after paying all prison & guard expenses'.[34]

During periods of concentrated activity, such as planting or harvesting, the island was short on manpower with all available hands fully employed. Work on prison construction ceased. The superintendent on more than one occasion requested that extra men be sent from mainland

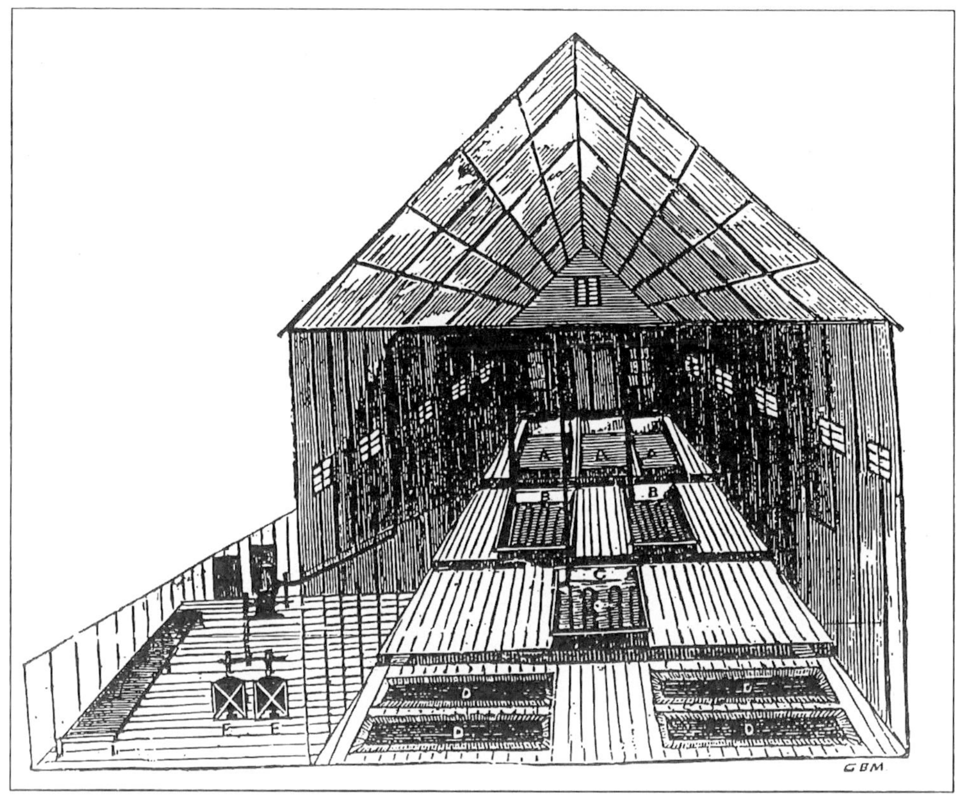


*3.2 Interior of the sugar house at St Helena,* Town and Country Journal *1871*

gaols, 'all the available prisoners that are not profitably employed, be forwarded to St Helena to enable me to plant all the arable land this season'.[35]

In late January 1870 McDonald asked for one week's leave to visit sugar plantations and study methods of production.[36] This was granted and, on his return, extensive plans were made for upgrading the facilities in the mill and sugar house. It must have been extremely difficult, in this time of rapid change and expansion in the industry, to be so isolated from other plantations and new ideas.

A new timber wing had been built on to the sugar house in November 1869 but the mill was unable to cope with the tonnage being produced. In May McDonald discussed obtaining a larger mill, three more horses or, for preference, a thirty horse-power engine from the Works Department to increase the working day of the mill.[37] In June he reported that foundations for a new sugar mill were 'being proceeded with all possible speed' and in July, that the woodwork was being erected.[38]

Alterations were made to the sugar mill again in 1871 and 1872, while in 1874 the old boilers were replaced. Continual upgrading occurred in subsequent years with a large Cornish boiler being installed in 1880. In 1882 McDonald was succeeded by a new superintendent, Captain William Townley, who carried on with the sugar production but understandably without the interest, enthusiasm and pride which McDonald had demonstrated for his own project.

The unpredictability of rain and the impossibility of using water from other sources meant that the island crop was at the mercy of the fickle seasons. Equipment was not upgraded as new and more efficient methods were introduced. Sugar production was part of an economic plan for the prison program and as such was not seen as a single business but as just one facet of the organisation of the institution.

In the 1887 'Enquiry into Prisons' the sugar-cane plantation was considered a possible security risk, 'being an excellent hiding place'. The cane also concealed some buildings, such as the armoury in the warders' barracks, from the view of guards. The combination of difficulties coincided with another change in superintendents when Captain Charles Pennefather took over the position on 14 August 1888. Having little knowledge of the industry, he was not inclined to continue the project, and production ceased. The last crushing took place in 1889. The machinery was adapted for laundry purposes and pumping water to the stockade. The sugar store was partly converted into the quarters for the master tailor.

So ended the major project on St Helena that had provided maximum involvement of the inmates, giving them productive occupation and the chance to learn valuable skills for use on their discharge from prison. John McDonald with his vision in 1867 had truly been one of the pioneers of the sugar industry in Queensland. As a prison training officer, his incentive had not been land control, monetary gain or political power, but the economic principle of profitable self-sufficiency at the penal establishment on St Helena Island.

*Chapter 4*

# 'A modified form of whaling': The Moreton Bay dugong fishery 1846-1920

**Murray Johnson**

In recent decades, growing public awareness has elevated the importance of environmental issues on the political agenda in many countries throughout the world. Perhaps nowhere is this more apparent than in those western nations where modern technology has impacted on the global environment in a manner out of all proportion to their population and geographical size. Many were also imperialist powers, whose legacy has often left former colonies condemned to the fate of over-exploiting dwindling natural resources in a desperate effort to balance flagging economies; neo-colonialism is far from defunct. Yet, how serious are Western politicians when confronted with dwindling numbers of biological species on their own doorstep? In 1997 Australia's federal environment minister, Robert Hill, announced that his country would 'lead the world' to terminate international whaling operations.[1] Senator Hill conveniently avoided any reference to Australia's role in devastating those marine giants in the historical past.

Barely three months earlier, Queensland's tourism minster, Bruce Davidson, announced plans to establish a game reserve in the northern state for the preservation of South Africa's endangered black rhinoceros. While the importance of international co-operation in confronting environmental problems should not be overlooked, it was left to one perceptive journalist to point out that Queensland was concomitantly ignoring the fate of many of its own resident faunal species – including a marine mammal, the dugong.[2] In relation to that species the historical past also joins with the present, for the dugong has been subjected to both indigenous and commercial exploitation over a considerable period of time. Indeed, continuing indigenous exploitation of the animal in Queensland has raised alarm among a number of marine biologists, who consider the species threatened with ultimate extinction. Nevertheless, there can be little doubt that the almost forgotten commercial fishery – which shared many close affinities with commercial whaling operations – contributed in no small measure to the precarious position of the species in Queensland today. It further emphasises that, as far as the preservation of marine mammals is concerned, Australia has been far from a shining example for the rest of the world.

Historical amnesia has ensured the obscurity of the commercial dugong fishery, which operated sporadically in Queensland from 1847 until the mid-1970s, although operations in the Moreton Bay region had largely terminated by 1920. Unlike indigenous exploitation, heed was seldom taken of diminishing numbers to ensure its long-term sustainability; it was, after all, 'a modified form of whaling', with the bounteous seas expected to appease commercial demands.[3] Conversely, as an important component of Queensland's indigenous coastal economies, dugong exploitation was carefully balanced and subject to strict guidelines enforced by law. As on land, colonisation in Queensland rapidly led to essential indigenous labour being grafted with European technology, a combination which almost invariably resulted in resource depletion, and analogies were drawn between the commercial dugong fishery and the pastoral industry. As with their terrestrial counterparts, Queensland's 'submarine squatters' were highly dependent on indigenous skill and expertise.[4] In both cases, exploitation was thus extended to utilise the human resource.

Commonly referred to as the sea-cow, dugongs (*Dugong dugon*) are closely related to the three existing species of manatee; together they form the biological order Sirenia. All have been adversely affected by human hunting activities. West African manatee (*Trichechus senegalensis*) have been exploited for their 'meat, skin, bones, and oil' – the same commodities which led to the depletion of their American cousins, the West Indian manatee (*Trichechus manatus*) and the Amazonian manatee (*Trichechus inunguis*).[5] The danger these animals face is best exemplified by the fate which overtook the giant member of the order Sirenia, Steller's Sea-Cow (*Hydrodamalis stelleri*). Attaining a length in excess of seven metres and a weight of 4,000 kilograms, this species was hunted to extinction in the Bering Strait within thirty years of its discovery in 1742.[6]

While anatomically similar to the aquatic manatees, dugongs differ in being strictly confined to a marine habitat. Found in the Red Sea and along the East African coast as far south as Mauritius, the range of the dugong extends eastwards throughout the Indian Ocean to Vanuatu in the Pacific.[7] In Australia, the species occurs from Shark Bay in Western Australia around the northern coast to Moreton Bay in southern Queensland.[8]

Many ancient Arab and Greek myths also surround the dugong. The Greek traveller Megasthenes described a creature resembling a woman in the sea near Taprobane or, as it is now known, Sri Lanka.[9] It has been suggested that later Portuguese and Dutch voyagers enlarged on this to create the myth of the mermaid, indelibly linked with the mysterious East.[10] Dugongs were also the sirens, whose singing lured unwary sailors to their watery graves.[11] The paradox was that it was human sea-rovers who decimated dugongs. Thoughout their entire range they have been hunted extensively, and so important has this been that specialised cultures, based around dugong hunting, developed as far apart as the Persian Gulf in the west and on Queensland's Cape York Peninsula to the east.[12]

Dugongs are relatively large animals, reaching over three metres in length and a weight in excess of 500 kilograms. They were once believed to be strictly herbivorous, feeding on a variety of seagrasses. Recent research has shown, however, that in southern areas this dietary intake is supplemented with marine invertebrates, particularly polychaete worms and molluscs.[13] Disclosures such as this also serve to demonstrate that while dugongs have been known and utilised for so long, remarkably little is known about their biology. Whether they are migratory or nomadic animals is yet another conundrum.[14] Certainly where food is plentiful they often remain, but their dependence on seagrasses has further ensured that they have a mandatory association with shallow coastal habitats, making them vulnerable to a range of human activities, including hunting.[15] In Queensland, two distinct methods of capture were practised by the indigenous peoples.

Torres Strait Islanders and Cape York Aborigines developed a sophisticated harpooning method for hunting dugongs. Up to five metres in length, the harpoons were manufactured from hardened mangrove wood and hollowed at one end to receive a detachable barb.[16] A rope made from Hibiscus attached the barb to either a bamboo framework (*neet*) built over dugong feeding grounds or, more frequently, a canoe. On Cape York the construction of *neets* – six bamboo poles lashed together – was rather limited and perhaps a recent introduction from Torres Strait.[17] As well, canoes were often of the outrigger type, thus confirming the strong Torres Strait influence.[18]

Unlike their northern counterparts, Aboriginal groups around Moreton Bay captured dugongs in nets. Manufactured from the internal bark of 'various species of Hibiscus', they were remarkable for both their elasticity and strength.[19] An early Queensland authority, Tom Petrie, recorded the process by which they were made:

> To get the bark the blacks would cut the vine in lengths, and then beat these well with sticks until it peeled off easily with the teeth. This they would then soak in water for several days, at the end of which time the rough outer bark would be thrown away, while with their thumb nails the men would split the inner bark up into fibre. This fibre was dried and then twisted on their thighs into excellent string, which was very useful in many ways. [Nets for Dugong] were formed of big meshes, and were sewn up in the shape of huge pockets; they were hand nets, and were finished off at the top by two pieces of stick ending in a handle. When making nets the natives used to measure to get the correct size of mesh.[20]

There may have been at least one variation on this construction. While exploring Moreton Bay in July 1799, Matthew Flinders appropriated a large net from an Aboriginal dwelling near what is now Woody Point, on Redcliffe Peninsula. It was described as being 'about fourteen fathoms long, the meshes of which were much larger than any English seine, and the twine much stronger; but its depth was much less, being not more than three feet'.[21] Equipped with a tapered pole at each end – to be driven into the seabed – it is generally recognised as having been manufactured for catching dugongs.[22] Although Flinders remained ignorant as to its purpose, he encountered a dugong seven days later in Pumicestone Passage, which separates Bribie Island from the mainland. Mistaking it for a seal, Flinders 'fired three musquet balls' into the animal, which promptly sank beneath the surface.[23] It was a prophetic meeting between Europeans and dugongs in Queensland waters.

For Moreton Bay Aborigines, however, dugong hunting was both a seasonal and communal activity. The appearance of a herd inshore signalled the launching of bark canoes, which were quietly paddled out to separate the dugongs from deeper water. Once the craft were in position their occupants generated as much noise as possible to frighten the animals towards a line of men – each equipped with a single net – in the shallows. Immediately an animal was ensnared, the hunter's colleagues rendered assistance, either by spearing the dugong or holding it beneath the surface until it drowned.[24] Their large size ensured that only a single animal was required to provide sustenance.

Netting was also carried out at specific locations, emphasising the dependence on environmental factors. Petrie recorded these sites as being in the vicinity of Fisherman and St Helena islands, Hays Inlet, Pumicestone Passage and near Dunwich, on Stradbroke Island.[25] The Quaker, James Backhouse, observed in the 1830s that dugongs were netted as they travelled up narrow creeks on Stradbroke Island.[26] This perhaps offers a solution to a problem which perplexed the later Moreton Bay authority, Thomas Welsby, who was unable to determine the affinity between dugongs and a stream on Stradbroke Island which bore the name 'Cooran-Cooran-pah' – an Aboriginal term for dugong meat.[27]

While the meat was largely sought by the indigenous people, the oil was also used for remedial purposes. It was the latter which attracted the attention of Europeans in colonial Queensland. The government health officer in Brisbane, Dr William Hobbs, has been credited with establishing the commercial dugong fishery in Moreton Bay during the 1850s.[28] While it cannot be denied that Hobbs actively and consistently promulgated the potential of an industry that revolved around the production of remedial oil, he was certainly not the founder. As early as August 1846 a European turtle fisherman with an Aboriginal crew had investigated the possibility of catching dugongs for their flesh.[29] While nothing appears to have eventuated from this initial attempt, 'several persons' were certainly engaged in hunting dugongs for their oil in Moreton Bay by January 1847. Based at Amity Point on Stradbroke Island, the fishery marketed dugong oil for a variety of purposes, 'ornamental as well as useful. It has been used in the frying of fish, and has been highly approved of by connoisseurs in cookery, who pronounce it to be quite equal to any salad oil. It is also said to be admirably adapted for the toilette'.[30]

Samples were forwarded to Sydney, it being envisaged that dugong oil would become 'a very valuable article for exportation, or for home consumption'.[31] Although the enterprise was still operating in October 1847, it did not achieve the expectations of its founders.[32] This was probably due to insufficient numbers being taken to make it economically viable. Harpooning was the method of capture and it was totally dependent on Stradbroke Island's Nunukul Aborigines. Moreover, the adroitness of the indigenous people with the harpoon was all the more remarkable given that the traditional method of capturing dugongs was with nets.[33]

Interestingly, a tombstone epitaph in Dunwich Cemetery on North Stradbroke Island records that Frederick Stiller 'Founded [the] Dugong Fisheries [in] Moreton Bay'.[34] A native of Poland and a former governor of the towns Olkusz and Slawkow in the Province of Cracow, Stiller did not arrive in Australia until 1863.[35] Until his death at Dunwich in 1883 he was indeed an active participant in the dugong fishery but, like Hobbs, Stiller was certainly not the founder of the industry.

For many of the early European fishermen the hunting of dugongs, or 'youngan' as they were more commonly known, was part of a broader sphere of activities. In October 1851, for instance, 'a party of three persons, engaged in the fishing trade at Moreton Bay, and chiefly employed in procuring youngan oil and turtle, recently had their attention directed to the value of the pearl oysters that abound in the bay, and in consequence, have for the last few days been procuring those animals on the beach at Calowndna [Caloundra], near Bribie's island'.[36]

Hobbs became involved in the industry from mid-1852, when a shortage of cod liver oil led him to experiment with dugong oil as a substitute.[37] Convinced that dugong oil was actually superior, Hobbs began prescribing the oil to his private patients suffering from stomach disorders.[38] Later it was perceived as a panacea for tuberculosis and a plethora of medical complaints.[39] Others were quick to capitalise on Hobbs' announcement, with Robert Graham of Cleveland advertising for contracts in August 1853. Importantly, Graham was an exporter, conveying mixed consignments direct to London, Liverpool and the Continent.[40] Nevertheless it was Hobbs who attempted to develop the industry on a sound basis. In 1854 he exhibited the oil in Sydney. The following year he embarked on a series of public lectures extolling the virtues of the product and also forwarded a sample to the Paris Exposition, where it was awarded a silver medal. This was also a clever marketing ploy. Along with numerous smaller requests, at least one British pharmaceutical firm ordered 1000 gallons (4,546 litres) at £3 3s. per gallon. This led to Hobbs entering into a partnership with the Brisbane grocer, wine and spirit merchant, Thomas Warry, to establish a commercial dugong fishery in 1856 on St Helena Island.[41]

Notwithstanding Hobbs' obvious entrepreneurial flair, the venture struggled from the beginning. Historian Clem Lack insisted that little capital was invested in the enterprise and due to other commitments neither partner was able to supervise activities.[42] Certainly Hobbs' interests were diverse. Apart from public and private medical duties, he was involved in experimental cotton-growing and the commercial production of mineral water.[43] It was further suggested that, while wages were high, European employees were of intemperate habits.[44] These are valid reasons to account for failure, but they overlook the prevalence of dugongs in Moreton Bay waters and the ability of the animals to modify their behaviour.

In October 1857 it was lamented that, despite orders for dugong oil 'to the extent of £100 or so', the two boats pursuing the animals had only limited success owing to the dugong's 'shy and wary' habits.[45] The following January, Hobbs and Warry fitted out a twenty-ton cutter, with two attached whaleboats, in a bid to increase productivity. Crewed by five Europeans and six Aborigines, the vessel was capable of holding seventy barrels of oil and remaining at sea for periods up to three months. The Aborigines in the whaleboats were harpoonists, and it was this mode of capture which negated success.[46] By September 1858 it was readily apparent that a new strategy was thus required:

> The success of the fishery was, however, very indifferent and not sufficient, I believe, to pay the current expenses. The dugong is so wide-awake a fish as to be a match in most cases even for the stealthy tactics of the blacks. At last nets were thought of, and since they have been employed the fishery has been vastly more productive. The party in the small cutter I have mentioned, since Wednesday last up to yesterday, had caught ten. Generally they seem to secure about two every night. The nets are thrown out in long lines in places frequented by the fish, and they get entangled in the meshes.[47]

Unfortunately, adulterated dugong oil was sold during this period of scarcity in quite substantial quantities. When this became known the price fell considerably.[48] The extent of adulteration was outlined by the *Sydney morning herald* in December 1858:

> During a given period, when there was being sold, in Sydney, fifty gallons weekly, and in Melbourne one hundred gallons weekly, for the space of twelve months, there was little more than one hundred gallons got from the Bay! This was adulteration with a vengeance.[49]

Adulteration of dugong oil was to remain a problem; but Hobbs worked tirelessly throughout 1859 in a bid to restore its reputation and place the industry on a firm footing. In January he was again lecturing in Sydney, this time bringing a preserved dugong foetus, which was displayed 'at the shop of Mr. Elliott, the druggist, in George-street'.[50] In March, the Sydney firm of Redford & Burrell were able to advertise that they were agents for dugong oil manufactured by Hobbs, and it seems clear that the partnership with Warry had now been dissolved.[51] By July 1859 the potential of the oil was being discussed in the prestigious British medical journal *Lancet*, but Hobbs also had formidable competition.[52] Brisbane merchant John McCabe appointed Younger & Son his Sydney agents in February 1859,[53] and began advertising 'genuine Dugong Oil' for both local consumption and export.[54]

Using nets, Hobbs no longer employed Aborigines, but smaller operators now entering the industry continued to rely on their labour.[55] Relations between the two groups were not always amicable. In January 1859 the body of Robert Collins, otherwise known as Bob Hunter, washed ashore at Luggage Point, near the mouth of the Brisbane River. Although badly decomposed, it was found that death had been caused by a tomahawk wound in the head. Collins had set out with two European companions and a number of Aborigines two weeks earlier, to procure dugongs around St Helena Island. No trace of his companions or the boat was found.[56] However, it was known that one of the Aborigines with the party was the notorious 'Dr Ballow', believed to have been responsible for the death of a European named Grant near the Caboolture River two years before. Moreover, it was stated that the Aborigines had a grievance against Collins; a warrant was issued for 'Dr Ballow's' arrest.[57]

Many years later, however, Petrie interviewed 'Billy Dingy', one of the three Aborigines involved in the killings. He told Petrie that the three Europeans had promised the Aborigines, who were accompanied by their wives, transport to Bribie Island. They landed instead at St Helena where the Europeans 'took possession' of the Aboriginal women and ignored the entreaties of the men. 'Billy Dingy' claimed that he subsequently killed the Europeans and dragged their bodies into the water, with the Aborigines making their escape in the boat, which they abandoned at the mouth of the Pine River. It was surmised that the bodies of Collins' companions were eaten by sharks.[58]

The increasing use of nets reduced the dependence on Aboriginal labour as well as inter-racial conflict within the industry. The first use of commercial dugong nets in Moreton Bay has been credited to Fred Foster, but whether he was employed by Hobbs and Warry remains unclear. Later moving north, Foster was operating a primitive dugong 'factory' near Cardwell in 1864.[59] By then, commercial operations were also being conducted in Tin Can Bay near Gympie – which name Raphael Cilento believed was a corruption of Dugong Bay through euphony.[60] In the Maryborough region, dugong fisheries were operating in both Wide and

Hervey bays, while there was another in existence at Rodd's Bay, south of Gladstone.[61] Later, a commerical dugong fishery was also established at Repulse Bay, near Proserpine.[62]

The nets used for the capture of dugongs varied only slightly. Generally manufactured from 1/2-inch manilla rope, they had large meshes diagonally measuring thirty-six inches between knots, a size which became compulsory in 1893 after an amendment to the Queensland Fisheries Act (1887).[63] Their length was in the order of 120 yards but the depth could be anything up to 30 feet. Weighted with anchors at both ends, a cork line ran along the surface, while the lead line kept the net vertical in the water.[64] Usually set at low tide, they were placed across channels at roughly a forty-five degree angle to prevent drift through excessive water pressure. As Welsby explained, even netting frequently drew on Aboriginal expertise to achieve optimum results:

> From [the] torn about condition of the [sea]grass; from the fresh uncovered dark coloured ground; from the ruffled or smooth bed of the passage, the native fisherman will tell you how old the track will be, whether one or more days; and will also tell if it is worth the setting of the net or not.[65]

Operations in Moreton Bay were concentrated around St Helena Island, where extensive seagrass beds allowed dugongs to 'feed and fatten like oxen on the plains; yet unlike them in requiring no stockmen to tail them, no stockyard to confine them, and no driving to the abattoirs'.[66] Despite the analogy with the pastoral industry, no cattle barons were involved here; in the 1870s the manager of the St Helena establishment was none other than a former Newfoundland sealer.[67] After enlisting the aid of the government resident, Captain J.C. Wickham, to obtain new export orders in October 1859, Hobbs faded from the scene.[68] Others soon took his place, but as an export commodity dugong oil had clearly failed to achieve his optimistic expectations. In March 1859, for example, a single case of dugong oil was despatched to London aboard the 'Gladiolus', an insignificant consignment among the vessel's manifest.[69]

In April 1859 McCabe began his endeavours in earnest, advertising that his stores held 'genuine dugong oil for sale, packed ready for exportation'.[70] Local demand was met by Thomas Drew, the Queen Street chemist, whose surburban agents were the grocers Reuben Oliver of North Brisbane and Messrs Peterson & Younger in South Brisbane. According to Drew, 'The wonderful properties of this oil and its superiority over the Cod Liver Oil are so well known and so generally recognised, that any recommendation of it would be superfluous'.[71] The advantage of dugong oil in the treatment of pulmonary complaints and general debilitation was two-fold. First, it contained no iodine and was therefore sweeter and more palatable – 'and does not produce nausea'.[72] Perhaps more importantly, it was considerably cheaper than the imported cod-liver oil.[73]

The upsurge in publicity prompted commercial activity elsewhere along the Queensland coast. In 1860 a dugong fishery was established near Maryborough when Lionel Ching entered into a partnership with F. Bryant and A.G. Crocker. Throughout 1860 and 1861 the Maryborough chemist, A.K. Bruce, sold substantial quantities of dugong oil to buyers in the southern colonies and it is also apparent that he began developing a market for by-products of the fishery.[74]

Nonetheless, commercial operations were primarily concerned with the extraction of oil, 'boiling down' being the usual method. In effect, large sections of butchered dugong were placed within a large boiler three quarters full of pre heated water, and continually stirred as the temperature rose towards the boil. Oil from the rendered flesh floated to the surface where, after cooling, it was either skimmed off or, more commonly, drained through a tap located at the appropriate height on the boiler.[75] It was then filtered through flannel bags and bottled.[76] Though largely sold as a local alternative to cod-liver oil, it was also used as a cooking oil and later for varnishing woodwork.[77] The stearine, a glycerol-based compound present in fats, was retained in the flannel bags during the filtering process and sold to soap-makers for £40 per tonne in the 1860s.[78] Indeed, dugong soap was awarded a medal at London's Great Exhibition in 1862, so well was it received. On the other hand, the highly-acclaimed oil merely received an 'honourable mention' at the same venue.[79]

Another method occasionally used for extracting oil was 'trying-out', whereby the flesh was rendered in its own oil. This was, however, a particularly delicate operation, requiring a very slow fire and extreme care so that the oil did not burn – in which case it was unmarketable.[80] There were minor variations in the process of oil extraction, including the selection of particularly suitable timbers for the fire, and much depended on the quality of the dugong.[81] As A.K. Bruce, the Maryborough chemist found, a demand could also be created for other dugong by-products.

Europeans involved in the industry appear to have followed the Aboriginal example and consumed copious amounts of dugong flesh, a diet which resulted in corpulence.[82] While it was also alleged to restore vigour, with Aborigines taking 'care to rub their persons with the grease',[83] it should not be overlooked that this provided indigenous people with some measure of insulation against the elements.[84]

The by-products of the industry were diverse. When butchering, the hide was first removed from the carcass. Up to one inch thick and 200 pounds in weight when fresh, it was sold for a variety of purposes. Sliced into lengths, the hide was tanned to make leather machine belts that were in considerable demand.[85] Yet another use was found for the tanned hide as vehicular brake blocks,[86] and it was occasionally rendered down to make a highly-digestible jelly for invalids or converted into glue.[87]

With the hide removed, bacon flitches were obtained from the flanks and, smoked or salted, they were a valuable commodity.[88] In 1864 Fred Foster was curing bacon as an adjunct to his dugong fishery at Cardwell in North Queensland.[89] Around 1860 Edward Wilson, editor of the Melbourne *Argus*, commented on dugong bacon he unwittingly sampled while staying at John Cassim's hotel at Cleveland, on the shores of Moreton Bay:

> In its fresh state it is something like tender beef, and salted it very nearly resembled bacon – so nearly, indeed, that I unconsciously ate it at friend Cassim's for bacon, and was rather startled by his assurance afterwards that the morning's rasher consisted of the flesh of 'young-un'.[90]

As late as 1912 dugong bacon could still be readily obtained in many Queensland coastal centres.[91] The remainder of the flesh was comparable to lean beef and, though not praised to the same extent as the bacon, it was occasionally offered for sale. Indeed, in 1906 there was an elaborate, albeit unsuccessful, attempt to market dugong meat as an alternative to beef and mutton in Australia.[92]

Devoid of skull and bones, the head could be cooked and pressed to make a potted brawn 'more rich and delicate in flavour than anything of the kind from ox or pig's head'.[93] Similarly, the flippers and tail flukes were made into a 'capital soup'.[94] Interestingly, Welsby insisted that Stradbroke Island's Nunukul Aborigines discarded the intestines.[95] Writing many years later, Aboriginal author and Stradbroke Island resident, Kath Walker, recalled how the intestines were a prized possession. Cleaned and packed with dugong meat they were eaten as sausages.[96] Walker, later known by her Aboriginal name Oodgeroo, referred to the intestines in the local dialect as 'gumpii' – a name which accords well with 'gumpi' – the locality near Dunwich where Petrie stated the Nunukul Aborigines traditionally captured dugongs.[97]

Adult dugongs are also endowed with tusks. Although they protrude in only a small proportion of females, those of mature males can reach a length of 20 centimetres.[98] How they benefit the animal is not yet fully understood, but they became another useful by-product of the commercial fishery, being polished to make ivory handles for carvery knives.[99] Less successful was an attempt to market the rib-bones, thirty-six in number, as knife handles. More than 500 kilograms of the bones were shipped to London in March 1859, when it was envisaged that the consignment might open 'an advantageous and profitable trade from the dugong fishery'.[100] However, it was found that the cost of production far outweighed the proceeds.[101]

Dugong bones were nevertheless found to be ideal for making the charcoal used in the refining of raw sugar.[102] Therein lies one of two important links between the dugong fishery and early sugar-growing in Queensland. As late as 1912, Marburg mill in southern Queensland was still using animal charcoal for refining, but whether or not they were dugong bones is not clear.[103] Far more certain is that a number of pioneer sugar-growers around Moreton Bay employed local Aborigines to procure dugongs as food for their Melanesian indentured labourers. This served a dual purpose, the meat being inexpensive and nutritious.[104]

One of the most damaging aspects of the dugong fishery was the refusal by all relevant parties to implement minimum size limitations. Juvenile animals were readily taken and, indeed, many preferred the flesh of calves to that of mature dugongs.[105] Strong bonding also allowed fishermen to boast that if a juvenile or one of a pair were taken, the parents or partner would soon be ensnared in the same location.[106] Although dugongs have a life-span of around seventy years, females do not give birth until over ten years.[107] Thus the loss of a number of juvenile animals almost certainly had a profound impact on resident populations.

Government inaction suggests that the dugong fishery contributed little to colonial revenue and was therefore largely ignored. In 1862 for instance the immigrant vessel, 'Erin-Go-Bragh', arrived in Moreton Bay with 'fever of a typhoid character' raging aboard.[108] St Helena Island was quickly taken over as a temporary quarantine station and the proprietor of the Dugong fishery at this time, H. Wenham, was refused access to his facilities. The fact that no warning had been given prompted Wenham to protest vigorously in the local press against the government's action.[109] Moreover the Reverend Dr John Dunmore Lang, who was an ardent promoter of Queensland's potential, made no mention of the commercial dugong fishery in 1861, merely referring to the importance of the animal in indigenous economies.[110]

The fishery certainly experienced a severe downturn in the 1860s, when it was discovered that shark oil was being substituted for that of the marine mammal.[111] As sharks were frequently ensnared in dugong nets it was not surprising that unscrupulous operators would eventually attempt to market an otherwise worthless commodity. In vain did merchants such as Henry Hockings of South Brisbane advertise their stocks as 'unadulterated' and 'warranted genuine';[112] once exposed, it not only resulted in the total cancellation of export orders, but also the exodus of all but one professional fisherman from Moreton Bay. By 1869, largely due to poor marketing techniques, even local outlets closed and all commercial activity temporarily ceased.[113] Yet it is remarkable that the substitution of shark oil was ever detected. Modern chemical analysis has confirmed that the vitamin content in both oils is virtually the same. Shark oil also offered an important economic advantage in being cheaper to produce.[114]

Hopes for a resurgence were nevertheless kept alive, despite the obvious signs that dugong numbers in Moreton Bay were beginning to fall. Rather than resulting from commercial activity, it was suggested that this was a consequence of increased boating traffic.[115] There were also economic considerations by 1871:

> The great obstacle to the developing of this industry has been that were an individual or company to expend the requisite capital in advertising the oil, and creating a sale for it, a rival company could at once invest its capital in the procuring of the oil, and reap all the benefits arising from the enterprise of the original company. So potent is this objective, that it has, up to this time, prevented the outlay of capital in this direction, so that, as we have already stated, no progress has been made in this industry in a space of twenty years.[116]

No doubt Hobbs would have readily agreed, and it is also apparent that throughout the 1870s and 1880s the dugong fishery functioned as an adjunct to other marine enterprises involving only small-scale operators. In view of later comments by Welsby that the dugong fishery was a winter pursuit,[117] it is interesting to note that this was not apparent in November 1871:

> The season for dugong fishing in and about Moreton Bay is just commencing, and considering the high favour in which dugong oil is held by the medical profession here, and the attention

> which it is attracting in England, it may be reasonably expected that the capture of the dugong will soon be developed into an important industry. The first of the season was caught a few days ago by men in the employment of Mr. Winstone, of Edward-street, and it yielded four and a-half gallons of excellent oil.[118]

The industry did not flourish, and it appears that no substantial catches were taken until late in the decade, when dugong fishing became a means to help finance Queensland's first Aboriginal reserve on Bribie Island in 1877. For their rations, the Aboriginal inhabitants were coerced into catching fish and manufacturing 'dugong, shark, and stingaree oils', with harpoons being provided for the hunt.[119] As Shirleene Robinson shows, the first Bribie Island reserve lasted only two years. During the following decade, Europeans dominated the industry but, once again, results were meagre. There can be little doubt that dugong numbers in Moreton Bay had been seriously depleted through previous commercial activities.

During a two-month period in 1884, for instance, only six dugongs were taken in Moreton Bay, despite being worth around £6 each.[120] There was also another threat with which dugongs were now forced to contend. The Moreton Bay oyster industry experienced considerable growth in the late nineteenth century, with dredges being introduced to procure the molluscs from submerged banks. This resulted in the destruction of many seagrass beds from siltation, thereby reducing the available dugong habitat.[121] By the late 1880s it was abundantly clear that government intervention was necessary to ensure the survival of the species in Queensland waters.

Prepared by Queensland's inspector of fisheries, Captain W. Fison,[122] a government proclamation in August 1888 prohibited the capture of dugongs in Queensland waters for a period of two years, commencing on 1 September 1888.[123] When this protection was removed in 1890 it was evident that dugong numbers had substantially increased, and this was aided by

*4.1 Dugong fishing in Queensland c.1886 (JOL)*

very little commercial activity. Throughout 1891, for instance, only three dugongs were taken for commercial purposes in Moreton Bay.[124] Dugongs had also modified their behaviour. As reported in January 1892:

> There is still a large herd of them in the neighbourhood of Moreton Island, between that and Mud Island, and these may be seen almost any day. They number 300 or 400, and roam about in this quiet and undisturbed place ... and as none have been harpooned for a number of years they will now allow a boat amongst them with perfect indifference; will even swim up within a few yards of it in an inquisitive sort of way, but they will not be taken by a net. They simply come up to it, take a look, and then sheer off in exactly the same way that a bullock would at a fence. It is only those that come in from the South Passage from the open ocean that will blunder into nets because they are wild ones and know no better.[125]

Presumably it was these 'wild ones' which allowed three separate fishing parties to escalate commercial activities during 1892. Based at Amity Point on Stradbroke Island, they consisted of one European crew led by the late superintendent of Dunwich Benevolent Asylum, James Hamilton, and two Aboriginal crews, one of which was headed by an Aborigine known as 'Colly Blow', while the other worked under an arrangement with 'Fernendez, a well-known fisherman'. Between May and October 1892, these parties captured at least forty-six dugongs.[126] Dugong oil was again readily available on the local market, but 'Brainerd Skinner, the meat preserver, and everything else preserver, of Brisbane' was also encouraging the consumption of dugong flesh.[127]

Fison, however, was still not convinced that dugong numbers in Moreton Bay had reached a sustainable level and argued once more for legislative protection. This was agreed, with a two-year closed season becoming effective from the beginning of 1893.[128] Protection abruptly terminated in June 1893, a decision which may have turned on the arrival of large dugong herds in Moreton Bay following the devastating floods which occurred in south east Queensland the previous February.[129] An explanation for this apparent migratory behaviour was not forthcoming for almost a century. Importantly, the Queensland government finally began regulating the dugong fishery in 1893. Under the plenipotentiary of the inspector of fisheries, a number of measures were introduced, including licensing:

> Any fisherman who takes or kills more dugong than can be utilised before waste accrues or the catch becomes unfit for use, shall forfeit his licence .... Every fisherman shall erect his smokehouse and keep his gear on one of the numbered allotments in the fishing reserve at Amity Point [Stradbroke Island]. Any person using a harpoon or implement of any kind other than a net of 36-inch mesh for taking dugong shall be liable to a penalty of twenty pounds, and shall in addition be debarred from fishing during the remainder of the season. Every person employed in taking, curing, or converting its fat into oil, shall pay an annual licence fee of ten shillings, and the owner of every boat employed in taking dugong shall, in addition, pay an annual licence fee of one pound.[130]

Henceforth, commercial activity in Moreton Bay was to be restricted to the period between June and September, a condition which Welsby considered unnecessary as fishermen themselves had confined their activities to those cooler months due to higher oil yields and the reduced risk of heat and flies putrefying dugong carcasses.[131] It certainly made sense, but dugong fishing was in fact carried out from September to March.[132] With the dugong breeding season extending from September to January, such a restriction, whether self-imposed or legislative, was clearly a wise precaution.[133] Nonetheless, the discrepancy between Welsby and earlier accounts may itself be indicative of learned response, environmental factors or migratory behaviour.

Dugong certainly do appear to have roamed widely. In March 1795 the Judge-Advocate of NSW, David Collins, recorded the discovery of skull fragments at Botany Bay which Captain William Paterson, 'the only naturalist in the country', identified as belonging to a 'Manatee'.[134] Subsequent skeletal fragments found at various localities along the NSW coast led mammalogist Ellis Troughton to assert that the range of the dugong had once extended as far south as Sydney.

From the presence of Aboriginal cut marks on many of these bones, Troughton then concluded that Aboriginal hunting activity had exterminated dugong in these southern regions.[135] Yet, dugongs still periodically stray into New South Wales waters. In 1959, for example, a solitary dugong washed ashore at Port Hacking, just south of Sydney, triggered considerable interest.[136] There can be little doubt that the intermittent arrival of dugongs provided a rare feast for coastal Aboriginal groups in NSW.

The reason for this southern movement was perhaps revealed in 1992, when severe flooding destroyed over 1000 square kilometres of seagrass habitat in Hervey Bay, near Maryborough. Within months, dugongs remaining in the region were found to be emaciated and many deaths occurred.[137] Concomitantly, dugong numbers in Moreton Bay to the south showed a considerable increase, while four dugong carcasses washed ashore near Sydney. The latter had evidently travelled too far south, while those in Moreton Bay had successfully relocated.[138] Similar environmental factors may have led to the presence of large dugong herds, one of which was estimated to be 'three miles in length', in Moreton Bay following the floods of 1893.[139]

By 1896, dugongs were again scarce in Moreton Bay, and despite 'oil being worth from 12s 6d to 15s per gallon', little commercial activity took place.[140] It was not until 1901 that yet another serious attempt was made to place the industry on a firm footing with the establishment of a new fishery station at Amity Point.[141] It was here that Professor H. Dexler of Prague University began compiling data on dugong anatomy and biology.[142] While Dexler was able to publish a number of important papers between 1902 and 1912, the fishery itself failed.[143] Not that it deterred others. Between 1901 and 1910 a series of attempts was subsequently made at the same location but, at best, only moderate results were achieved.[144] In 1908, for instance, seventy bottles of oil were obtained for the Franco-British Exhibition in London, though it does not appear to have elicited anywhere near the same level of response that was shown over half a century earlier.[145]

Lack argued that the advanced ages of fishermen with essential knowledge of dugong fishing limited commercial activity in the twentieth century. As well, younger men showed little interest in acquiring the skill necessary to prepare the oil.[146] It could be added that Aboriginal expertise, on which the industry had depended so heavily, was also virtually non-existent. Nor should it be overlooked that it was an expensive industry to enter, with no guarantee of recovery costs. As pointed out in 1912, a dugong net alone was worth £40, while substantial expenditure was required for the fishing vessel, smokehouse for curing bacon, boilers for extracting oil, and various other expenses necessary to carry out fishing.[147]

The outbreak of the First World War in 1914 did revive the industry to some extent when supplies of cod-liver and other essential oils normally imported were severely curtailed, resulting in local substitutes being eagerly sought.[148] By 1917, dugong oil was again readily available, with one Queensland fisherman netting seven animals in as many days.[149] On the national level, however, the dugong fishery remained a 'minor' industry of little consequence.[150]

Hopes were nevertheless kept alive that the industry could be resurrected. In July 1920 a dugong display figured prominently in the Fisheries Court being prepared for the Brisbane Exhibition:

> A frozen dugong weighing about 6 cwt. will also be a centre of attraction .... Close by the dugong are samples of the many commodities of great commercial value that it yields. Leather and oil are the foremost, but interesting also is the dugong bone, the handsome ivory nature of which is excellently shown. The Inspector of Fisheries [J.H. Stevens] points out that the dugong is a really remarkable mammal of the greatest commercial value. There is no waste in it. All its products are of use, and enthusiasts are confident that the dugong products industry will gain important proportions in Queensland.[151]

Few responded, however. Though Bert Levinge was supplying dugong bacon from his base at Amity Point on North Stradbroke Island in August 1923,[152] by the end of the decade there were grave fears for the survival of the species.[153] Intermittent hunting nevertheless continued elsewhere along the Queensland coast until the mid-1970s, by which time it was restricted solely to Torres Strait and was once again entirely dependent on the indigenous people.[154] Indeed, while the dugong had received legislative protection in Queensland from March 1969, Torres Strait Islanders were virtually forced to appease the limited commercial demand.[155] Conversely, the hunting of dugongs for traditional purposes was drawing increasing criticism from marine biologists, many of whom considered this to be the greatest threat now facing the marine mammal.[156]

On the other side of the ledger it cannot be denied that from time immemorial the species provided Queensland's indigenous coastal communities with an easily sustainable resource; commercial exploitation was a major factor in it becoming unsustainable. Indigenous hunting also fades into insignificance when compared with environmental despoliation and shark-meshing, both of which have had a devastating impact on dugong populations.[157]

An obvious inability to counter such problems reveals that Queensland, and by extrapolation Australia, has thus far exhibited little initiative to 'lead the world' in the preservation of marine mammals. It requires considerably more than rhetoric and legislation to guarantee their survival. Nor should it be overlooked that initial European settlement in Australia was largely built on the exploitation of marine mammals.[158] As a maritime nation, Australia clearly has a moral obligation to safeguard these animals. That it can also be economically viable is shown by the public interest in 'whale watching', already generating around $50 million dollars per year in tourism.[159] Whales provide spectacle and, as Bruce Davidson demonstrated, visibility has a high priority with politicians – even if large animals have to be imported into the country. For dugongs, the lack of visibility, of spectacle, has thus far worked to their detriment.

*Chapter 5*

# 'Nothing beyond myself and Mr Watkins': James Hamilton and the Dunwich Benevolent Asylum 1865-85

**Joseph Goodall**

Tuesday 29 July 1884: In committee room number one of Queensland's Parliament House, four members of the Legislative Council were meeting in a committee for the first time. The agenda: an inquiry into the management of the Dunwich Benevolent Asylum, initiated by its recently appointed chairman, the outspoken William Henry Walsh. With him were Andrew Thynne, George King and Postmaster-General Charles Mein. They met seven times between then and 27 August when they presented a preliminary report, and on another ten occasions until 19 December. At various times other members were present: Dr Kevin O'Doherty, William Graham and William Power.

Included in the committee meetings were three trips to Dunwich to inspect the benevolent asylum and talk to people there, although the chief witnesses were brought to the committee in Brisbane. If they arrived on one of the sixteen times the committee did not have a quorum, their attendance was wasted. Sometimes Walsh used the time informally with the witness to gain a greater insight into the benevolent asylum, but more often than not there was nothing for it but to call the day off.

What prompted the inquiry? Walsh had moved for it in the Legislative Council in July on the basis that the benevolent asylum had been subjected to no scrutiny and no controls over the years. Perhaps the committee could find ways of improving the management of the institution? There was a general murmur of agreement: one councillor had visited Dunwich and not heard any complaints, while finding the superintendent a 'humane man'; another praised the improvements which had taken place, though an inquiry would do no harm 'and might do much good'. It was pointed out that no complaints had been received but there still might be abuses.[1] So, in a general atmosphere of polite goodwill, the committee of inquiry was established.

Notwithstanding the honeyed words in the previous July, the findings of the reports were hardly stumbled on by accident. Criticisms abounded and letters were written by inmates to Premier Samuel Griffith in June. Walsh hinted to the Legislative Council one of his own purposes: the fear that some inmates were undeservedly living off charity at Dunwich. As soon as he had established that there was no regulation or supervision of the asylum he started to find ways of hunting the freeloaders out.

When news of the inquiry got around to the inmates at Dunwich, a small rush of complaints emerged. Some were concerned with the quantity and quality of food, others the treatment of inmates. There were accusations that Superintendent James Hamilton ran a store to sell items to the inmates which were theirs by right, or the items were government property, or government property was sold to people outside the institution. It was alleged that Hamilton maintained, at government expense, inmates who had left the asylum to do work for him; that he appropriated money belonging to people who had died; and that he had claimed a pony on Peel Island that belonged to someone else.

As a result, in August, Walsh received permission for the committee to report from time to time and in December he presented an interim report.[2] The committee, he explained, had found 'their labours much more arduous than they expected, and to some extent more painful than they expected'.[3] The final report was even more ominous: 'Grave and serious abuses have crept into the administration which demand the immediate attention of the Government'.[4] The completed report recommended:

1. The removal of all female inmates to a separate and distinct institution not situated in the vicinity of the asylum, and under separate control.

2. That the management of the Asylum be placed in the hands of an experienced medical practitioner.

3. The increase of the accommodation for the inmates, to be especially available in the day-time and in inclement weather; and the connection by covered ways of the several wards with the mess-rooms.

4. The making of such regulations as will provide for the more effective inspection of the institution, for its internal good order and government, and for the recovery from the inmates or their relatives of some contribution towards the expense of their maintenance.[5]

The recommendations were symbolic of the attitude that existed throughout the benevolent asylum's existence: the rhetoric of pity painted over a belief that their destitute condition reflected inmates' personal faults and the suspicion that they may be getting a free ride at public expense. Historian Ross Fitzgerald paints a picture of Queensland's ethos of development at any price.[6] The strong prospered, the weak were unsympathetically pushed to one side. In 1891 the *Brisbane courier* acknowledged that people were forced into Dunwich through economic problems: 'It arises from the industrial distress which tells first on the aged, the infirm and the disabled'. It was still their own fault: 'It would probably be found that drink and unthrift were the largest factors in bringing men to the point of helplessness in which Dunwich is the only resort'.[7] It would not do to make life at the benevolent asylum too easy for people who, through their own failings, had not managed to keep up with the march of progress.

Hamilton was in the firing line. If the accusations were true he could be found incompetent, possibly even criminally responsible. Even if they were partially believed he would at least remain under suspicion, and an opportunity would be found to dismiss him. If the fault lay elsewhere, he, as superintendent, would be held responsible, a scapegoat for his superiors. After seventeen years in the position he could not claim inexperience, the abuses of a previous incumbent, or lack of time to effect change. He would have little defence. At that stage Hamilton and the Dunwich Benevolent Asylum were as one. In the distant past there had been other superintendents at Dunwich, but they had not lasted. Before Dunwich, the benevolent asylum was located in the Brisbane Hospital as a ward, which the hospital committee had been trying to unload.

The Benevolent Asylum Ward Act of 1861 funded hospitals to set aside wards as benevolent asylums. In the General Hospital (once the convict hospital in George Street) the wards provided 'indoor relief'.[8] Neither the accommodation nor the money was adequate and the hospital committee continually asked for more funds. In 1862 the benevolent wards cost £1200, the total estimate for the entire hospital.[9] In 1862 the hospital asked that the government take over the benevolent wards.[10] In 1863 the hospital committee resolved 'that the Brisbane Hospital and Benevolent Asylum be dissociated, and be converted into separate and distinct institutions'.[11]

The colonial government hesitated. They were considering a far more sweeping solution to the hospital's many problems, of which the cost and overcrowding of the benevolent wards was only one. They planned a completely new hospital, with a benevolent asylum as a separate building.[12] The only difficulty was that the hospital was already overcrowded. 'At the present moment there is not a vacant bed for either a male or a female patient, or for a Benevolent Asylum inmate'.[13] As a temporary measure it was agreed to house the benevolent wards in government accommodation using government staff, freeing personnel and space for hospital patients.

So the benevolent asylum passed into the hands of the Immigration Department, who had beds and people to deal with numbers of people who needed only accommodation but not medical care. The most extensive facilities were at the quarantine station located at Dunwich on Stradbroke Island since 1850. For another dozen years tents were the order of the day, until 1862 when a small complex of wood and brick buildings was proposed.[14] By 1865 the quarantine station buildings were described as 'five in number, stand[ing] in a line fronting the beach ... the superintendent's house ... and at back a large store room, cooking kitchen and offices. A large brick building ... which was the hospital. Next were two wooden buildings about twenty yards apart and a third about a hundred yards away'.[15]

There was a slight delay in getting the asylum inmates out to Dunwich, due to the 'Hannah More' occupying the quarantine station and the necessary clean-up. On 13 May 1865 the benevolent asylum moved in – at least in part.[16] It was clear that the arrangement was not intended to be permanent as seen in a letter from the surgeon which referred to the 'temporary station – Dunwich'.[17] It was also clear that the benevolent asylum remained a hospital responsibility. Medicine, clothes and supplies were to be provided by the hospital 'out of funds placed in their hands for that purpose'.[18] However things were not quite as clear-cut as they first appeared. The buildings remained in government hands and staff were government employees, not hospital people. Moreover, Dr Jonathan Labatt, the surgeon, who thought he was employed by the government, found he was responsible to the hospital committee when he tried to apply for leave.[19]

The weakness in the scheme was that the quarantine station might at any time be pressed back into its original use, as it was three months later. A deal was arranged after some last minute negotiations that cut the time so fine that the sixty inmates were left, wet and cold, on the 'Platypus' moored in the Brisbane River, with nowhere else to go. The hospital accepted the women and children while the men were to be housed at the old Commissariat Stores building deemed unsuitable back in 1858. From the children's placement at the Green Hills Fever Hospital grew the colony's orphanage.[20]

In October 1865 the quarantine station fell vacant and in November the benevolent asylum moved back there.[21] In December it returned to Brisbane, this time in the old immigration department building on the south side of the river, a structure so dilapidated that complaints from a subsequent group of immigrants shamed the government into putting up a new building as quickly as possible.[22]

For most of 1866 the benevolent asylum remained in Brisbane while an increasing number of inmates arrived from regional hospitals: Ipswich, Gayndah, Warwick and Toowoomba. Meanwhile the Select Committee on the Hospitals of the Colony brought down its report, recommending 'that a benevolent institution for the whole colony be erected at Dunwich, or some other suitable locality, to which the benevolent patients from the outlying districts should be forwarded'.[23]

This was Hamilton's first contact with the asylum. Born in Suffolk, England, in 1825 he had originally emigrated to Victoria in about 1850, found his way to Queensland and set up business as a lime burner near Wynnum.[24] He was appointed wardsman in February 1866 under immigration agent John McDonnell as acting superintendent although McDonnell himself was not resident at the asylum.

Towards the end of the year Hamilton left the benevolent asylum and was posted to St Helena Island, where plans for a quarantine station were well under way. Between 29 October and 4 November an advance party under Hamilton's replacement, John McFarland and his wife, went out to Dunwich to prepare once again for occupation by the benevolent asylum. Later in November, the inmates, numbering between eighty and ninety, moved in. Whether it was the intention to accept the recommendation to make Dunwich the benevolent asylum site is not clear, as £5000 had been set aside to erect buildings at the new hospital on Bowen Bridge Road.[25] However, there was no need for quarantine for some considerable time and the colonial government found itself in financial hardship: the asylum stayed put.

In May 1867 the Colonial Secretary's Office assumed complete control. McDonnell was replaced by Henry Nicol who soon died and in turn was replaced by Richard Watson in July.[26] At the beginning of 1868, Watson and the McFarlands were replaced by James and Brigid Hamilton, no longer needed at St Helena which was now to be used as a prison.[27] When Brigid subsequently died, James remarried. In 1871 George Watkins was appointed as an assistant.

Finally in 1874, with Peel Island declared the quarantine station, the benevolent asylum became permanently located at Dunwich.[28] In January there were 97 inmates living there, of a total number of 159 over the year. The 62 admissions comprised 55 men and 7 women, 38 percent of the annual total. Sixty-two also left: 18 deaths – 11 percent of the total inmates and 44 discharged – 27 percent of the total. Full-time staff remained at 3. Weekly reports were confined to bare statistics while the needs of good order and health were served by a visiting justice and visiting surgeon respectively.

So it was in 1884 when Walsh's committee started its inquiry. There were still three staff, now supervising an average of 381 inmates per week and a total of 663 in the year, though inmates took on a range of responsibilities including wardsmen, nurses, cooks, growing food and tending animals, even teaching Hamilton's children. A total of 663 admissions outweighed the 257 inmates who left (179 discharged, 8 sent to the Woogaroo Mental Asylum, 70 died) ensuring that the growth of the last decade continued. 1884 and 1902 shared the record for the number of admissions, although admissions in 1902 was greater than the total number relieved.

The average age of inmates was sixty-two but this arithmetical mean concealed a wide range. The annual report for 1888 showed 6 people being under twenty years old, a further 17 under forty and 164 between forty and sixty (almost 40 percent of the total).

To accommodate inmates, wards were built progressively along the ridge of land which the quarantine station had first occupied and around the vegetable gardens further inland. There was never any spare space. The best that could be expected was adequate for the demand, but frequent requests went in for more wards. The women's division was next to the superintendent's quarters. A variety of works was built or recommended to cater for the growth in numbers including a cook house, bake house, mess room and outhouses. Such was the rate of growth that these buildings quickly became inadequate. Though the need for a bathroom and laundry was raised in 1872 they were not constructed until 1880. At the same time a kitchen and bakery were built. By 1884, however, they were too small. In 1878 water was being supplied, but in 1884 Hamilton warned that the quantity was insufficient and in the following year with a drought in progress, it failed altogether. Apart from the messroom built in 1871 there was no day room. Inmates were turned out of their wards in the morning and not allowed back until evening, virtually the only shelter being the verandahs. This state of affairs was pointed out by Hamilton but there was no response.[29]

When Hamilton, his assistant George Watkins, Visiting Surgeon Dr Wray, and Visiting Justice Colonel Ross were examined at the inquiry it became clear that no instructions had ever been issued for the administration of the asylum. Letters of appointment said very little. Watkins admitted that he guessed what his job was supposed to be by 'the very name of my office'.[30]

*5.1 Preserved ward, Dunwich Benevolent Asylum (AHC)*

Nor were there any regulations by which Hamilton could govern the benevolent asylum. They probably continued to use the regulations prepared when the asylum was still part of the hospital in 1861.[31] As early as 1867 the first superintendent, McDonnell, asked for an act of parliament to regulate the benevolent asylum and was told that it existed and the regulations he really needed were on the way.[32]

They were still on their way in 1871, when the Inspector of Public Institutions reported that 'Regulations are in course of revision, and will shortly be submitted for approval'. Nothing happened.[33] In 1874 Hamilton made another appeal: 'At present the rule is personal and arbitrary'.[34] He submitted regulations for approval in 1877, almost identical to those of 1861 and therefore possibly a resubmission of those referred to by Manning in 1871. Despite the support of Visiting Justice Barron, the result was the same – nothing happened.[35]

The request for rules backed by some sort of authority was instigated to deal with troublesome inmates. The situation was further complicated by the fact that the colonial under secretary in Brisbane admitted inmates but the superintendent in Dunwich discharged them at their request. As Dunwich was a voluntary institution, inmates could not be forced to remain there. With no rules to be broken, there were no grounds for dismissing inmates, although in practice it was possible. Hamilton made short work of one inmate who had been the bane of the McFarlands' lives when they were responsible for the asylum in 1867. His exploits included following a woman into the privy where he 'closed the door, raised her clothes and put his hand on her person'. She screamed and hit him with her wooden crutch. As Mrs McFarland responded to the commotion, she saw the assailant running away 'with his pants down and his person exposed'.[36] The following year he climbed into the women's ward in the middle of the night – responding to an invitation, he said. Hamilton, newly appointed, had him out of Dunwich forthwith.[37]

Other cases of 'disorder' were not so clear-cut. Elizabeth Melville, who featured at the 1884 inquiry, ran away twice and continually applied to Hamilton to be discharged. She wrote letters and pestered visitors. Finally she left: 'Woman Melville gone off this morning I believe to Amity Point to try to get up in a boat from there', wrote Hamilton to the under secretary.

Hopefully: 'Do you want me to follow her and bring her back?' 'Yes' was Gray's laconic reply.[38] Melville's problems were interpreted as alcoholic and menopausal, causing major disruptions to her family, but little sympathy was shown for her difficulties. The approach to dealing with her focused on 'obedience' and 'misbehaviour'. The process by which her family enticed her to go to Dunwich by promising she could return home if things did not work out and then reneging, forcing her to go back to Dunwich on Christmas Eve, was never considered as contributing to her state of mind at the asylum. After months of continual agitation and conflict she ended her days at Woogaroo Mental Asylum.

Regulations could also deal with two groups of inmates who were seen as a drain on the public purse. The first group was those people capable of paying for their keep, either because they or their relatives had money, or because they could earn something. A blind inmate, William Townson, was capable of earning fourteen shillings a week by making halters if he had the materials. Unfortunately, Hamilton explained, he did not have the authority to lay hands on Townson's income. Another man made some money by selling 'matches, tobacco, lollies and biscuits'. Most, however, did nothing. Hamilton was keen to find work for them (and accept their income).[39] In addition he advocated the hunting down of relatives who could contribute to inmates' board, or seeking out their bank accounts. Of course, he pointed out, this would require legislation.[40] Hamilton produced a list of these people, along with those who in his opinion should not even be in the benevolent asylum. His comments included:

> An able-bodied woman who should be able to support herself.
>
> A very bad character and frequently in gaol.
>
> Has grown up children.
>
> Somewhat defective sight but not sufficient to prevent him supporting himself.
>
> Paralysis. Has wife and children in Toowoomba and I believe able to support him.
>
> Admitted with £13-£14 cash.

Hamilton followed this up with 'List of blind inmates who might be taught suitable trades &c, to assist them to support themselves'.[41] In this he echoed the sentiments of most of the officials who appeared at the inquiry, a belief which persisted over the years. In 1889 Theodore Unmack advocated to parliament their wholesale dismissals: 'Many of them were there from the effects of drink and are their own worst enemies'.[42] Matthew Reid MLA referred to the inmates during the economic crisis of 1893 as 'a burden on the state'.[43] On the face of it there were people who seemed to have nothing wrong with them: inebriates, tuberculosis sufferers and diabetics for example. There was a time when the benevolent asylum housed people looking for work but this was impractical at remote Dunwich.

Others had more obvious disabilities: epilepsy, dementia, cancer, missing limbs or physical deformities. They were the ones who 'deserved' to be there. Least deserving were those who were proving problematic to the administration. One young man, a diabetic, was accused of behaviour probably associated with hunger as a reason for discharging him:

> He robbed my house at night, robbed the huts, robbed his fellow inmates in the wards, robbed the gardens, sucked the quieter cows at night ….[44]

Most problematic were the inmates, like the occupants of the 'dirty ward', who were obviously so incapable of looking after themselves and therefore could not be discharged. They were also socially unacceptable for reasons ranging from not bathing to masturbating, but did not do anything illegal enough for them to be sent to gaol.

The admission registers and the application forms received from potential inmates show a consistently unhappy life pattern. Elizabeth Smith had the dubious distinction of coming to

Dunwich for its first use as quarantine station in 1850 aboard the 'Emigrant', and returning fifteen years later for its first use as a benevolent asylum. She was by then sixty-six years old and widowed. After she had been some time in service, her husband had tried his luck on the diggings but died. She went to New Zealand but things did not work out. Now the Brisbane Hospital had done all they could for her but she was suffering from paralysis. So to the benevolent asylum she went.[45]

James McCloskey, native of Ireland, came to Australia fifty years previously without his wife. He lost track of his son. He was a seventy-three year old illiterate itinerant labourer on the Darling Downs who now suffered from 'old age and debility'.[46] Gympie Hospital sent 'A boy aged 14 years (an imbecile).... He is at present an inmate of the Hospital. His father has been an inmate of the Woogaroo Asylum for the last ten years and his mother is unable to support him'.[47]

John Brockett, fifty-two, was a bridge builder on the Logan railway, with a wife in the Lunatic Asylum, no children or assets, but with rheumatism. He was applying for admission after a month in the Brisbane Hospital.[48] Another man, single as many were, was a Maryborough resident and stationer, who was in Brisbane Hospital suffering from heart disease. At thirty-five he had been in the colony for six months and was destitute.[49]

The last word should go to Dr Patrick Smith, who would take up duty as medical superintendent at the end of 1885: 'My first impression with regard to the inmates are that they are well fed, decently clothed and that not many of them are physically able to earn their living outside'. Later he observed: 'most are not fit for hard work', although they could take on some light duties.[50] After eleven years in which he had time to reconsider his first impressions, following numerous attempts to get productive labour from inmates, he still concluded that 'the institution is principally occupied by those for whom it is intended'. Furthermore all of the inmates under forty years of age had identifiable medical conditions.[51]

Subsequent to the inquiry, an attempt was made to weed out the freeloaders and extract money from the secretly wealthy. The entire operation was, however, unsuccessful – as it would be on future occasions when attempts were made to act on allegations. In the debate on the Public Charitable Institutions Management bill in 1885, Henry Jordan showed a jaundiced view of filial ties:

> In common life it was really wonderful to see how children would allow their parents to almost starve, and how fathers and mothers would not look after their children, and he was exceedingly glad that they would be compelled to do so.

Jordan's colleague, John Donaldson, regarded a person getting into Dunwich as fraudulent if any member of his or her family could pay something. Accordingly, when someone applied for admission, investigations were initiated to ensure that neither the applicant nor members of the family had any assets. If the money was there, they could be forced to pay.

After further vigorous debate, siblings were exempted from payment.[52] With the backing of the new act and after two years of trying, the Colonial Secretary admitted that, 'It was difficult to get at those who would not pay. The law provided for it but it was very hard to put it into practice'.[53]

It seems to have escaped everybody that Dunwich was a last resort which people did their best to avoid. Inmates lived in overcrowded wards, with nothing to do but wait for the next routine meal. Contact between men and women was limited. The attraction of walks in the bush and fishing off the jetty paled after a while. For all its beauty, Stradbroke Island was remote. There was little chance of visitors from home in Brisbane and virtually none if home had been elsewhere in Queensland. If people had the money or could get the support for their disabilities, they stayed well away from Dunwich.

There were some (whom the inquiry stimulated to action) who spoke up against real or perceived wrongs. Allegations were raised of ill treatment to inmates. Hamilton, it was also claimed, interfered with the mail, pilfered money from the pockets of deceased inmates and even laid claim to a pony by stating that it had died. He sold government stores to inmates and outsiders, or had inmates work for him. He was given or took a wide range of official duties. He was a justice of the peace, and the visiting justice, Colonel Ross, supported Hamilton in the event of a conflict with inmates, on one occasion haranguing them for their approach:

> I'm an old soldier man: I'm a man and I like man to man: If you gave me your complaints I'd have taken them down to the Colonial Secretary. But there is some underhand work going on here! There are some mean men here! Why don't you come to me if you have any complaints instead of writing anonymous communications to the papers? You're a mean lot of men![54]

A lack of independent judgement was also shown by Visiting Surgeon Charles Wray, giving rise to a situation in which inmates' deaths were not explained. He visited once a week and could get out to Dunwich if there was an emergency – but there never was. In the event of a death of a patient under his care he prepared a certificate at his next visit. If a patient whom he had not seen at his previous visit died, he relied on the notes made by Hamilton in the register, 'if he was a patient under my charge'. Otherwise Wray would not certify death in the usual form – but he never held a post mortem nor an inquiry into cause of a death.[55] In other words, the doctor made himself dependent on the information of the supervisor of the institution, who did not have the medical training to elicit what had happened, what the medical symptoms were and whether medical instructions had been followed. 'There is nothing beyond myself and Mr Watkins,' asserted Hamilton confidently.

When inmates died, it was likely that Hamilton presided at their burials. The catholic priest, Father Joseph Canali, explained that having Dunwich as part of the Logan parish was unworkable. Yet, having been placed under his control, an inmate even stated that in the event of a burial 'it would be impossible' for Canali to officiate.

A carpenter, John Simpson, was sent to Dunwich to do some work. While he was there an assistant was sent to help him. The man arrived with a letter of introduction addressed to Simpson and asked George Watkins for the foreman. 'I am the foreman and master at the present time, Mr Hamilton being in town', Watkins replied as he opened the letter. A few days later Hamilton discharged the assistant carpenter although he was employed by the Works Department rather than Hamilton. Inmates told Simpson that the opening of other people's mail was common practice.[56]

This minor incident reveals a lot about the way Hamilton and Watkins perceived their position of dominance at Dunwich. Watkins opened the letter as acting head of the institution; it was an expectation that correspondence in government institutions goes 'through the manager'. It was also an expectation that outsiders sent to do a job should not interfere with the workings of the institution; but it was obvious Simpson had considerable contact with the inmates and passed on their complaints. To ensure good order and management, Hamilton and Watkins considered it their right to monitor communication to and from inmates, a practice that was not confined to Dunwich or to the nineteenth century. No matter who it was – worker, visitor or inmate – Hamilton was totally in control. His requests for rules were not so motivated by a wish for structure as to legitimise his power.

Simpson also accused Hamilton of giving him private work while on government pay, and of' having him use government-owned timber to make items for himself. To support this he showed copies of his diary to the committee.[57]

Two inmates confronted George Thirkill, manager of the nearby oyster lease, and then made a written complaint to Visiting Justice Ross. They claimed that Hamilton was selling him government stores. There was evidently quite a lot of commerce going on, with inmates operating stores or growing food which Hamilton sold to other inmates or outsiders. Another accusation was that Hamilton had a house at Amity Point to which he sent inmates to look after while they were still receiving government rations. The problem was one of delineation. Lucy Hamilton, who was keeping poultry and selling the eggs to inmates, was employing a legal way of earning some pin money. Hamilton's use of inmates supported by government funds as a private labour force was fraudulent. Between the extremes lay a spectrum of situations of varying legitimacy.

Jacob Schindler also ran foul of Hamilton because he did not keep to his station in life. Though he was admitted as an inmate, he did not consider himself as such because he taught Hamilton's children. He accused Hamilton of cutting his rations and not supplying him with clothes.[58] In his defence, Hamilton claimed that clothing was ordered but not supplied. 'We are ashamed to look the people in the face,' Hamilton said. 'They come to the window and ask for clothes'.[59]

Finally there was the strange case of the Timor pony. This had been landed off the German ship 'Gazelle' while quarantined at Peel Island. The commander gave the pony to the German Consul, Sigmund Berens, who went to collect it, only to be told by Hamilton that it was dead. As he had sold an identical pony to Sir Arthur Palmer, all the evidence pointed to the two ponies being one and the same.[60] This seemingly deliberate lie was an extreme example of Hamilton's autocratic rule of his kingdom.

The inquiry was over and reports were tabled in parliament. The recommendations started to be implemented, including a new female division – but at Dunwich rather than another location. By the following July the Public Charitable Institutions Management Bill was passed. Regulations were prepared and Hamilton was empowered to collect the cost of board from inmates or their relatives if possible. Roomier accommodation, day rooms and covered walkways took longer to materialise, however. More staff began to be employed: from three in 1884 to seven by 1886. A new superintendent, a medical man, was sought.

To Hamilton fell the task of implementing the changes in the benevolent asylum, and here he fell into trouble. He was given the authority he had asked for, to have inmates make financial contributions to their support either personally or through relatives, but ran into immediate and considerable resistance. Hamilton reported in March that he was having difficulty in getting inmates to do the work in the benevolent asylum.[61] Later, when the regulations were promulgated, Visiting Justice Ross reported on those inmates who would not sign. Nine were 'imbeciles', had religious objections or were leaving. Eight had property or a pension. Forty-eight were 'insubordinate' or 'influenced by men antagonistic to the regulations'. Ross commented that most 'object to handing over small sums of money that they may occasionally get from friends'.[62]

Hamilton's adversaries among the inmates began to complain again. William Gardiner started pushing ancient complaints and raking over the coals until another inquiry was mooted. Desperately Hamilton wrote: 'Such investigation should I contend be final when once brought to a conclusion otherwise there is no protection to officers against malicious accusations'.[63]

Simultaneously, Colonel Ross received complaints from the inmates and accusations of insolence and insubordination from Hamilton. The complaints were directed at the cook, John Duggan, who had 'made himself offensive' and 'frequently used most objectionable language'. There were also complaints about poor quality and inedible food. 'In my opinion', commented Ross, 'it has been drawn up in malice, by some eight to ten men, whose names are among those appended to it'. He observed that some signatories had only just arrived within a couple of weeks, while others were incapable and would sign anything. Ross accused the ringleaders of stand-over tactics and bullying to get the 138 names.[64] He could also have added that the complaints were the same as had come before the inquiry the previous year. A week later more complaints were received by Ross.[65] Francis Praeger continued to pursue the case of the appropriated pony. 'I shall yet bring Hamilton to justice', he wrote to inmate-teacher Jacob Schindler.[66]

Emboldened by his successes, Gardiner spoke out: 'I am the man here. Don't be surprised if you see two policemen coming to take old Hamilton away in the steamer'.[67] He was unaware that George Thirkill had made his own complaints about 'improper proposals' by Gardiner and

Praeger to the Aboriginal women working for him. Ross had responded with the advice: 'Unless some serious notice is taken of their conduct it will be almost impossible to maintain proper discipline in the Asylum'.[68]

Accordingly it was Gardiner and not Hamilton who was on the steamer – dismissed by Ross.[69] Hamilton did not last much longer. More inmate complaints began in September. The new superintendent, Dr Patrick Smith, arrived in November, Hamilton took twelve months leave and retired.[70] His wife Lucy, who acted as matron, and assistant superintendent Watkins, went with him.[71] An era was over.

It seems hard on Hamilton that his time at the benevolent asylum should have ended so ignominiously. Even if he were guilty of the accusations levelled at him, he had been left unsupported and unsupervised on an island in Moreton Bay for seventeen years. How an ex-lime burner could be expected to run an increasingly complex institution under these conditions defies understanding. It is ironic that every one of the recommendations from the inquiry that would fix the abuses had already come as requests from Hamilton on several occasions.

For all the activity that went with the inquiry of 1884 there was little interest in the benevolent asylum, and surprisingly little real change. The committee of inquiry hardly ever had all its members together at a sitting and frequently had no quorum. Though Hamilton was replaced by a medical practitioner, this did little to relieve the health problems of the inmates, and replacement of the whole staff did nothing to improve the general management of the asylum. Regulations were first issued in 1885, and increasingly from then on. The idea of getting from the inmates 'some contribution towards the expense of their maintenance' was embraced and demanded off and on for the next eighty years. Recommendations involving expenditure, such as the day rooms, were not acted upon. Anything beyond the most basic of needs was a long time being met. Complaints about the treatment of inmates continued, resulting in another major investigation in 1906. It is hard to avoid the conclusion that no one really cared.

Of all the benefits that Dunwich may have had as a site for a benevolent asylum, the greatest was its remoteness, so that the flotsam and jetsam of society – the weak, the incapacitated, the unfortunate – could be kept safely out of sight and out of mind.

*Chapter 6*

# 'Keep them away from Brisbane': Bribie Island Aboriginal reserves 1877-79 and 1891-92

**Shirleene Robinson**

In June 1877, following two commissions into Aboriginal matters and sustained agitation by Duncan McNab, Premier John Douglas, along with several ministers of his cabinet, accompanied Tom Petrie to Bribie Island to inspect a potential site for an Aboriginal reserve and fishing station.[1] However, this Aboriginal mission, with Petrie installed as a visiting superintendent, scarcely outlasted the Douglas McIlwraith Ministry in March of 1879.[2] Notwithstanding its failure, another Aboriginal mission, this time with a school attached, was set up on Bribie Island in 1891. This mission also failed, with Aboriginal children and adults being removed from Bribie Island to Peel Island in November 1892.[3] To a large extent, the failure of both missions may be attributed to the lack of freedom for Aboriginal people and the negative impact of the missions on traditional culture.

Both reserves were established during periods when the government wanted to remove the Aboriginal presence from Brisbane, and also when many selectors were loath to grant land to Aborigines. Moreover, both colonial governments were reluctant to provide funding for Aboriginal causes, and an overview of the two Bribie Island missions reveals how these complex factors interacted.

Bribie Island, the most northerly island in the Moreton Bay area, is believed to have supported an Aboriginal population of at least 600 people before European intrusion.[4] They were members of the Joondaburri, a sub-group of the Undambi who inhabited the Sunshine Coast.[5] The Joondaburri spoke a dialect of the Gubbi Gubbi language and interacted closely with the Ninghi Ninghi people of Sandgate, Redcliffe Peninsula and Toorbul Point.[6] Though Bribie Island consists largely of sand, it abounded with natural resources, and archaeological evidence confirms an Aboriginal presence from a least 2000 years BP.[7]

The Joondaburri first came to the attention of Europeans in 1799 when Matthew Flinders sailed up Pumicestone Passage, the waterway between Bribie Island and the mainland. This visit began badly when an Aboriginal man was shot after a spear was thrown.[8] Nevertheless Flinders managed to repair relations well enough to trade with the Joondaburri and witness a musical performance before leaving fifteen days after his arrival. Until the establishment of the first Aboriginal reserve in 1877 European contact with the Joondaburri was frequent enough for Archibald Meston, judging the island by its European history, to later declare Bribie Island to be 'historically, the most interesting island on the Queensland coast'.[9]

There are two differing explanations as to how the island came to be named. One maintains that 'Bribie' was a corruption of 'Borabee', as the island was known to Moreton Island Aborigines.[10] The second explanation holds that Europeans named the island Bribie after a convict who resided in the area from about 1839 to 1842.[11] The Joondaburri themselves referred to the island as 'Yarun', meaning 'hunting ground'.[12]

In the colonial period, Brisbane newspapers such as the *Moreton Bay courier*,[13] and commentators such as Archibald Meston,[14] described the Joondaburri people as violent and fearsome; yet those Europeans who interacted closely with this group found them to be friendly and generous. Two ex-convicts, Thomas Pamphlet and John Finnegan, who had been shipwrecked in the area, were supported by the Joondaburri for five months. Pamphlet observed that the men treated women well and that dishonesty was unknown amongst the tribe.[15] Members of John Oxley's Moreton Bay expedition of 1823, who removed Pamphlet and Finnegan, also found the Joondaburri to be friendly and 'both in their disposition and manners far superior to those in the neighbourhood of Sydney'.[16] European intrusion was devastating. In May 1877 Petrie estimated the population at only 53,[17] but the mission was not established to protect this vestigial group; rather, it was to remove large numbers of indigenous people from the area around Brisbane.

By the 1870s, when the colony was industrialising and developing rapidly, dispossessed Aboriginal people, often residing in fringe-camps on the edges of towns, served as a reminder of a violent past. There are many letters to the editors of various newspapers and articles from the 1870s complaining about visible Aboriginal people who refused to act like white people or who had alcohol problems.[18] The *Week*, for example, cited a Bowen meeting where the best plan 'for improving the condition of the blacks and ridding the town and district, not only of the great begging nuisance, but also of the cause of a great amount of the grossest immorality' was discussed.[19] The message from such incidents was clear. Aboriginal visibility offended the sensibilities of the white community, while serving to remind them of the unpleasant past.

The opening of the Bribie Island reserve in 1877 coincided with the development of these attitudes, and it is crucial to place it within this broader context. Many Europeans expressed offence that Aboriginal people dared eke out an existence where settlers had to see them, yet they still wished to exploit Aboriginal labour. A scheme officially begun in Mackay in 1871 provided a means for the continued exploitation of Aboriginal labour without them being visible to settlers. George Bridgman, a grazier and later plantation owner, who actually maintained positive relations with local Aborigines, was given permission to run a reserve.[20] By 1873 it was so well regarded by local settlers that several of them, under the name of the Association for the Employment of Aborigines, drew up a petition urging the Queensland government to extend the scheme across Queensland.[21] The subsequent Drew Commission readily concurred, as did the Hale Commission in May 1876.

Another strong agitator for the expansion of the reserve system, although for very different reasons, was Reverend Duncan McNab, who spent three months at the Mackay reserve in 1875. He strongly believed that, if given land, Aboriginal people could be taught to support themselves in a European manner by taking up agriculture. It appears that McNab first suggested the idea of establishing the Bribie Island mission to the government. He further recommended that Tom Petrie should be involved. Petrie was a practical choice as he had spent much time with Aboriginal people as a child, spoke several Aboriginal languages and used the labour of the local Aboriginal population on his station 'Murrumba', near Caboolture. On 10 October 1876 McNab wrote to the governor advising that a number of Aboriginal people, including 'Prince William' of Bribie Island, had requested that reserves be established on their traditional land.[22] The change of government was also important for the establishment of the mission, as the new Douglas ministry proved to be more amenable to expanding the reserve system than the earlier Palmer ministry.

However, such schemes still met considerable opposition from both parliamentarians and the public. While Europeans wished for Aboriginal people to be removed from visibility, questions were still raised over the amount of money the government should provide for missionary ventures and reserves. Furthermore, many believed that Aboriginal people should be given poor land, keeping the best for settlers. In 1877 John Douglas was confronted in the Legislative Assembly by the member for Durundur, John Pettigrew, who asked him if any government money was being spent on 'Christianising' Queensland's Aboriginal population and if there were plans for any more reserves.[23] Pettigrew, who was being pressured by selectors, then asked Douglas why he had reserved for Aboriginal use 'rich, flat country, destitute of game, and given to agriculturists scrubby ranges overrun with marsupials and a longer distance from a market'.[24] Douglas responded by denouncing the leading nature of Pettigrew's questions.[25]

Notwithstanding such criticisms of the Aboriginal reserve movement in the 1870s, there was also a considerable amount of support. As a result, in October 1876 the Queensland government officially set aside 1000 hectares for the purposes of an Aboriginal reserve and fishing station at Bribie Island. In April 1877 Petrie wrote to the Minister of Lands, setting out the conditions he believed necessary for the success of the venture.[26] The following month he spent four days assessing the island and with the help of the Aboriginal inhabitants, found a suitable site for a reserve at an area called 'Taranggeer' by the indigenous population,[27] later known as White Patch by Europeans.[28] Petrie himself did not wish to manage the reserve, instead preferring to inspect operations on a monthly basis. This resulted in the commissioners appointing Frederick Redman as the live-in manager.

Perhaps the strongest indication of the government's motives in establishing this Bribie Island reserve can be found in a note scribbled by a commissioner in 1877. It advised those involved in the mission to 'Procure supplies for two months in want to avoid the necessity of blacks visiting town'. Furthermore, the note mentions that 'the police magistrate has been advised of the annoyances and requested to assist in keeping the blacks out of Brisbane'.[29] Despite the philanthropic pretences of the reserve movement in the 1870s, it is clear that the prime moving force behind it was a desire to shunt away the indigenous population from the main centres. In May 1877, reporting on a plan by which the government intended to relocate the Brisbane Aboriginal population, the *Queenslander* stated:

> ... the usual distribution of blankets to the aborigines did not take place at the City Police Court yesterday, but the blacks of the district received them this year at Durundur and Bribie Island. This is in consequence of a regulation lately issued, with a view to keeping the natives out of town as much as possible. It is well known that in many instances the 'Queen's gift' has been exchanged for rum to some town or suburban politician, and thus turned into an injury instead of a benefit to the aborigines. The present action of the government will commend itself to most people as a practical solution to the evil mentioned.[30]

Petrie also believed that the Aboriginal population should be removed from Brisbane.[31] However, this was mostly due to his belief that Europeans were endangering the Aboriginal population by supplying them with alcohol.

By the middle of 1877 the Bribie Island population stood at 50 people, but was boosted sizably over the coming months when more than 12 Aboriginal people from the Pine River and Fortitude Valley areas moved to the reserve.[32] Naturally the newcomers to the mission had an impact on the culture of the Joondaburri people. Reports from the Bribie mission recorded that the Aboriginal population had killed dolphins, yet traditionally the Joondaburri people had used dolphins to round up fish.[33] It is highly unlikely that they would have engaged in such a practice.

The inhabitants were supplied with a boat, fishing net, and harpoons to catch and cure fish and to manufacture dugong, shark and stingray oils.[34] Along with turtle, they were then sold in Brisbane. Two months after the establishment of the mission, Petrie submitted a report to the commission. He wrote that the Aboriginal people residing on the island appeared happy and healthy and that they had delivered two consignments of dried fish valued at £7 11s 2d to Brisbane, which had been exchanged for rations.[35]

In October 1877 McNab also submitted a report on the Aboriginal settlement. While McNab considered that the population worked well while Petrie was in residence, he noted that after Petrie left the reserve they became 'indolent', did not respect manager Redman and spent time hunting and begging, as well as fishing. Furthermore, McNab noted that they were selling fish on the mainland for flour and money, the latter being used to purchase tobacco and alcohol.[36] While the Aboriginal population respected Petrie, who spoke their language, they had little time for McNab, who tried to convert them to Christianity, or for Redman, the resident superintendent. There is clear evidence that they viewed McNab as a comic figure. Constance Petrie cites an occasion when Tom Petrie found 'Prince Willie' impersonating McNab to other Aboriginal residents:

> There was an old book, from which he pretended to read, jabbering away like a parrot, and he had water at his side in which he dipped his hand, and then sprinkled the blacks he was about to name. He made the latter cross themselves and then the others he married with a ring. The white man had to laugh till his sides were sore at the way the absurd fellow went on, although he felt he should not, and there were the rest of the blacks simply rolling on the ground with laughter.[37]

Petrie's report to the commission in January 1878 mentioned both the frequent movement of the Aboriginal population away from the island and the lack of respect shown for Redman.[38] Meston also asserted that they could not be induced to stay permanently on the island, instead choosing to exercise freedom of movement and using the island as a base.[39] While Petrie was sensitive to many Aboriginal requirements, he did not fully appreciate the need of the indigenous population on Bribie Island to participate in cultural activities on the mainland. There was also an incident in 1878 where Petrie offended the Aboriginal people on the island by trying to obtain the skin of a dead Aboriginal elder for the Queensland Museum.[40]

Despite these setbacks, by the end of 1878 Petrie felt more optimistic about the future of the Bribie Island reserve. He reported to the Aboriginal Commission that 'in furnishing an asylum for the old, in breaking off the wandering habits of the young, and teaching them habits of providence and industry, [the reserve] is succeeding to a degree that justifies the expenditure involved in its maintenance'.[41] Similarly, the *Queenslander* asserted that 'it certainly appears but reasonable, if we exclude the blacks from the towns, that reserves should be established to which they may be directed and have a right to resort'.[42] McNab, however, became increasingly disillusioned with the Aboriginal Commisssion and tendered his resignation in January of 1879, citing a lack of progress in Aboriginal welfare as being due to 'the opposition of some bigots, of envious selectors and interested publicans; to the late Ministry of which some members opposed the Premier's desire of carrying into effect the resolutions ... for the benefit of the aborigines of Queensland; to the heads of religious denominations ... who neglected to supply them with missionaries; and to the misconceptions and prejudices of the commissioners'.[43]

Petrie's optimism in 1879 was severely misplaced. According to Raymond Evans, the new McIlwraith government 'began playing its parsimonious hand' with regard to the Aboriginal reserves in the colony.[44] Funding was withdrawn not only from the Bribie Island reserve but also from Mackay, Townsville, Bowen and Durundur reserves.[45] Matthew Hale wrote to the Colonial Secretary in March 1879, noting that the government had already instructed Petrie to break up the Bribie Island settlement and dispose of property held thereabouts. Hale considered the withdrawal of funds 'likely to cause serious distress especially to the old and infirm'.[46]

The government had wanted Bribie Island to serve as a remote settlement where the Aboriginal population could be removed from visibility, permanently. However, during the existence of the first mission, most remaining members of the Joondaburri and relocated Brisbane Aboriginal people resisted restriction on their movements and instead chose to use the island as a base, with wider contacts being maintained. This was not the case for older Aborigines, who were almost permanently based on the island and largely dependent on government subsidies. These older people and the relocated Brisbane Aborigines who were not entirely familiar with the area were particularly affected by the withdrawal of government funding for the mission. Constance Petrie recorded that when 'the news had to be told to the blacks, [they] were all very miserable about it'.[47]

Aboriginal people residing in Brisbane had been compelled by the government to obtain supplies from Bribie Island Yet a changing political climate only two years later led to the relocated people being abandoned on the island and left to fend for themselves. Some indication of how this act resonated in the collective indigenous consciousness can be viewed in a telling aside made by the European settler D.A. Tripcony in 1963. He remembered 'an aborigine having a dog called 'Government' and when asked how they arrived at the name they said, 'He was a greedy b_____, just grabbed everything'.[48]

Thus, a lack of commitment to the improvement of Queensland's Aboriginal population by the McIlwraith government, combined with a lack of freedom for Aboriginal people, led to the eventual collapse of the mission in 1879. The following decade saw an even greater decline in government and societal interest in the welfare of indigenous Queenslanders, perhaps due to decreased activity by the native police and the policy of 'letting in' Aboriginal workers on stations.[49] On the other hand, the 1890s saw interest in Aboriginal welfare regenerated. This was due in part to the increased public awareness of the condition of northern Aborigines. The most visible indication of this trend was the passing of the Aboriginals Protection and Restriction of the Sale of Opium Act in 1897. Six years before this legislation was passed, Bribie Island once more became the site for an Aboriginal mission.

While details are available concerning the first attempt, there is a distinct paucity of information regarding the second Bribie Island Aboriginal mission. Established in February 1891 under the auspices of the Queensland Aboriginal Protection Association,[50] it was located on the western shore of Bribie Island at a place called Sydney Camp opposite Goat Island.[51] Like the first, this second mission was not established to protect the indigenous population of Bribie Island, whose numbers had by now dropped alarmingly, but to resettle Aboriginal people from Dunwich on Stradbroke Island.[52] The steamer 'Miner', on its first trip from Dunwich to Bribie Island, took 13 Aboriginal people, 10 of whom were children, from Dunwich to the island.[53] While the first reserve had been expected to become a self-sufficient fishing station, the second was established with an Aboriginal school as its focal point.

The opening of a school is also indicative of the general change in attitude towards the indigenous people. Ideologies which stressed the 'civilisation' of the Aborigines through the 'improvement' of their children were quite influential at this time.[54] Members of the Queensland Aboriginal Protection Society espoused this argument when they asserted that the mission would 'raise the few blacks now remaining with us to a position far removed from their present intolerable depravity',[55] as the adults 'love their children, and it is argued that if the children are once induced to settle on such a reserve, their elders in the desire for their children's companionship will gradually learn to appreciate and adopt the habits of civilisation'.[56] Children formed the majority of the population at this second mission. A report from 1891 indicates that there were 9 female children, 6 male children, 3 men and one woman residing at the reserve.[57]

The Aboriginal school was run with Mr Tyson, Secretary of the Queensland Aboriginal Protection Association, as superintendent, Mrs Kerr as matron and a Mr Balliston as a schoolmaster.[58] The children residing at the mission led an austere existence. In May 1891 the *Queenslander* urged its readers to donate to the mission as 'the children, of whom there are now seventeen, are in urgent need of warm clothing'. As at the first mission, efforts were made to convert the Aboriginal people to Christianity. For these purposes, and ignoring traditional indigenous religious practices, Tyson held a religious service twice a day on Sundays and every evening during the week.[59]

6.1 Bribie Island Aboriginal school c.1892 (JOL)

Thomas Welsby has written that the second mission, like the first, grouped together several Aboriginal clans without respect for traditional animosities or the number of clans who could reside in one settlement.[60] Furthermore the mission experienced problems right from the outset, as those people from other areas felt uncomfortable about residing on Joondaburri territory.[61] Newspapers did not focus heavily on problems the mission experienced, concentrating instead on the 'good work' the mission was doing for Aboriginal children.[62] Stories appeared concerning the success of a lecture Meston gave to raise funds for the mission in September 1891,[63] and the happy Christmas the children enjoyed at the end of that year.[64] In what appears to be an extraordinarily insensitive move by both Meston and the Aboriginal Protection Society, the lecture featured children acting in a play where they were fired at by an authority figure hunting for an Aboriginal criminal.[65] Meston's performance was so popular that it was repeated the following night.[66]

There is very little information about the closure of the mission school in November 1892. Apart from the animosity between members of the various clans grouped together on the island and the discomfort of Aboriginal people residing on Joondaburri territory, a strong contributing factor towards the closure may have been the death of the school master, Balliston, who fell from the mission boat, 'Dayspring', while going for supplies.[67]

In November 1892 the *Week* reported that the 'Bribie Island blacks once more "move on", this time temporarily to Peel Island' where they were to be housed until their removal to Stradbroke Island.[68] This is confirmed in the 1905 report from the Protector of Aborigines, which asserts that 'Fifty acres of land in close proximity to Dunwich were proclaimed as a

"Reserve for Mission Station" on the 26th November 1892, on account of the site for Bribie Island mission having being found unsuitable'.[69] The children were being shunted back to where they had been removed from the previous year. On the other hand, the Aborigines Protection Association was assured by the superintendent of Peel Island that work could be found for the older boys from the mission.[70]

By this time the number of Joondaburri had been seriously depleted, with Meston asserting that only four remained alive in 1891.[71] Kalmakuta, generally believed to be the last of this group, died six years later.[72] Perhaps ironically, she is commemorated by a cairn at Toorbul Point, opposite her island home.

The strategy of the government was also changing direction, with consolidation of the reserve system. In practical terms, lack of government support, combined with an insufficient understanding of indigenous culture, were the major factors leading to the failure of both Aboriginal reserves on Bribie Island. They nevertheless serve to illustrate the motives behind attempts to ameliorate the condition of Queensland's Aboriginal population, and the impact of colonisation. Put simply, they were based more on a desire to remove the indigenous people from urban centres, rather than any compassionate ideals. Once removal had been accomplished, interest in their future rapidly dwindled.

## *Chapter 7*

# 'Leading lights': The first Moreton Island lighthouse communities

**Rosemary Ahearn**

The establishment of Moreton Island settlements from the mid-nineteenth century to the early twentieth century was based on the fulfilment of mainland requirements. The minimalistic approach adopted to the expansion of Moreton Island as a Brisbane outpost resulted in stunted community development and cohesion. Much of the sense of community revolved around a feeling of loss for a closer-knit past. This is reflected in attempts of community members to create or uphold the standards of the old world – which proved the most successful way to retain direction and focus within a community that shared no prospects of specific long-term goals or future. While many perceived their residency on Moreton as semi-permanent, their common points of interest as a community focused on the available employment, their own families, and day-to-day survival.

Early development of Moreton Island was dictated largely by mainland navigation requirements and activities in the quest for the safe passage of ships through Moreton Bay to and from Brisbane. The first organised settlement was precipitated by the wreck of the 'Sovereign' in 1847, in which forty-four lives were lost. This occurrence highlighted the dangers of the South Passage bar and prompted the transference of the pilot station at Amity Point on Stradbroke Island to Bulwer on Moreton Island in 1848.[1]

Thereafter ships generally proceeded to sail around Cape Moreton following a carefully charted course. A need soon emerged for a conspicuous light marking the entrance to the bay following the wreck of the 'Venus' in 1855 and the 'Aurora' in 1856.[2] In 1857 the Cape Moreton lighthouse was built, the first of seven erected on Moreton Island. The lighthouse and keeper's cottage were constructed of sandstone quarried from the immediate area for an original capital cost of £7,616.[3] At Comboyuro Point, North Point and Cowan Cowan, lights were established with large kerosene burners fitted with dioptric apparatus and housed to ensure they were not blown away in heavy gales.[4] Coastal steamers continued to use the South Passage during the day. Consequently red beacons, visible from Flat Rock, were placed on the extreme south of the island.[5]

Reinforcing the temporary nature of the settlements dictated by jurisdiction of mainland authorities was the continued effect of erosion on the island and displacement of sand in the Moreton Bay channels. Through this movement the forces of nature controlled the establishment of settlements and structures on Moreton Island. At Yellow Patch the lighthouse was shifted ninety metres to the north east in 1882 due to movements of the channels, and by 1891 had been moved for the fourth time. By 1898 the Cowan lighthouse was endangered by the encroachment of the sea washing away the point, and in 1901 was successfully moved back under the direction of the department's inspector of works.[6] At Comboyuro Point in 1890, the light and keeper's cottage required moving back sixty metres under threat of the encroaching sea. Many other navigational aids on and surrounding Moreton have since vanished, including most of the lighthouses, pile lights and signal lights.[7]

*7.1 Cape Moreton Lighthouse 1856 (ML Frederick Korff collection)*

Improvement of services on the island was based on upgrading navigational amenities in Moreton Bay for the benefit of increased mainland needs. They included the establishment of a signal and telegraph station at the South Passage in 1873 and its subsequent extension in 1878 to the pilot station at Bulwer. This enabled the pilots to obtain information regarding shipping movements at any time, and a lookout no longer had to run well over a kilometre to Bulwer to alert the pilot, although it was reported to have been a full-time job just keeping the line clear of vegetation.[8] Facilities at the Cape Moreton settlement and Bulwer were maintained or upgraded only in accordance with the demands of the small but expanding populace.

When the pilot station was moved from Amity to Bulwer in 1848, 'it was recorded by 1860 to have in residence two pilots, nine boatmen and others, all living in wretched conditions'.[9] By the late 1860s, as community and services increased, a visitor depicted the pilot station as consisting of some 'eight or nine buildings, used as a boathouse, church and school house, and the dwellings of the pilots and a school master'.[10] At the Cape, galvanised-iron roofs replaced those of leaking shingle; rainwater storage facilities were upgraded with a water tank sunk into the rocks, and a school room was built in 1879.[11]

The population on the island was diverse, with employment providing the only real thread of common interest. Aside from the more senior employees, many were unskilled and unable to find work on the mainland. They considered their positions there as temporary, regarding Moreton island as a relatively undesirable and isolated outpost. This led to a temporary existence applying the same minimalistic approach adopted by the authorities, and forming a community devoid of shared goals or values.

The nature of temporary residence continued throughout the first period of settlement on Moreton. This is reflected in correspondence from Georgina Nordling, a resident at Cape Moreton from 1910 to 1916. She recalled the initial announcement by her father that he had a job on a lighthouse, and her mother's reaction, thinking it was in the middle of the ocean but promising to go for three months.[12]

Remnants of the Aboriginal Nooghie tribe of Moreton Island were moved to Stradbroke in 1846. Some of the remaining people served the lighthouse communities and were employed to row the boats to and from the ships, while the women worked as domestic servants for pilots' wives. Relationships between European and indigenous people at the lighthouse settlements were reported to have been good.[13]

Another aspect of the shared social experience was the school. By 1906 there were twenty-six students attending class at the Bulwer school. Education index files provide a good insight into the developing thoughts and principles in the small and isolated communities of Bulwer and Cape Moreton. Correspondence between teachers, residents and authorities reflect commonly held values and also exhibit the frequent fluctuations in community discipline.

At Bulwer, complaints from teacher James McLeod indicate the lack of social structure and future vision and the need for defined and organised social formation. Calls for his dismissal in 1881 due to low grades, and his subsequent reply, indicate attitudes prevailing among the Bulwer population. McLeod complained that there was rarely any sustained attendance, with the exception of the pilot's children, whom he claimed turned out to be 'fair scholars some of whom were, and some now employed in the government offices'. Efforts to induce parents to enforce attendance failed, with the frequently repeated retort that 'the children were their own, that they fed them and clothed them, and could use them as they pleased'. McLeod also protested that at the time of his dismissal there had been more regular attendance owing to the recent pressure brought to bear by the Port Master and Harbour Master, and 'that the school was in as prosperous a state as ever I have had it'.[14]

James McLeod would appear to represent the first and last teacher actually discontented with his removal from the Bulwer posting. Education files are thereafter littered with repeated requests for transfer for reasons ranging from a poor supply of fresh produce to the unfriendliness of the locals. Records pertaining to teachers posted to Moreton Island indicate their inferior educational qualifications and skills. Any lack of previous commitment to their vocations rarely improved on Moreton, with the temporary nature of their postings affecting their level of commitment. In their letters the teachers exhibited a general yearning to leave – presenting the Department of Public Instruction with a host of reasons for discontent.

Numerous letters were written by Louisa Blunt requesting transfer with her children to a more convenient situation. In 1884 she complained that by the time supplies arrived, they were not wholesome:

> The potatoes are bad, the meat tainted, the butter rank, and this at the beginning of the month, so that long before the next store day, my children and myself who have always been accustomed to a town life and able to get food as we wanted it, and fresh vegetables, feel very much at a loss.

Blunt explained that what little milk and vegetables were produced by the local population was used by them, and that her children's strength was failing for not receiving sufficient nourishment.[15]

In subsequent correspondence, she expanded her argument to include her concerns as to her sons' future educational requirements, including that of a 'good master', the unavailability of 'a good servant' to perform the more arduous household tasks and the total disregard of the community for Sunday 'and or any other day'. Blunt claimed that the last protestant minister on the island left nearly two years previously and she feared the children would lose their 'habit of attendance' at church.[16] Her comments reflect the notable fluctuations in community discipline throughout the early decades of settlement.

It appears Louisa Blunt's years on Moreton may have affected some of her higher principles and values. A letter in 1891 written by her replacement, Emily Hulme, claims that 'the men in removing Mrs Blunt's goods from the house and boat were as overcome with the stench arising therefrom, that they were obliged to stop two or three times and only with great difficulty managed to accomplish their work'. After the men had cleared the house, Hulme borrowed caustic soda to remove the dirt from the floors and walls.[17] Possibly the condition of the teacher's residence at the end of Blunt's occupation indicates that a relaxation in housekeeping only applied as a result of her Moreton posting.

Such abandonment of prevailing social standards appears a frequently repeated occurrence amongst generations of Moreton inhabitants. This supports the theory that for many of them the perception of their residency as semi-permanent, in conjunction with Moreton's isolated position, made the island communities seem less connected with the outside world and its normal social regulations.

The frustration of isolation and the inability to progress beyond a certain point in social development was regularly reflected in self-destructive antagonistic community behaviour jeopardising the successful progress of the school, a principal focus of community interest. Relationships between teachers and residents at Bulwer were often fractious.

In 1894 M. Cloherty resigned from her teaching position on the basis that boatman 'Major' and his family had rendered her life 'very disagreeable'. Cloherty expressed her doubts that any teacher would receive a day's peace while 'Major' was on the island and claimed other residents had told her that he made it a point to make life as unhappy as possible for the teacher.[18] The often inferior quality of new appointments to the school and the adoption of relaxed standards by teachers further reduced community spirit and enthusiasm, and provided a cause for public discontent.

Upon the resignation of Cloherty, the Bulwer school closed from December 1894, but was re-opened with the appointment of F.N. Newnham in April 1895.[19] While Newnham, staying nearly eight years, proved a popular choice, his replacement in 1904, G.H. Cooke, did not appear to have quite the same heart for Moreton island. In a letter of complaint to the department from a resident by the name of Blackburn, Cooke was accused of not only taking every opportunity to play truant teacher but also of falsifying his scholars' attendance records to indicate otherwise. Closing school and running away to Brisbane for a long weekend appeared an early favourite of his, degenerating as time passed to unexpectedly closing the school at midday on any given day of the week and, at one stage, disappearing for a full week.

Despite Cooke's concerted efforts to indicate through his records that he had not missed a moment's duties, he was eventually foiled by the fastidious Blackburn, who provided the department with a precise account of Cooke's activities over a twelve-month period, including a reluctance to pay his bills to the local Chinaman.[20] Cooke responded by offering the only noble and face-saving action available – an application for transfer – a popular move in Bulwer academic circles. Like teachers before him, he blamed the isolation, unavailability of supplies and irregular mail communication for his discontent. However, he was required to make several applications before the department took pity on all concerned and transferred Joseph Hirst to the Bulwer school in 1903.

Hirst and his family provide an example of the successful application of independent principles. Unlike their predecessors, they grasped and developed some fundamental skills required for comfortable survival at an outpost. His daughter, Eleanor Beck, provided the author with an account of their life on Moreton at the turn of the century.

In Joseph Hirst's immediate favour was his wife's enjoyment of fishing – she was quite a fanatic, and would take baby Eleanor out on her rowboat to fish all day. Every inch the practical settler, Mrs Hirst established a smoking room for fish and meat – the meat rations largely comprising wild pig, which she shot herself. There were seven children in the Hirst family and they also grew their own vegetables.[21] In later years when asked by the daughter-in-law how she acquired yeast to make bread, the remarkable lady revealed that it was made from lemons.[22]

Perhaps lacking some of his wife's more practical characteristics, Joseph Hirst is reported upon his final transfer in 1909 to have become so emotionally attached to the family cow that he made it swim out behind the whaleboat though shark-infested waters to be loaded aboard the passing ship.

*7.2 Pilot Station, Bulwer 1899 (JOL)*

Though spared the swim and the ropes, his wife, eight months' pregnant, also endured the undignified loading progress en route to give birth in a Brisbane hospital. Unfortunately the passing ship turned out to be a passenger liner: it is reported all on board watched the rope ladder ascent in bemusement.

Eleanor Beck's youthful reflections include an account of nature dictating the structure of a Moreton day. When a school of fish was spotted close to shore, the school bell was rung and the children waded out to sea with the nets. All dined on fish that evening.[23]

The Hirsts' adaptation to their circumstances, and application of self-discipline and self-reliance, proved a success formula in maintaining an acceptable lifestyle and set of social values. This was achieved in a society that had become adept at dismantling standard codes of behaviour. The Hirst couple focused on family and principle, and avoided undue preoccupation with the psychologically undermining influence of local inhospitality and abandoned order.

The replacement of Hirst by Lizzie Carpenter Weston in 1909 was followed by a letter to the department wherein she complained bitterly of the locals' inhospitality. She quoted recent correspondence with Hirst where he apparently stated that the Blackburn family gave him nothing but bother, and that in the first three months his wife was ostracised for wearing gloves on the beach. Weston claimed Hirst reported to her that 'the locals would do nothing for her, but this had not bothered his family as they were independent of them'. The Hirst family had got on particularly well with the Normans and the Rogers, who had departed before his transfer.[24]

Lizzie Weston provides an example of the antithesis to Hirst's successful application of independent social survival. She sought to maintain familiar standards of community interdependence and failed to accept the lack of existing social cohesion. Weston complained of the locals being 'a most selfish people', never offering fresh fish or the produce from their cows or goats. The children, she claimed, 'are bold and their rudeness surpassed only by their elders'. Her efforts to get them to clean up the school-yard under the bribe of lollies was responded to by the parents advising the children 'not to do anything the teacher tells them'. Weston claimed that when she asked Mr Palmer if he would put the wood he was delivering closer to the house, he looked at her savagely and growled; 'I'll put it where Hirst had it', and then proceeded to deliver it fifty metres further away.[25]

Several letters were exchanged with the department during the following year, with relationships reaching an all-time low when Miss Weston hit young Polly Blackburn over the head with a slate. The locals claimed Weston held herself aloof from the people, and that her previous work in the Torres Strait led her to expect services. Weston retorted by referring to the locals as rude and ill-mannered. Somehow a version developed through Mrs Blackburn that Weston believed the Bulwer students to be 'no better than niggers'.[26]

After the stormy schoolroom 'brawl' ensuing between Weston and local residents, it was no doubt of great relief to the department that student attendance numbers had diminished to such an extent as to warrant closure of the Bulwer school. By 1911 most of the Bulwer families had been removed, signifying the end of the community. Attempted arrangements were made for the education of lighthouse keeper Palmer's four children by the Cape Moreton Provisional School teacher, Frances Lee, with the suggestion she travel the sixteen kilometres once per week to set and correct lessons.[27] By the end of 1912 the school was closed and its structure removed to Dunwich on Stradbroke Island for use by children with eye problems.[28]

The smaller community at Cape Moreton enjoyed more balanced progress, due in part to stronger leadership and the example set by its prominent role models. Communal society at the Cape was represented by individuals who inspired and reflected commonly-admired values. They included the first appointed keeper of the light, James Braydon, who resided with his family at Cape Moreton as superintendent for thirty and a half years until he retired in 1887 and was replaced by Walter Powell.[29]

In 1879 a school-room was built at Cape Moreton, providing a better opportunity for the children to make progress, comparable to those placed in the more accessible position of Bulwer. At one stage the school had up to twenty-one children within a community comprised of five families.[30]

A welcome product of the new educational facility was another community role model, Henry Ward, who commenced his duties as first teacher of the Cape Moreton Provisional School in 1876. In a letter of report to the under secretary, Ward described his arrival at Bulwer, fourteen kilometres from the Cape, 'through sand and water', and the newly-fitted out school room that previously served as sleeping quarters. Ward proclaimed that 'the men seem determined nothing shall be wanting on their parts to make a success of this undertaking'.[31] He conveyed his approval and high regard for the lighthouse keeper and his wife, Mr and Mrs Braydon, and the establishment they had provided for the education of twenty-one students including the Braydon, Griffin, Pascoe and Jones families, whom Ward claimed to be an 'intelligent lot'.

This intelligence is reflected in an impressive letter, published in 1879, by thirteen-year-old Robert Poole Braydon, who wrote to his uncle in England stressing, among other things, the educational opportunities provided:

> It is but three years since a school was established at Cape Moreton and this letter is a fair specimen of what I and other pupils are doing. How strange it seems when one thinks of it that the people who lived four centuries ago in Europe were acquainted with such a very small portion of the earth's surface, and that the vast continent of Australia should have laid dormant for such a lengthened period.[32]

Much reference is made to the popular teacher in other Braydon family correspondence, and to his enthusiasm in providing educational and cultural experiences on a par with those afforded to larger settlements. These included the arrangement of a Queen's Birthday sports day on 24 May 1878. Florence Braydon referred to the event as a 'monster entertainment' with 'Old English sports, foot racing, running in sacks, and throwing the cricket ball for prizes'. For the occasion, Ward organised prizes of fishing lines, hooks, sinkers, and two books, with a special prize presented to the girl who could make the ugliest face through a horse collar.[33]

Children's accounts, though frequently lacking in precision, provide useful material to examine people at leisure and perhaps determine more accurately the degree of pride and community identity not always evident in official correspondence. A well-known long-term resident Jessie Wadsworth (nee Hill) recalled in her memoirs of life on Moreton since the turn of the century, travelling from Yellow Patch to the Cape by horse and dray, and the Sunday picnics where, after eating, everyone loaded the wood upon the horsecart to last them for the week.[34] The highlight of recreational activities for permanent Moreton inhabitants during this period was the weekend picnic. Residents travelled by horse and dray to Ocean Beach, then known as Pig Beach, or as far as Clifton (Blue Lake) where duck shooting made for good sport and a variation in diet. Other regular recreational activities evident from photographs of the period included fishing and boating excursions, model boat races at Lake Clifton and organised community celebrations.

Former resident, Betty Bell, while sympathetic to adult complaints, fondly recalled her time, from the age of four, on Moreton island:

> Our small house had no power, not even an ice chest. None of this could have been much fun for my city bred mother, but the whole of Moreton was all magic to me ....including the heady mixture of terror and delight when a wild pig got under the school and couldn't get out.[35]

Bell further recalled the stout little boat that delivered their supplies:

> Matthew Flinders days held a special magic with parcels to open and picnics on the beach with the crew. The Matthew Flinders brought me a fox terrier, a kitten, the very smallest size working hurricane lamp, so that I could help my father on his rounds, day old chicks which stay day old and delightful in my memory, and fresh bread.[36]

Accounts such as this are invaluable in determining daily pleasures and events not otherwise documented, and the degree of community participation and enthusiasm.

In other Braydon correspondence the family-centred nature of the Cape community's existence is reflected, with the focus of daily interest generating around its members. Letters written to her sister Carrie in Brisbane express the sameness of the days and their hopes for Carrie's return. Florence writes of her fear for 'the light of the household' – young Master William – following the capture of two snakes close to the house. A highlight in Florence's week was the acquisition of new reading books, and learning to sing 'Home Sweet Home' at school.[37]

After the transfer of Henry Ward from Cape Moreton in 1890, succeeding teachers' performances proved less satisfactory, with repeated resignations and transfer applications. Following the loss of this much-admired role model, community relations deteriorated with Captain Braydon referring in his reports to constant quarrelling. In departmental letters it was noted that 'at lonely places difficulties arose with mothers causing problems'.[38] Often women appointed to the school left for health reasons, claiming the sea air did not agree with them. As with Bulwer, the Cape Moreton inhabitants did not always prove hospitable towards the teachers. Frances Lee, appointed in 1907 and regarded as patient and hardworking, was refused accommodation until the minister stepped in, threatening closure of the school.[39]

Ructions similar to the Bulwer debacle occurred in 1912 when the wife of first assistant Harper established herself as teacher for the Cape Moreton school. In this instance, however, venom against the new teacher was well-established prior to her appointment due to the Harpers' behaviour as residents. A letter to the department from assistant lighthouse keeper Lockhardt indicates both Harpers to be poorly regarded, the first assistant having been found 'the worse for drink and sound asleep lying on the lighthouse floor' while on duty. Lockhardt accused Mrs Harper of 'schandilas talk about me and mine' and her designs to see him and his family off the hill, thus making impossible the likelihood that his children would get fair play in the school- room. Lockhardt also questioned the legality of a man and wife drawing separate salaries from the state.[40]

In the following year the Cape Moreton superintendent George Byrne wrote a similar letter of complaint about Mrs Harper using, among other words, 'mischiefmaker, unscrupulous, crafty, conniving and incompetent'. He denied the allegation that there was prejudice against her as a Roman Catholic, assuring good relationships had been maintained with the three previous teachers of that denomination. Byrnes introduced some sound muckraking, namely the desertion of Mr Harper from his wife prior to the Moreton appointment. He alleged that at a previous teaching post, Mrs Harper regularly abandoned her class to attend to domestic duties, and claimed that 'Everyone in Moreton Bay speaks of this woman with great disrespect'. On her decision to send two of her children to Brisbane schools, Byrne seethed: 'It appears though incompetent to teach her own children, yet anything is good enough for people of another denomination'.[41]

After removal of the 'unscrupulous, conniving and crafty' Mrs Harper, the Cape Moreton Provisional School continued operations under a number of teachers until 1926, though there were rarely more than nine children in attendance. While relationships between the teachers, Cape families and Yellow Patch families remained affable, there were the usual requests for transfer from teachers owing to isolation and lack of fresh food. In 1923 the remaining families with school-age children were the Hendersons, Clohertys and Greens.[42] At the closure of the Cape school in 1926 it was suggested to the families that the remaining children enrol in correspondence classes.[43]

In the meantime, development of the South Passage lighthouse settlement halted when navigational services were shifted to the northern end, encouraging passage around Cape Moreton. In 1906 a holiday village site was planned for the southern end of Moreton on the ocean side, opposite what is now the village of Kooringal. This was intended as a holiday spot for 'adventurous Brisbanites', in an endeavour to open up Moreton to less officially-oriented settlement.

The proposed settlement of Booloong was quite elaborate with the old diagrams of the town showing sites for a number of buildings including a government residence, private beach houses,

*7.3 Cape Moreton State School c.1913 (JOL)*

stables, a beach pavilion and bathing sheds, with the lagoon accessible from South Passage providing a safe anchorage for boats. A Booloong town plan shows the proposed development of Rous Esplanade, with at least thirty large building allotments, and the position of the electric telegraph line running through from the signalling reserve station at South Passage to Cape Moreton.[44]

As with most ventures on Moreton, nature dictated the success of the future development. Later described as 'the lost city of Atlantis', the entire settlement site has completely disappeared into the sea and continuing South Point erosion problems now threaten the small town of Kooringal, with residents fearing a catastrophe similar to that at Amity Point on Stradbroke Island.[45] Photographs taken in 1912 and 1913 show the encroachment of the sea at the signal station settlement at South Passage. At this period it appears to have consisted of a signal tower, four houses, a number of out-buildings including a 'refreshment' pavilion and a jetty. By 1920 this lighthouse at Reeders Point was one of seven on Moreton Island in operation.[46] Though few records exist pertaining to the actual demise of the settlement, based on the traditional speed of South Passage erosion the buildings were probably destroyed by the early 1920s. The remaining population at the signal reserve station faded away in keeping with reduced employment as the South Passage channel became increasingly unpopular as a shipping route.

Moreton Island communities prior to 1920 did not establish a distinct identity or culture that may otherwise have encouraged their continuance after the increased demanning of navigational services. While the island's wilderness was admired, it failed to compensate for lack of amenities, inaccessibility and natural hazards. These were significant deterrents to a recently-settled white population aiming primarily to emulate the commercial prosperity and lifestyle of past European associations rather than appreciate and develop a sense of belonging as a community in the existing environment.

*7.4 Cape Moreton Post, Telegraph and Signal Station c.1920 (JOL)*

*Chapter 8*

# Patrick Roche and HM Prison Farm on St Helena 1926-31

## *Yvonne Reynolds*

As the 1920s drew to a close, the worsening economic depression meant that life became a battle for many people. This was often all the more ironic and cruel when compared with what had been achieved just a few years earlier.[1] For those who had taken the gamble of acquiring quick gain from crime and found themselves in prison, life had little hope for improvement. Often these were men who had prided themselves on their ability to provide but had then resorted to robbery for sheer survival of self or family. Their self-esteem and confidence had thus disappeared leaving an angry bitterness. St Helena Island prison farm in Moreton Bay mirrored the hard times with 380 men confined there in 1929. The most prevalent offences were larceny (162), fraud (67), and burglary and housebreaking (25).[2]

The prison had been established in 1867 and reached its maximum efficency in the 1890s. By the 1920s it had become quite outdated. The buildings were predominantly of timber, and successive superintendents and comptrollers-general of prisons had written to the authorities expressing their fear of a fire outbreak in the cell blocks where men were locked at night.[3] To make the danger more acute, carbide gas lighting was used throughout the complex until 1925.

The prison facilities were therefore far from ideal. The water supply on the island was a continual problem, and the length of time staff were required to be absent from their families on the mainland caused much concern. The living conditions in the warders' barracks were spartan and the distance to the mainland in times of emergency also created a major disadvantage.

As well, prison accommodation was outdated. It fell short of the new penological philosophy of providing single cells. The continued use of the old aggregated wards, where men were housed six or eight together, had caused the comptroller-general to comment in 1919 that 'such a system is really an incubator for crime'.[4]

Members of the community were also agitating for closure of the prison. Since 1910 some influential citizens of Brisbane, led by Thomas Welsby MLA and the Moreton Bay League which he formed, applied pressure for their vision of St Helena as a public reserve or holiday resort island to be adopted.[5]

After several years of complaint, His Majesty's St Helena Penal Establishment was reclassified as a prison farm on 21 September 1921. The long-sentence prisoners and workshop facilities were moved to Brisbane Prison and a small group of trustee prisoners was selected to maintain the farm and demolish the buildings, ready to hand the island over to the people of Brisbane. The salvaged materials were used in other government constructions. One problem had been eliminated: there was finally enough single-cell accommodation (93 cells) for the remaining men.[6]

In 1925 the staff was reduced from seventeen to nine officers due to the continued winding-down of St Helena in favour of institutions on the mainland. The remaining warders, being completely familiar with the management of the prison, maintained a degree of continuity

*8.1 Graves on St Helena (AHC)*

despite the changes. One warder, however, was to make this period of down-grading and decay into a worthwhile and valuable time for the prisoners in his care.

Patrick Roche, a quiet, congenial Irishman from County Cork, had been assigned to St Helena as a warder during the 1914-18 war. The last superintendent, John Alexander MacDonald, was appointed in January 1916 and Roche served under his leadership until MacDonald's death on 12 June 1924.

Due to the proposed closure of the institution, the prison department took the opportunity to leave the senior position vacant. Roche was promoted to acting chief warder on 1 July 1924 with W.H. Cranch as acting superintendent.

After fourteen months service, Cranch retired and was 'presented with an armchair and a walking stick'.[7] Roche was promoted to acting superintendent after a short period during which G. Locke held the office. Roche was finally in a position to continue and expand the 'Honour System' which he believed was the answer to rehabilitation for the confinees. The staff was reduced to four, with two on duty, and sixty men in their charge. The challenge to introduce new methods was one of great courage under such conditions.

Roche's family has in their possession a number of newspaper cuttings and letters from released prisoners dating from 1926 to 1934 which he had kept in 'his own little desk'.[8] The men wrote as if to a friendly uncle telling him their family news, their struggles and successes at finding employment, and generally seeking approval for their efforts at trying to 'make a go of it'. Relatives wrote thanking him for the help he had given to sons and husbands:

> I thank you Mr Roche, and that means more than words.[9]

> You indeed have fired my determination to do better in the future and live a clean life and never again go wrong.[10]

> The system under which we were there has mended a broken spirit and given me another lease of life with a complede [sic] different outlook.[11]

> I once again take my place in society with my head in the air, due no doubt to the good influences prevailing under the Honour System.[12]

> I am sending you a little token of gratitude which I hope you will axept [sic] & like the cross opens & contains the relics I know you are a Roman Catholic by the lovely prayer book and sacred heart you gave Wally.[13]

> I hope to be able to do some good, for the sake of the System that done so much for me.[14]

> I am determined to do well ... I owe my altered views of life definitely to you and your humane ways.[15]

> ... attributes of manhood that were fast slipping away, and any success or happiness that may come my way in the future will be solely the result at bottom of the 'Good Samaritan' principle behind the Honour System.[16]

> I am writing to thank you for your kindness to my brother James Casey while he was a prisoner under your care.[17]

> I will of course return the two pounds you so kindly gave me as soon as I find employment.[18]

> We thank you for your information recently sent and also the good advice you've given Stan.[19]

Each letter shines with praise and hope, and shows the incredible success of the 'Honour System'. The idea of this scheme was first introduced to St Helena in the mid-1920s from the United States of America. It was there, in particular, that a new sensitivity had developed in penology, which was in line with new movements in education that rejected negative-reinforcement through punishment. Alexander Sutherland Neill had developed an education system in England which gave the students the responsibility of forming their own rules and also the authority to administer them with minimal supervison. Such ideas brought administrators and those in their care into closer relationships but were regarded, until recent times, with great suspicion in institiutions that were traditionally highly regimented and authoritarian. In 1930 'Friend' Taylor wrote:

> We have all looked upon you as a father always ready to sympathise with and help the poor unfortunate boys – joining in our sports, coming to our Entertainments and supervising us as tho you were our elder brother.

On 21 December 1828 the Brisbane *Telegraph* reported that in August 1926, 'an Honour Club was voluntarily formed by the prisoners to carry out the principles of the system'. Roche had placed a large placard on the wall of the library which read:

> To Supporters of the Honour System: The present honour system, installed by the Queensland Government, is in the experimental stage. It has for its object the uplifting of the unfortunate. Remember, the system is only in its infancy; its success probably depends on your good conduct and industry. Any man who misconducts himself not only will injure himself and his comrades, but also the men who come after him.

The article also reported that attached to the walls was 'a code of rules drawn up by the men themselves for the upholding of the system'. A committee from among the trustees was appointed to advance the work of the club and to provide education and recreation opportunities.

A wireless set, 'costing a considerable sum', was installed by Roche. On 3 February 1927 he had requested permission from the comptroller-general to have the radio on the island, with the reasons clearly set out: 'This concession would have an elevating effect on the minds of the men, it would be a benefit to them, and consequently a benefit to the State'. He recommended that the prisoners be allowed to hear church services when a chaplain was not available and to hear any entertainment that the superintendent 'may deem education'. This innovative addition was praised in newspaper reports and remembered with obvious gratitude in letters from the discharged prisoners.[20]

For off-duty hours the men had cricket and football with equipment provided by the Salvation Army; the privilege of an 'evening dip in the bay' and supervised gambling with their tobacco ration as the stake.[21]

*8.2 Ruins of the smithy, St Helena (AHC)*

Roche's daughter, Mary Bell, stated that her father felt strongly that the cause of their negative attitudes was the environment in which they grew and was acquired behaviour. His frequent argument was: 'Have you ever seen a bad baby? They are all good boys,' and if 'given a go' they would be alright.[22] Extending a helping hand with understanding to men 'down on their luck' was apparently most effective with the trustee prisoners sent to St Helena.

For the hardened criminals and pathological cases confined in other gaols on the mainland, a much higher degree of security and planned precaution was a necessity. Roche, with his ideas, was placed in the right place at the right time where maximum benefit could come to those who were capable of responding positively. An item appeared in the *Brisbane courier* in December 1926 symbolised the new attitude in announcing that the cat o'nine tails from St Helena had been presented to the Home Department Museum. Brutality on the island was now outdated.

The fact that the men were regaining their self-worth was reflected in their letters in which many mentioned endeavouring to live an honest life. T. Purcell wrote to Roche in January 1927 to show 'my appreciation for any treatment at your hands'. He continued: 'if the system extends it will only be a matter of time when there will be less of the criminal element. That old saying "Man's inhumanity to man make countless millions mourn" will be a thing of the past'. These are thoughtful words from a former inmate of an antipodean gaol. Many of the men compared the scheme with the treatment they had received in Brisbane Prison:

> One only has to visit the prison at Brisbane and see on the faces of the men the expression of dogged and sullen hatred, as compared with the joyous and well contented look on the faces of the men in your care.[23]

> What a contrast hard iron rules under which a man is almost compelled to live a life of slavery and goes out with vengeance and vindictiveness in his heart to all mankind. And a system of love where a man is made to feel he is still a man and that he <u>still</u> may hope for bettering his conditions when he goes out.[24]

> Had I to finish my time at the Road my outlook on life could have been prejudiced to such an extent that I would not have been able to write as I am doing now ... P.S. If possible would you transfer my stamps to Dallas Gooham.[25]

> I dread to think what the consequence would have been had I completed my sentence at Boggo Road.[26]

> Harsh and Callous rules of treatment I have found out, the time I happened to have the misfortune to be in prison at Boggo Rd. would out of 100 cases, I do honestly believe, make 90 real criminals.[27]

The men continued to worry about the island after they left and wrote to Roche reminding him of the tasks they had been working on when discharged:

> Has he touched the piece on top up near the light that we cleared? & had the lads got much more wood out?[28]

> Trust that one out of the numbers of the men will take pity on the state of affairs of both cemeteries and nail the loose palings on ... I trust you will find also a man, who will be so good & look after the 2 banana plants I have put in ... also the 7 peach trees are getting watered.[29]

In the 1930s a report in the *Daily mail* mentioned the 'great work done by the instigator of the "honour system" in Australia, Superintendent Roache'. J.B. Walcot, the Queensland agent for Fox Film Incorporated, invited Roche to a viewing of the film 'The Honour System' which was shown in the suburbs of Brisbane in 1927. Roche replied that 'The Picture has been described to me as wonderful ... it may be a great assistance to me in the Prison work on which I am engaged' and that he felt honoured 'by your kindly consideration re my admission to view the film'.[30] It is not known how Roche came to develop the system. His daughter said he studied the American honour system but could not recall whether this was before or after his system was operating.

In 1934 Roche, then superintendent of Rockhampton Prison, wrote to the comptroller-general reminding him of his work on the island and recommending the system as a worthwhile penological practice. He stated that the basis on which he worked was the second paragraph of the Prison Rules and Regulations 'framed by you'.[31] On 8 October 1927 the *Queensland government gazette* included the 'Rules and Regulations – HM Prison Farm St. Helena'. Paragraph two reads:

> It shall be understood distinctly that the system in operation is to be essentially one of a reformative nature, and that all prisoners are to be given to understand that they are placed on their honour to perform their duties faithfully and to best of their ability, and not to attempt to escape.[32]

It is possible that Roche had argued for the system to be included in the new regulations. In many newspaper items the scheme is reported as having been instituted by the government; having it officially recognised certainly validated his work as an accepted system. However, the attention it drew did not endear him to fellow officers entrenched in the existing prison system outside St Helena. Whether through jealousy of his publicity or a fear of the unknown or different, he was not formally recognised for the work so widely acclaimed.

Working with a small number of selected men established the conditions in which his success rate was more likely to be high. The warders on the mainland would certainly have resented his opportunities to try out new ideas while they coped with hardened criminals under a restrictive and non-rewarding system. His media image as an independent iconoclastic reformer, set apart from the faceless-many struggling with difficulties, encouraged a desire to 'cut down tall poppies'.[33]

Roche remained unmarried until he was almost sixty, which gave him an enormous advantage with the amount of time and dedication he could give to his ideas without the added distractions and responsibilities of wife and family.[34] He had the ideal setting for his work: a small group on an isolated farm out of reach of the onlooking authorities. With his Irish background he was sympathetic to the cause of the 'underdog' and lacked the cynicism and insensitive qualities of the politically-minded who indulged in power struggles for promotion and advancement.

*8.3 Disused commandant's house, St Helena (AHC)*

The Salvation Army, with whom he worked closely to rehabilitate the men, recognised his good work. Brigadier Thomas Scotney wrote in 1931:

> I have appreciated your friendship more than I can express. You have been a great help to us in our work amongst the men. I shall ever remember you as one of the most humane and tactful of men, and I have greatly admired your sterling qualities which have helped you make such a grand success of the Honour System. Not only by the Salvation Army Officers who have come into contact with you are you remembered with affection but the many hundreds of men you have assisted, have a very warm regard for you.[35]

Roche's daughter remembered him being rather bitter sometimes about his treatment within the prison system and the feeling that later, after being transferred to Rockhampton and then Palen Creek, he viewed an appointment to Brisbane Prison as a demotion. He was never given official recognition of his ability in proving that positive reinforcement could be a successful reforming method. Prison authorities continued to emphasise punishment rather than rehabilitation. Roche left St Helena in mid-1931, and without its mentor the 'Honour System' faded away:

> Your leaving was felt by all the boys and of course more by the older ones and has created a blank time itself cannot fill. Altho Mr R. is a thorough gentleman and has the good of the boys at heart he is not the father and elder brother that you were. He does not come to the Services (divine) nor concerts or sports as you did and the feeling has grown that the honor system is no more. Even what was known as the honor club has been abandoned.
>
> I was the last chairman of the Club. This is not because he (Mr. R.) has purposely set his face against it but because he has not travelled in your footsteps. Then again Messrs. Hills & Hegarty are transferred to the Road and places filled by temporary warders and one of them an autocrat indeed so much so that he is not respected by anyone.[36]

The Irishman 'with the large heart' who delivered 'a little homily to the newly arrived men' had to be content with his past successes on St Helena and was not encouraged to develop his methods further.[37] The letters from discharged men are his testimony:

> A good many hungry days passed for me but I still fought, and the spirit of <u>Roche</u> and <u>St Helena</u> were my greatest aids.[38]

> I can tell you Mr Roche that I am sure you have not a single enemy in the whole of the world. God grant that you be spared for many years to come for I can assure you that every man who has passed through your hands knows fully well that you can never be replaced.[39]

Perhaps the free tickets from Walcot of Fox Films should have gone to those in charge of the Prison Department and not to the man who lived and carried out the ideals of the 'Honour System' and modern penology, decades ahead of his time.

The work of Patrick Roche influenced the lives of many by changing the attitudes of both the men and their families, extending through them into our community today. The reformed young man in 1930 may have become a great-grandfather who hopefully reflected on his past and could actually be thankful for the time he had spent on St Helena Island, when his life was redirected.

# Chapter 9

# 'The leper shall dwell alone': A history of Peel Island lazaret

**Thom Blake**

Leprosy has been one of the most feared diseases of mankind. No other disease has invoked such a sense of apprehension, dread and horror. Yet leprosy is neither very contagious nor has it swept the world in epidemic proportions like smallpox, influenza, measles, typhus or plague. Furthermore only some sufferers have experienced the terrible disfigurement commonly associated with the disease. About nine in ten persons infected with the leprosy bacterium show no physical signs of the disease, and of the remainder some exhibit only a mild and self-healing infection.[1]

Nevertheless it has been the minority of cases, where terrible mutilation occurs coupled with the foul smell that develops from gangrenous parts, that has made the leper an object of horror and so inflamed the popular imagination for millennia. A consequence has been that the leprosy sufferer has been, at least in the Judaic-Christian tradition, the ultimate social outcast. The victims of irrationality, ignorance and fear, the leper has been forced since biblical times to 'dwell alone'.

## Leprosy in Queensland

The first recorded case of leprosy in Queensland was in 1855 when a Chinese labourer, Oun Tsar, was admitted to the Brisbane Hospital.[2] Isolated cases were reported throughout the colony in the 1860s and 1870s. Throughout the 1880s a small but growing number of leprosy cases was detected. The disclosure of each new case caused some degree of public consternation, but while the disease was restricted to Chinese and Pacific Islanders and the sufferers could either be sent back to their homeland or removed to an island off the Queensland coast, the dominant white population was not overly concerned.[3] In 1889 a lazaret was established on Dayman Island in the Torres Strait for a number of non-European sufferers.

When a young European male, James Quigley from Rockhampton, was diagnosed with the disease in late 1891, public concern about this 'loathsome and dreaded disease' increased. Quigley was removed to Stradbroke Island and isolated in a tent near the benevolent asylum. Concern about the legality of this action, and also the establishment of the Dayman Island lazaret, prompted the government to introduce a bill in April 1892 'to provide for the Treatment and the Detention and the Isolation of Lepers'. The bill gave wide sweeping powers to the Colonial Secretary who could order the removal and indefinite detention in a lazaret of any person suspected of having the disease. The rationale for such draconian measures was encapsulated in the remarks of the Hon F.T. Brentnall:

> The danger of the disease, its loathsomeness, and its objectionable nature rendered it desirable that lepers should be treated ... It was repugnant to the eyes, and lepers were glad to get out of sight. Whether it was a danger or not, it was in the interests of the community that there should be complete isolation.[4]

Opposition to the bill was led by Dr William Taylor who was well qualified to debate the issue. Taylor had worked with leprosy patients in England and visited lazarets in India. He also held a Diploma in Public Health. He argued that it was an 'inhuman Bill' and that it would 'frighten the life out of people'. Taylor asserted that the complete isolation of leprosy patients was not warranted or appropriate. In his view, it was most important to provide the best possible medical treatment because it 'was want of care ... that made leprosy such a terrible disease'. Taylor was also concerned about the extreme powers in the bill. In particular, he was worried that a person could be incarcerated for life simply on the judgement of one medical practitioner who may never have seen a case of leprosy.[5] Taylor's pleas were ignored and the legislation was enacted in July 1892, denying any suspect all forms of natural justice. Indeed, leprosy suspects had fewer rights than a person accused of murder.

Soon after the bill was passed, a lazaret was proclaimed on Stradbroke Island to accommodate white patients, and in the north a lazaret was established on Friday Island in the Torres Strait for all non-white or 'coloured' patients. The Friday Island lazaret replaced that at Dayman Island, which had proved to be a most unsuitable location.

The government showed little interest in either institution, hoping that only minimal expenditure would be necessary and that any problems would remain out of sight and out of mind. However, during the following decade the government was confronted with a litany of complaints from the patients about their accommodation, food, lack of medical care and harsh treatment by staff. A number of those appointed to care for the patients either lacked the necessary skills or were temperamentally unsuited for the task. Both lazarets were badly situated in low-lying sites and close to swamps. The death rate, particularly on Friday Island, was alarmingly high. The government became further embarrassed when several white female patients were sent to the Stradbroke Island lazaret in the early 1900s, and there was a public outcry about leprosy patients engaging in sexual activities.[6]

Though the government continually tried to evade taking any substantial remedial action, by the early 1900s the cumulative effect of ongoing problems forced consideration of new and more appropriate arrangements for leprosy patients in the state. Several plans were considered including housing the non-white patients on Peel Island and moving the white patients to a new lazaret at Amity Point on Stradbroke Island. Another plan involved the establishment of a lazaret on Mud Island near the mouth of the Brisbane River. Eventually Peel Island was selected as the site for a multi-racial lazaret. Despite the possible problems, the main benefit from the government's perspective was that it would result in an overall decrease in expenditure on leprosy patients.[7]

Peel Island had been proclaimed a reserve for quarantine purposes in 1873. A station was established on the southeast corner of the island and was in regular use throughout the 1870s and 1880s as the colony received a constant stream of immigrant ships. With a sharp decline in immigration in the 1890s and a general improvement in public health, the quarantine station fell into disuse. In 1906 an area of 160 acres [64.75 hectares] on the north-western corner of the island was gazetted as a reserve for lazaret purposes and the remainder was proclaimed a reserve for the purposes of a benevolent asylum.[8]

Peel Island had indeed been used unofficially as a lazaret prior to this time. In 1895 a white male who was suspected of having leprosy, but tested negative, was detained on the island. In the following year, when the first white female was diagnosed with the disease, it was thought unwise to place her on Stradbroke Island in close proximity to the male patients. She was sent to Peel Island to live in one of the disused quarantine station buildings and spent two years there.[9]

9.1 Peel Island Lazaret 1955 (JOL)

## Establishing the lazaret

The site chosen for the new lazaret was on the northwest corner of the island. It was on one of the higher ridges and well away from the old quarantine station buildings. Construction began in late 1906 and the lazaret was completed by June the following year. The buildings for the white patients and staff were erected by a Brisbane contractor, Messrs Hooper & Ross, for £2,600.[10] The huts for the coloured patients were erected by Aboriginal workers from Myora on Stradbroke Island and Barambah (now Cherbourg) Aboriginal Settlement.[11] In early July 1907, 26 patients were transferred from Stradbroke Island and 30 inmates from Friday Island were brought south on the steamer 'Otter'.[12] Fifteen other patients from Cooktown, Cairns and Halifax were also admitted later in the month, making a total of 71 patients when the lazaret commenced operation.[13]

The overall plan of the site and the design of the individual buildings was based on the 'isolation' principle, which meant that the more effectively patients could be isolated from each other, the greater the possibility for controlling the disease. The system of accommodating patients in wards or barracks as practised on Stradbroke and Friday islands was dispensed with. Each patient was accommodated in a separate hut, and huts were grouped in separate compounds according to race, sex and severity of illness. There were three main compounds – male, female and 'coloured'. The isolation principle, however, was not limited to certain medical views on the most appropriate treatment of leprosy. It was also influenced by prevailing ideas of sexual morality and race. Female patients were well segregated from males and all non-white patients placed in a separate compound. Within the coloured compound the division into male and female was not enforced.

The lazaret buildings were designed by architects in the Department of Works under the supervision of Thomas Pye, the district architect.[14] They were typical utilitarian government buildings of the period – timber framed, clad with weatherboards and roofed with corrugated galvanised iron. In common with other contemporary government buildings roof ventilators were provided. This inclusion on all of the buildings reflected prevailing ideas about the importance of ventilation and fresh air, particularly in institutions for the sick.

*9.2 Kitchen and new lazarette 1907 (JOL)*

The huts for white patients were simple one-roomed structures measuring ten by twelve feet [3 by 3.6 metres] and ten feet [3 metres] high. Each hut had a window on the back wall, french doors and fanlight, and a roof ventilator. A total of 11 male and 5 female huts were constructed, and each hut was furnished with a bed, chest of drawers, table and chair.[15]

Other buildings included bath houses (one female and two male), dining rooms (one female and two male), kitchens (male and female), nurses' cottage and attendant's quarters. The caretaker's residence, which was originally part of the Stradbroke Island lazaret, was dismantled and re-erected on the new site.

Approximately 100 metres from the white compound and staff quarters was the coloured section. These buildings were noticeably different from the huts for white patients.They were of rudimentary construction, being framed with bush timber, clad with cypress pine slabs, roofed with tea-tree bark, and simply provided with an earth floor.[16] The contrast between the two types of huts was also apparent in the cost of construction – £3 for each coloured hut versus £55 for the white hut. Sixteen coloured huts were built and measured approximately ten by twenty feet. The principle of isolation which was so rigidly adhered to in the white compounds was not enforced in this compound. These huts were of similar dimensions to those in the white section, but were intended to accommodate two patients each.[17] A larger hut of similar materials was also constructed for a married couple.[18]

The divisions within the lazaret, evident in the building types and spatial relationships, were reinforced by fences and paths. Within the male compound, there was a further division between mild and advanced cases. The two groups were provided with separate dining rooms and bath houses. The huts for the advanced cases were positioned further apart than the mild cases.

**Development of the site**

Additional buildings were erected as more patients were sent to the island. In 1908 an additional male hut was built, and another in 1910. Four male huts were constructed in 1911. A hut to accommodate two patients was erected in the female compound in 1910.

A small but noticeable change to the form of the huts occurred in 1908. Immediately they were occupied, the need for greater protection was apparent and awnings were added to the

*9.3 Male hut, Peel Island 1992 (TB)*

front of the huts for greater shade and protection from the weather.[19] All huts built subsequently had awnings incorporated.

More significant changes occurred in the coloured section in this early period. Three huts, of similar materials and form to the male huts, were erected for females in 1908. The general condition of the huts quickly deteriorated, and the suitability of the bark cladding as a temporary measure became more and more obvious. The patients became increasingly discontented. In April 1909, 28 coloured patients wrote to the Home Secretary complaining about the conditions they were forced to endure and requested 'decent houses'. They explained:

> ... the winter season is begun and we are left unprepared to meet the winter how are we to live, we shall most of us perish with the cold for the want of a warm and comfortable place to sleep in.
>
> At the present time we are having our meals under a tents fly & it is no use to us, because when it comes on to rain we all have to stand up and eat our meals for everything gets wet. Since we have lived on this island we are dying away fast about fifteen have died already here and only one white, the reason why there has been so many deaths amongst us coloured patients it is because we are not looked after as well as the whites & as far as our bodies concerns they have all the comfort they are kept in warm houses away from the cold & wind & rain & us poor sufferers who suffer the most cannot get what we ask for.[20]

The government agreed to improve the conditions in the coloured compound, but there was no suggestion of upgrading the accommodation to the standard enjoyed by the white patients. Instead, the existing huts were simply reclad with corrugated galvanised-iron sheets fixed to new sawn timber battens which were in turn fixed to the existing bush posts.[21]

Although an improvement, conditions in the coloured compound were still unsatisfactory and the patients continued to complain about their huts and lack of facilities.[22] After they had been forced to eat their meals under a tent fly for almost three years, a dining room was finally erected in 1910.[23] At the same time the floors of the huts were concreted.[24]

In 1908 a church was built adjacent to the coloured compound. When the patients from Friday Island were being transferred to Peel Island, the Anglican Archdeacon Le Fanu suggested that a church be provided for the lazaret as a large number of the Friday Island patients were 'earnest Christians'.[25] The church was constructed partially out of materials from buildings

9.4 'Coloured' hut, Peel Island 1992 (TB)

demolished on Stradbroke Island. Though intended to be non-sectarian, it became recognised as an Anglican place of worship, and was later known as the Church of the Good Samaritan.[26]

Following the initial increase in the population of the lazaret, the number of patients steadily declined between 1912 and 1919. Few improvements occurred and no new buildings were erected during this period.

A resurgence in the number of new cases in the 1920s resulted in a significant increase in the population of the lazaret. Between 1919 and 1926, patient numbers rose from 41 to 76 – an increase of 85 percent. Thirteen male, 7 female, and 4 additional huts were erected in the coloured compound. During this period the procedures for cooking meals were altered. The kitchen in the female compound was closed, and female patients were required to cook their own meals. The female huts adopted a new form, with enclosed kitchenettes incorporated on a side verandah.

Other buildings erected during the 1920s included one new kitchen, store, nurses' quarters and surgery or treatment room. The surgery, a two-room building with verandah on three sides, was built in 1925. Remarkably, although the lazaret had been in operation for almost twenty years, this was the first building specifically built to provide medical treatment for the patients. Improvements were also undertaken in the coloured compound. Four timber huts similar to those in the white compound, were erected in 1924 for female coloured patients. In an attempt to regulate their behaviour an eight-foot high fence was erected around these huts. During the 1930s, as the number of white female patients decreased, several unused huts were moved to the coloured compound. The only major new building in this period was a six-bed hospital built in 1937.

In January 1940 the coloured compound was closed when the patients were transferred to a newly-constructed Aboriginal lazaret at Fantome Island near Townsville. Efforts to establish a separate institution had begun several years earlier when Dr Raphael Cilento was appointed director-general of Health and Medical Services. He brought to the position extensive experience in tropical medicine, including an interest in leprosy. Cilento also had firm views about race and the problems which Aborigines posed to white development. He was a strong advocate for the creation of a separate lazaret for Aboriginal patients, and after investigation of various island locations in North Queensland, Fantome Island, near Palm Island, was finally selected in May 1939.[27]

In the early 1940s the remaining white patients formed a welfare committee with one of its main objectives to improve conditions on the island. They were strongly supported by Dr Eric Reye when he was appointed Medical Officer in 1944. On several occasions Reye threatened to resign if improvements were not forthcoming. Four new huts were built in the male compound in 1945. Although retaining the same form as the earlier ones, these huts differed in the use of asbestos cement sheeting for the internal walls and roof.

A new recreation hall was built in 1945, replacing an earlier building that had been destroyed by fire in 1941. A system of reticulated electricity was introduced in 1948 and three new buildings were erected: a power house, battery shed and engineer's hut. Three alternators (two 20 KVA and one 5 KVA) driven by diesel engines supplied power to all the patients' huts and staff buildings, and provided lighting throughout the site.[28]

With the appointment of a resident medical officer, a timber hut from the former military camp at Redbank was purchased, relocated and converted into a duplex residence. Five other huts were purchased and used for a patients' dining room, staff dining room, staff recreation room, hospital annexe and patients' barracks. This latter building, erected on the southeast corner of the male compound, signalled a departure from the isolationist approach.

As the number of patients began to decline in the 1950s, more and more huts became vacant. Rather than repair or renovate any huts, patients were moved into those in better condition. Until this period, all work on the buildings had been undertaken by Department of Works tradesmen, but in the 1950s patients began to undertake their own repairs and alterations. The last major building activity was new accommodation for male staff in 1955.

## The patients

The probability of being infected with leprosy in Queensland in 1900 was approximately one in 200,000. The rate of incidence did increase in the following decades, but the probability of contracting the disease and being admitted to the lazaret was extremely low. In the early

*9.5 Female hut, Peel Island 1992 (TB)*

1900s the group most affected by leprosy were Melanesians who had been brought to Queensland as indentured labourers in the sugar industry.

The lazaret opened with 71 patients: 16 Europeans, 3 Chinese, 1 Indian, 4 Aborigines and 47 Melanesians. There were 64 males and 7 females.[29] Disparity between the number of females and males continued throughout the life of the lazaret, as there were always substantially more male than female patients.

Between 1907 and 1959 there were a total of 572 admissions to the lazaret. This figure includes a number of patients who were discharged and later re-admitted. In total, there were approximately 400 individuals who were inmates of the lazaret, of whom 250 were to die on the island.

The number of patients quickly increased to 84 in 1910 and then gradually declined in the following decade. This decline was attributed to the termination in 1906 of the indentured labour system, resulting in a large number of Melanesians returning home. There was a resurgence in patient numbers in the 1920s, both among whites and coloureds. The latter group by this time consisted principally of Aboriginal people. Indeed, by the 1930s the coloured compound confined only Aboriginal inmates.

Patients admitted to Peel Island varied greatly in age and occupation. The average age of white patients was 41 years, and of coloured patients 34 years. The oldest patient sent to the lazaret was 92 when admitted, while the youngest inmate was aged 7.[30] During the 1930s several children aged under 12 years were admitted including a 7-year-old girl from Woorabinda, an 8-year-old girl from Mona Mona, and an 8-year-old boy from Palm Island.[31]

The occupations of patients included labourers, farmers, students, tailors, housekeepers, clerks and police officers.[32] Though inmates came from all parts of the state, the disease was more prevalent in some areas. Leprosy was endemic in several regions in Queensland, notably around Rockhampton, Mackay, Bundaberg and Mona Mona Mission near Cairns.

## Conditions in the lazaret

When the lazaret opened in 1907, the facilities were described by the Commissioner for Public Health in enthusiastic terms.[33] Two years later the commonwealth Chief Quarantine Officer visited the island and observed that 'the treatment is generous in the extreme'. The patients saw the matter very differently. Throughout the life of the lazaret, they complained constantly about the conditions on the island. Their efforts to improve the situation included a barrage of correspondence to the Home Secretary, the formation of a patients' welfare committee, letters to the press, the enlistment of support from outside groups and even undertaking a clandestine trip to Canberra.

The first four years were the most turbulent. Both the white and coloured patients protested bitterly about the conditions that they were forced to endure. The coloured patients in particular had every reason to complain. They were deprived of basic amenities including decent food and shelter. A number were forced to live in tents while huts were erected.[34] In March 1908 Sam Wright, a Melanesian patient, wrote on behalf of other coloured patients to the Home Secretary, urging him to do something about the living conditions. He suggested that if nothing could be done 'the best thing to do was to send us all home to our own countries & then we would be sure to find better accommodation for ourselves'.[35] In 1910 Aboriginal patient Thomas Moreton wrote to the Home Secretary about the treatment of the coloured patients:

> ... we have suffered here for little over two year for want of a better accommodation to you the truth when it come on to rain here the dining place under a fly is get worse than a pigs sty & we have to stand & eat our meals its a disgrace to leave us like we are & we want a hospital ward for the sick & blind who cannot take care of themselves you dont know all the difficulty we have in helping the sick and blind if you will get a hospital ward put up for them it would be better.[36]

The white patients, despite better accommodation, were no less discontent by conditions. Water was, at times, in short supply and strict rationing was necessary. They also complained about the quality of the food they were served and the lack of medical attention.[37] The patients also rebelled at the restrictions on their movement in and about the lazaret. Concerned about the moral behaviour of the patients, strict measures were introduced regulating patients' activities, particularly the women. They objected to these impositions and one patient, Rose Donovan, complained bitterly about the restrictions. She wrote to the Home Secretary:

> Sir, I won't be locked up like a criminal .... Why are we being treated in such a harsh manner. . . What crime are we supposed to be guilty of .... If these rules continue there will more die of broken Harts than Leprosy.[38]

Within two years of the lazaret being opened, not one but two inquiries had been conducted into the management of the lazaret. The magistrate concluded that at one stage the 'institution was in a state of anarchy'. The general attitude within the lazaret was described by one patient: 'the place is nothing but a living torment to us'.[39] Although the initial discontent did dissipate after some improvements were made, the basic problems remained. The disregard for authority prompted the visiting medical officer to report in 1921 that 'The half-castes have an idea that being leper patients the law cannot touch them, in consequence of which they are impertinent and defy everyone on the island'.[40]

In the following year the Australian Labor Party produced a report detailing many of the old grievances about poor food, a lack of medical care and bad management.[41] During the 1940s the patients became more organised and formed a patients' welfare committee to agitate for better conditions. A member of the committee travelled secretly to Canberra and lobbied the commonwealth minister for health to establish a royal commission.[42] The committee was supported off the island by the Relatives and Friends Association. Conditions on the island began receiving public attention and criticism. At the 1946 Country Womens Association Annual Conference, delegates were informed:

> Patients there are living under the most shocking conditions. They have not even the ordinary amenities of civilisation. There is no electricity on the island, there is no telephone, and inmates with infectious leprosy are living among patients with another and milder type of the disease.[43]

These criticisms, along with other pressures prompted some improvements, notably the introduction of electricity in 1948. Conditions nevertheless generally remained inadequate. In March 1950 the lazaret featured in several articles and letters in Brisbane's *Courier-Mail* newspaper, and an article entitled 'New deal needed for State leper patients' highlighted deficiencies in the food and quality of the medical care.[44] Again the government was prompted to remedy some of the more severe and embarrassing problems but no substantial changes were made to the operation of the lazaret. Only in the closing period of the lazaret, when few patients were left, was there less cause for complaint about the conditions.

A contentious issue among the patients was visitor access. The possibility of never returning to one's home meant that patients looked forward to visits from friends and relatives, though visits to patients were strictly regulated. In the early period of the lazaret the regulations stated that visitors were not allowed to 'kiss or embrace or allow himself or herself to be kissed or embraced by a patient', nor could they shake hands with any patient that had sores or a wound on the hand.[45] Visitors had to obtain a pass from the Health Department to travel to the island. Access became more liberal in the latter part of the life of the lazaret.

**Everyday life**

Unlike the inmates of other government institutions such as prisons, reformatories, asylums and Aboriginal settlements, the inmates of Peel Island were not expected to work or contribute to its operation. Some patients were employed as carpenters, labourers, attendants and seamstresses but generally they were treated simply as hospital patients and left idle and alone.[46] The inmates had to devise their own means of overcoming the boredom and despair of confinement on the island.

Gardening was a popular activity and remained so throughout the life of lazaret. During the 1920s prizes were offered for the best kept gardens.[47] The 1924 annual report noted that the patients' huts 'in many instances have pleasing parterres and in which much taste is displayed in the cultivation of choice flowers'.[48] Patients also occupied their time reading, painting and tending animals such as goats and fowls. Boating and fishing were popular pastimes; the patients constructed their own jetty and several owned boats which they used for fishing.

A focal point for social activity was the recreation hall. Soon after the lazaret opened, a male dining room was converted into a recreation hall and it contained a small library, pianola and billiard table. This building was destroyed by fire in 1941 and replaced four years later by the present recreation hall.

The advent of radio broadcasts in the 1920s provided a new form of contact with the outside world for the patients. A 1920s photograph indicates an array of masts scattered throughout the lazaret. The introduction of electricity in 1948 expanded the range of social activities for patients. A movie projector was purchased for the lazaret and regular screenings of feature films occurred. Patients were also entertained by occasional visits from bands and concert parties.

Sporting activities included cricket and tennis, the latter being the most popular. A court was constructed for the patients during the 1920s at the northern end of the site. When the new recreation hall was erected a new court was built in the centre of the lazaret between the staff quarters and male compound.

**The treatment of leprosy**

When the Peel Island lazaret was opened, leprosy was a disease still shrouded in mystery, ignorance and misunderstanding. There were diverse theories as to how it was transmitted, and new cures and treatments were regularly promulgated. One of the few aspects agreed upon was that the disease was caused by a rod-shaped bacterium *Mycobacterium leprae*. It had been identified by Gerhard Hansen in Norway in 1873, and the disease was later called Hansen's

*9.6 Caretaker's cottage and men's hut, Peel Island 1907 (JOL)*

9.7 Peel Island grave 1989 (AHC)

disease.[49] With no cure available until the 1940s, for the patients on Peel Island there was little hope. They were doomed to spending a lifetime on the island, their health slowly but surely deteriorating while surrounded by others sharing a similar fate.

When the first patients arrived at the lazaret, the commissioner of public health, Dr Burnett Ham, was optimistic that research on the disease could be undertaken. The lazaret provided, he claimed, 'an opportunity for study unique in character'.[50] If the patients thought that this meant they would be well cared for, they were soon to learn the opposite. The history of medical care on the lazaret was one of neglect, indifference and ignorance.

The first medical officer appointed to the lazaret was Lindford Row, who was also the medical superintendent at the benevolent asylum at Dunwich. Due to the latter duties, Row was only able to visit Peel Island once a week at the most. The task proved to be beyond him, and on one occasion he privately admitted that he knew nothing about leprosy.[51] Following constant complaints by both white and coloured patients about the lack of medical attention, Row was relieved of his duties in April 1912.[52] He was succeeded by J. Irwin Moore who visited the island on a weekly basis. Other medical officers appointed included J. E. Thompson (1914-19), C. D. H. Rygate (1921), J. Coffey (1922-28), J. G. Drew (1931-38) and D.W. Johnson (1939-44). These officers had a great concern for the patients' welfare, but the amount of time that they were able to spend on the island was extremely limited. They were given the task of medical responsibility for the lazaret along with a myriad of other duties. At best they were able to visit the island only once a week; often it was much less frequently than that.[53]

It was not until the 1940s that patients had more than a weekly visit from a medical officer. In 1946 Eric Reye was appointed medical officer to both Peel and Fantome islands. As a result the patients received medical attention more regularly than previously. The first full-time medical officer, V.J.B. Lennon, was finally appointed in 1949. He was replaced by M.H. Gabriel in 1951. Gabriel remained as the medical superintendent until the closure of the lazaret in 1959.

The lack of concern for the welfare and health of the patients was reflected in the delay in building dedicated medical or nursing facilities on the island. Though there was no cure for leprosy, the patients still needed day-to-day medical attention and facilities where such care could be administered. As early as 1910 the patients had requested a hospital, resident surgeon and small surgery, but they had to wait another fifteen years before a two-room surgery was built.[54] The Health Department finally acknowledged in 1937 that a hospital was necessary for 'patients who could not look after themselves', and in the following year a six-bed hospital was erected adjacent to the surgery.[55]

For the first patients on Peel Island, the intention to undertake research on the disease had unfortunate consequences. In 1909 some patients underwent treatment with a new drug, Nastin. After a year, the results were more than disappointing. Several patients undergoing the treatment died and the experiment was suspended in 1911.[56] On the advice of Dr Anton Breinl, director of the Australian Institute of Tropical Medicine, chaulmoogra oil was introduced as a remedy.[57] This oil was derived from the seeds of Asian trees and had an extremely nauseous taste.[58] It remained the standard treatment for more than thirty years, although there was no evidence that it arrested the disease among patients.

Despite the lack of an effective cure, for a minority of patients the disease did go into natural remission. According to Reye, medical officer for the lazaret between 1944 and 1949, the diet and lack of stress probably contributed to remissions rather than any treatment such as chaulmoogra oil.[59] All patients were regularly tested as to the state of the disease and until the 1920s any patient who gave bacteriologically negative smears for two years could be discharged. In 1929 this period was reduced to eighteen months, and in 1937 to fifteen months.[60] Between 1907 and the late 1940s, when an effective cure became available, an average of four patients were discharged each year.

The 1940s were a turning point in the treatment of leprosy. In 1940 researchers working at Carville leprosarium in the USA began experimenting with a variety of drugs that could arrest microbacterial diseases. Initial results were not promising, but in 1941 a group of patients were given the drug Promin, a sulphone derivative. Within a year it was evident the drug was effective in halting the disease, prompting the trial of related sulphone drugs.[61] News of this success soon reached Australia. As there were difficulties in obtaining supplies of the drug, it was not until January 1947 that Peel Island patients first received a course of Promin. Within months the effectiveness of the treatment was obvious. For patients, the commutation of their life sentence on the island became a distinct possibility. Promin did have certain side-effects as well as the disadvantage of having to be administered intravenously. It was soon replaced by other more effective sulphone drugs including Diasone, which could be administered orally.[62]

The success of drug therapy became increasingly apparent as a growing number of patients were discharged – 39 of them between 1951 and 1953. A decade of treatment saw a five-fold decrease in the number of patients. By 1959 with less than a dozen patients and effectiveness of the drug treatment well established, the lazaret had finally become redundant.

### The campaign to close the lazaret

The push to close Peel Island began in an indirect manner in the 1920s. Although a cure for leprosy had yet to be discovered, some members of the medical profession in Australia increasingly questioned the appropriateness of the strict isolation of leprosy patients.[63] In the *Medical journal of Australia* in 1926, E.H. Molesworth, a lecturer in skin diseases at the University of Sydney, suggested that there was no scientific basis for continuing the practice of compulsory segregation. He argued that such an approach was based more on prejudice and ignorance:

> What is the reason that leprosy alone of all the chronic infective diseases is treated this way by internment and deprivation of almost all civil and human rights? Is it because it is so dangerous to our community? ... No? is it because of the horror inspired by the disease and the ignorance of its appearance, course and possible cure ....
>
> What is the rhyme, reason or justice in continuing the existing practice and condemning fellow countrymen to an indeterminate incarceration, to a fate which they fear with some reason to be worse than that reserved for a convicted burglar or in New South Wales at least for a convicted murderer?[64]

Molesworth contended that one of the major problems with strict isolation was that it discouraged sufferers seeking medical attention in the early stages of the disease. Citing Peel

Island as an example, he also argued that patients, when isolated, did not often receive satisfactory treatment.[65]

Molesworth received strong support for his arguments from Sir Leonard Rogers, who was internationally recognised for his research into leprosy.[66] He cited several examples, including Nauru, where leprosy patients had been successfully treated only as out-patients. He concluded that 'the contrast between the rapidly successful results at Nauru with the failure of three decades of compulsory segregation in Queensland is too evident to require further emphasis'.

Neither Molesworth nor Rogers persuaded health authorities in Queensland or elsewhere that the closure of lazarets such as Peel Island was desirable. The isolationist argument was strongly defended by two senior medical officers, Cecil Cook and Cilento. Both men were regarded as experts in the field, and while arguing that white patients could be less strictly isolated, maintained that leprosy was still increasing among Aboriginal groups and that the only way of limiting its spread was to continue a policy of strict segregation.[67] To maintain that Aboriginal and not white patients should be isolated was simply too difficult to argue – and too overtly racist – even in the 1930s. Nevertheless, when Cilento was appointed Director-General of health and medical services in Queensland in 1934, any possibility of a new, or less isolationist approach evaporated. Instead, within Queensland's health bureaucracy, the isolationist stance became more entrenched than ever. In 1939 Cilento proudly boasted that the 'strict measures practised here for the segregation of lepers' had put Queensland 'for many years ahead of the rest of the world'.[68]

Agitation for the closure of the lazaret intensified in the 1940s. The efforts of the patients' welfare committee and the Relatives and Friends Association eventually forced the government to consider building a new lazaret. A site approximately one kilometre to the south of the existing lazaret near the south-west corner of the island was selected and plans drawn.[69] The design of the new complex bore little resemblance to the existing lazaret. All buildings were to be of brick construction, patients were to be accommodated in dormitories, and the buildings were to be arranged around gently sweeping curved paths and roads.[70]

The proposal never eventuated and the department continued to attempt to answer the criticisms of the lazaret by improving conditions. It did not answer, however, the specific issue of why the lazaret was required at all. The Relatives and Friends Association began publishing a magazine, the *Moreton star* which aimed at 'radiating the true light on Hansen's Disease'. It vigorously challenged the validity of isolation of leprosy patients:

> In Sweden, the disease has disappeared, but then Sweden, a most enlightened civilised and christian country, never had COMPULSORY SEGREGATION which causes cases of Hansen's to hide away from medical care for years, until they are very advanced indeed. Hansen's is only very feebly, if at all, communicable, and it is a Public Disgrace to know that cases remain away from medical help – for years AND without infecting other people – because they know they will be COMPULSORILY SEGREGATED as soon as they ask for help![71]

The Association received support from a freelance journalist, F.G. Gladen, who in 1950 published a pamphlet, *The case against compulsory segregation of leprosy in Australia*. The campaign, although not completely successful, did have some impact on the Health Department. While not accepting that leprosy patients could be treated as normal hospital patients, the department did agree that it was no longer necessary to isolate patients on an island. A site was selected at Burpengary for a new leprosarium. The project advanced to the stage where prefabricated buildings were ready for shipping to the site when it was suddenly abandoned, principally due to public pressure.[72] The Peel Island patients were forced to endure yet more years in isolation through public ignorance, political indifference and bureaucratic inertia.

Despite the obvious success with the sulphone drug therapy, the Health Department was not prepared to act quickly in embarking on a new approach in the care of leprosy patients. The eventual closure of the lazaret was principally due to the efforts of the medical superintendent,

Morgan Gabriel. In November 1958 Gabriel attended the Seventh International Congress on Leprosy in Tokyo and presented a paper advocating the 'abandonment of strict isolation of Hansen's Disease sufferers, especially in the case of white patients'.[73] Following the conference, Gabriel recommended the closure of Peel Island and that the patients be transferred to an annexe at one of Brisbane's hospitals.

On 5 August 1959 the ten remaining patients were transferred to a ward in the newly opened Princess Alexandra Hospital at Annerley.[74] Eventually it seemed leprosy patients were to be treated no differently from any other person with an infectious disease – but not quite. In a last act of prejudice and ignorance, all the patients' bedding, together with all floor coverings, mats, and curtains, was burnt. All buildings that they had occupied or used were fumigated with formaldehyde gas. The medical superintendent commented following this action: 'In my opinion no further action is necessary!'[75] That most 'loathsome and dreaded disease' had finally been expunged from the island.

**Subsequent events**

Following the closure of the lazaret, the government began investigating new uses for the island. The gazettal of the island as a reserve for lazaret purposes was rescinded and it reverted to vacant crown land. Organisations such as the Girl Guides Association and the Queensland Sub-Normal Childrens Welfare Association expressed an interest in taking over the lazaret buildings.[76]

The government, however, placed economic considerations before acts of charity. The island had obvious potential as a tourist resort and in February 1960 applications were invited for a lease of Peel Island for tourist development.[77] The idea met with little enthusiasm as applications were called for twice, and on the second occasion only one proposal was submitted from a Californian doctor. It was a grandiose scheme involving the construction of a scenic ring road around the island, an air strip, a golf course, a sanctuary for wild life, a hotel and motel.[78] The scheme lapsed through lack of finance.

In 1964 the government proposed a new scheme involving the construction of an esplanade around the island, setting aside 145 acres (58.6 hectares) for residential development, twenty-seven acres (10.9 hectares) for a tourist resort and the remainder of the island as a national park.[79] Again the idea failed to attract public interest and the government decided to offer the former lazaret buildings for sale. Many of the buildings were sold but the task of removing them from the island was more difficult than anticipated. Some buildings were removed, while others were simply dismantled, with timber and other materials remaining either on the stumps or stacked together.

The government made yet another attempt to develop the island as a tourist resort in 1967. Expressions of interest were called and an area three chains [60.3 metres] wide around the perimeter of the island was gazetted as an esplanade. Three applications were received but none were considered suitable.[80]

The following year the Church of England Grammar School offered to lease a portion of the lazaret site. The government accepted the offer, and granted the school a special lease for twenty-five years over an area of two acres (.8 hectares) which included the recreation hall, nurses' quarters, matron's quarters and superintendent's quarters. In 1970 the lease was extended on the eastern border by nine metres and included five male huts and the male bath house. The school used the area for educational camps.[81]

When the lazaret was closed in 1959, the site became the sole responsibility of the Department of Works. A caretaker was appointed to the island to maintain some oversight of the buildings. The department dispensed with a caretaker when the Church of England Grammar School obtained their lease in 1968, and appointed their own caretaker. In 1989 the island was proposed as an Environmental Park and responsibility for its day-to-day management was transferred to the Redlands Shire Council. The island is currently managed by the Department of Natural Resources and is subject to a native title claim by the Quandamooka people.

*Chapter 10*

# The whalers of Tangalooma 1952-62[1]

## *David Jones*

In contrast with the other Australian colonies, Queensland had little early contact with the whaling industry. Whaling vessels occasionally worked offshore waters in the first half of the nineteenth century, well before European settlement along the coast. In 1800 the British whaler, 'Speedy', searched for sperm whales as far north as Point Danger. Some whalers were among the earliest wrecks, such as the 'Duke of York' on Port Curtis in July 1837. Queensland waters were not productive for these ships, however, and only isolated catches of sperm whales were taken, far off the southern coast or beyond the Great Barrier Reef in the Coral Sea. The range of the southern right whale, common around southern Australia, did not extend beyond northern NSW and thus little shore-based whaling took place during the nineteenth century.

The first record of a whale being taken by this means occurred on 12 December 1872, when a ten-metre specimen was taken off Sandgate in Moreton Bay. Thereafter they merely provided the occasional windfall for individuals involved in other maritime activities.

At the beginning of the twentieth century, modern techniques began to make whaling more efficient and lucrative. Steam chasers using harpoon guns had removed many of the dangers for those involved in the industry, and made the kill more certain. At the same time, the Antarctic Ocean began to be systematically harvested. Modern whaling was also being organised in Australian waters. In 1912 Norwegian whale factory ships, accompanied by chasers, operated from Jervis Bay in NSW and in Western Australia. An Australian concern also operated from Point Cloates in the latter state between 1922 and 1924.

After the Second World War an unprecedented demand for whale oil revived the industry once again. Australian companies commenced whaling off Western Australia from Albany in 1947 and, two years later, a station was re-established at Point Cloates. The commonwealth government was interested in establishing whaling on a permanent basis because of its immense potential for improving the nation's balance of overseas trade. Information was sought as widely as possible about whale distribution and habits.

As well as carrying out their own investigations, the government sought the advice of professional whalers and in 1948 brought Captain Alf Melsom to Australia as a consultant for envisaged development. A Norwegian whaler with more than forty years' experience, and an internationally-recognised authority, Melsom visited all potential sites around the Australian coast and made recommendations. The Australian whaling commission was established the following year and operated a large shore factory at Carnarvon in WA from 1950 to 1955. By 1953 whaling in the west was at its height; three stations took a combined total of 1300 whales.

The postwar research by the commonwealth government revealed that whales were plentiful along the east coast during winter and early spring, and could be economically viable. Accordingly, on 15 December 1950 Whale Products Pty Ltd commenced operations from Sydney, with extensive research being carried out on the feasibility of operating a whale factory ship and possible sites for a shore-based station. A decision was subsequently made to construct

*10.1 Tangalooma whaling station 8 June 1952 (JOL)*

a station at Tangalooma on Moreton Island, and thus began Queensland's first and only whaling station.

The site offered dichotomous advantages: proximity to the migration track of humpback whales, and to the facilities of the port and city of Brisbane. A thirty-year lease was arranged with the Queensland government over an area of 12 hectares. The company engaged Melsom as manager and gained the benefit of his expert advice and organisation. He made two trips to Norway in 1951 for purchasing whale chasers and the factory plant, and to have the necessary plans drawn up. While in Norway, Melsom also engaged experienced personnel for the chasers and flensing decks. By the end of the year construction was underway.

The following year Whale Products Ltd was registered as a public company, with a nominal share capital of £1 million. Melsom was appointed to the directorship in recognition of his services, and the company took over the shares of Whale Products Pty Ltd, which retained responsibility for catching and processing whales. Two other subsidiary companies were concerned with the refining and marketing of margarine and whale bone – the main products of the industry.

After negotiations with both the commonwealth and state governments a licence was obtained for a period of five years, which allowed the company to harvest 500 humpback whales annually, with the season extending from 1 May to 31 October. The area of operations extended in a radius 240 kilometres north, east and south of Tangalooma, but over the next few years it was not necessary to venture far beyond the immediate vicinity of Moreton Island.

Construction progressed rapidly, and in seven months the station was operational. It comprised a large factory surmounted by a flensing deck, with a log ramp running into the sea to land the captures. As well, a jetty had been built, a steam generator installed and accommodation for staff almost completed. In the meantime, a number of employees were forced to live under canvas.

Three whale chasers were purchased, and these were brought to Brisbane along with fifty-one experienced Norwegian whalers. It was envisaged that the Norwegians would fill key positions and train Australians in the intricacies of the industry. In the long-term, Australians were expected to replace their teachers.

The first of the whale chasers, KOS VII, berthed in Brisbane on 14 May 1952, having travelled 19,500 kilometres in just seventy-six days. Before the end of the month she had been joined by her sisters, KOS I and KOS II. The organisation of Queensland's first commercial whaling venture had been most enthusiastic. Whale oil was in high demand and prospects looked very promising for the company as it approached the beginning of its first season.

KOS II made the first foray on 6 June. Around noon two whales were sighted just north of Cape Moreton lighthouse and the vessel gave chase, with Melsom at the harpoon. The hunt was successful, with both whales, around 13.7 metres in length, being taken. By late afternoon they were being cut up on the flensing deck and Tangalooma was in business.

Just over a month after the season commenced the Tangalooma whalers scored their first century. The hundredth whale was taken by KOS I on 7 July, a day in which five whales were captured. At this stage low tides at Tangalooma were delaying the landing of whales and two left overnight were mauled by sharks.

In August the company's quota was extended by 100 after the Byron Bay whaling station in NSW failed to commence operations in time for the 1952 season. These were taken in little more than a fortnight and Tangalooma's first season thus closed successfully on 7 October, having lasted 124 days.

In 1952 the average humpback whale was worth around £1000 in terms of the products which could be rendered from its carcass. The most important product, of course, was whale oil, which was particularly valuable at the time operations commenced at Tangalooma owing to a world shortage of fats. The oil, whilst found throughout the whale, was heavily concentrated in the coat of white blubber, about 25 centimetres thick, when the animal was in good condition. This could yield as much as fourteen tonnes of oil, although yields as low as two tonnes were not unknown. Seasonal factors were also important, and the average was around nine tonnes.

Top grade oil was used for edible fats, particularly margarine. The Tangalooma product was manufactured and sold by Farm Margarine Pty Ltd. In the first year, all the margarine was exported to Europe, but over subsequent years large quantities were sold locally. Lower grade oil was used for tempering steel, pharmaceuticals, soap, as a base for cosmetics and for making glycerine. Of the secondary products, meatmeal and bonemeal were the most important. The intestines, bones and meat residue were also processed into a meal of high protein for cattle, pigs and poultry, or used as a fertiliser. Marketed by Hi-Protein Pty Ltd, meatmeal and bonemeal were intended for the domestic market, but in some seasons surplus was exported.

Approximately 4 or 5 tonnes of whale meat could be recovered from the carcass, and this was utilised for both human consumption and pet food. Most of the latter was exported to America and Britain. Whale steaks were served as a novelty at Tangalooma once or twice a week, and were comparable to beef. The whalebone, which was so valuable in the nineteenth century, was still used in the overseas fashion industry. So, once the whale had been fully processed, only a wheelbarrow load of gristle remained to be dumped.

As time progressed, however, the whalers found their industry undermined by substitutes. When vegetable oils came on the market the demand for whale oil fell dramatically. In 1952 it was worth around £100 per tonne, but ten years later realised only £45 per tonne. Whale meat, bonemeal and meatmeal were also replaced by similar products from cattle abattoirs, and these substitutes were the main factors leading to the global collapse of this maritime industry.

These problems were certainly not envisaged at the outset. After the first successful season, activities settled into a regular pattern, and little trouble was experienced in filling the quotas allocated to the station. During the second season a record 700 whales were taken, and this was accomplished quicker than the catch of the previous year. In 1954, however, when whaling began at Byron Bay, the quota was reduced to 600. This remained unchanged until 1959, with no difficulty being experienced in catching the set number of whales.

In 1954 extra equipment was installed to speed processing. Unfortunately, the season was hampered by adverse weather conditions and finished only four days earlier than the previous year. At one stage the chasers were weatherbound for five consecutive days as a cyclone threatened the coast. Earlier there had been great excitement when KOS II sighted a blue whale a few kilometres north east of Cape Moreton. After a three-hour chase the female animal was taken, but it measured only 20.4 metres and proved to be an embarrassment for the company. Though it was the largest whale ever processed at Tangalooma, she was still under the legal limit set by the International Whaling Commission.

The new factory equipment paid dividends in the 1955 season, which was completed in record time – just over two months. From then until 1960 this was the normal duration, with a new record of sixty-three days being set in 1957. From 1955 the chaser captains also exercised a high degree of selectivity in their choice of targets, taking the largest specimens and leaving the young. Wherever possible males were taken in preference to females, and usually two-thirds of the catch consisted of males. Lengths averaged about 12.5 metres.

The factory and processing installations at Tangalooma represented the most modern available and provided a continuous mechanised process through all stages. It was designed to handle 9 whales every 24 hours, but at the outset this could not be achieved. With extra equipment, efficiency steadily improved, and processing rose from a low of 4 whales per day to a peak in 1959, when 10 animals were processed every day of the season.

A Norwegian whaling engineer, Chris Christophersen, was engaged as factory engineer and he supervised the installation of equipment. About 120 factory staff were normally employed and they worked two twelve-hour shifts for seven days a week.

The factory building was the centrepiece of the establishment. Built of reinforced concrete surmounted by the flensing deck, a turpentine log slipway led to the latter in two stages. The ramp was a dangerous place for sharks and men working on the lower ramp had to undertake their tasks while keeping careful watch for these marauders. Indeed, even the higher ramp which held the whales until they were ready to be processed was not safe from intrusion by sharks. It was not uncommon for them to slither up the ramp to take a bite before sliding back down. On occasions they became stranded or caught in the railings, and were despatched with

*10.2 Captured whale on the loading ramp, Tangalooma 1953 (JOL)*

a gun; some measured up to five metres in length.

The flensing deck itself was built of concrete to prevent seepage and measured 49 metres long by 20 metres wide. Timber decking was bolted to the concrete and taken up at the conclusion of each season for cleaning. Three winches were fitted at the rear of the deck with another on each side. A steam-driven saw was also installed to deal with the bones left when flensing was completed. Hatches in the flensing deck led directly into the Kvaernar cookers and Huse shredder plant below.

Two cookers were installed on the southern side of the factory and commenced the process of extracting oil. In effect, they were pressure cookers, each with a 29 tonne capacity. The blubber was cooked for four hours at 60-pound pressure, which reduced it to oil. After passing through the separators which removed impurities, the oil was pumped to measuring tanks and then stored. Sharples Lassen separators for decanting and reducing solubles were installed after the first season, and in 1954 a spare boiler was added.

A Huse plant was located on the north side of the factory for shredding the meat to meal without going through the Kvaernar cookers. This was the first Huse plant in Australian whaling and was claimed to produce a high quality meal. It was a large rotating drum with a capacity of 300lb and contained numerous blades. The shredded meat was then transferred to the rotating meal drier, and was later bagged and stored in an adjacent room.

Steam power was provided from an oil-fired boiler, originally from a navy destroyer, located in a separate building just south of the factory. When the second boiler was fitted, voracious demands were made on the available fresh water supplies. This was obtained from eight bores, while seawater was used for washing out the factory and cleaning floors. An Allan steam generator supplied electricity and this was supplemented by three Ruston diesel generators of 800hp, 600hp and 120hp respectively. All four units were required to operate the factory at full capacity.

Oil was stored in two tanks, with a capacity totalling 1,137,500 litres, well to the north of the factory building. A nearby jetty carried a pipe for conveying the oil from factory to tanks, while a second pipe was used to transfer the oil onto the lighter 'Centipede' for cartage to Brisbane. The lighter was owned by Moreton Navigation Company and was kept busy shuttling stores to Tangalooma and eighty tonne loads of oil back to Brisbane. Staff and perishable stores were conveyed to Tangalooma thrice-weekly by the fifteen-metre launch, 'Norman R Wright'.

A blacksmith at the factory repaired harpoons, which were invariably twisted and sometimes bent double during the kill. Such was the strength of this unnamed individual, that he was reputedly able to lift a 160lb harpoon with one hand and slide it down his test gun barrel.

For three or four months the factory was expected to work at full pressure and without a break to make the most of the season's catch. Only running maintenance was possible during this period and it was essential that all machinery was brought up to peak efficiency for the start of the next season. At the close of each season a small maintenance staff of fifteen to twenty remained at Tangalooma repairing, refitting and replacing the many items of equipment in the factory. Maintenance personnel lived at Tangalooma but were able to return home to Brisbane on weekends, leaving the factory in the hands of a supervisor.

The life of a whaler both at sea and on land was not easy and a seven-day week and long hours were demanded throughout the season. At the close of the season they returned to other jobs or went whaling elsewhere. In 1952 the key employees on the chasers and in the factory were Norwegians, but as the years unfolded crews gradually became more cosmopolitan.

Norwegians were far and away the best and most experienced whalers of the century, and many were flown from their homes in Norway every year at the company's expense. Most valuable were the chaser captains. They were also harpoon gunners and their expertise could not be matched anywhere in the world. For the first season the chasers were commanded by Captain Engels (KOS I), Captain Bredo Rimstadt (KOS II) and Captain Bjorn Laurentsen (KOS VII). All were very experienced, with 3000 whales and twenty Antarctic seasons each to their credit. They earned around £5000 per season, as well as an incentive bonus 5s. a head for their catch. Taken together, it was enough to allow them to live comfortably for the rest of the year.

After the first season an Australian, Captain Stan Sheridan, took command of KOS I, which was used as a towboat until the 'Firern' arrived. Sheridan then took command of this boat while Laurentsen transferred to the KOS I, as his vessel had gone to WA. These three captains remained in command of the three chasers until the station closed down.

The crew of a chaser was arranged in two shifts, consisting of a mate, an engineer, a fireman and two deckhands. Shifts lasted four hours during the day and six hours at night, but during the chase it was 'all hands on deck' until the kill had been effected. They lived aboard the chaser during the season, setting foot ashore only when an opportunity arose, and then only briefly. Understandably, accommodation was cramped. The captain enjoyed a small cabin in the bridge superstructure; the mates, engineers and cook were accommodated in the hull aft; while the deckhands, firemen and messboy berthed in the bows under the forecastle. Though the watch officers and engineers had their messroom near the galley, the deck and engine hands had theirs located in the hull adjacent to their sleeping quarters. Meals were carried along the open well deck forward from the galley to the messroom regardless of the weather.

Competent teamwork was a prerequisite for a successful catch. So too was patience. At times the whales proved elusive, and when they turned out to be undersized after a long wait, frustration often surfaced. Experience alone taught the patience required. With any sort of sea running, the chasers had a very lively motion, and a strong stomach and good sea-legs were also essential. Only during exceptionally bad weather would the chasers be forced to withdraw from the hunt and anchor inside Moreton Island.

After the day's quota of whales had been captured the chaser's crew usually spent the rest of the day fishing or playing cards. During the early years, when the factory could only handle a limited number of whales, the crew had considerable leisure time. Later, when the factory

*10.3 Whale chaser KOS VII off Tangalooma 1952 (JOL)*

became more efficient and the whales became more difficult to catch, leisure time disappeared.

The chasers could operate at sea for periods up to a fortnight, when they would have to re-enter the Brisbane River to restock their fuel bunkers. To minimise interruption of the hunt this was usually undertaken at night.

Despite the constant work, everything possible was done to make life comfortable for employees. The factory was clean and modern, and after work the men retired to twin rooms, warm showers and clean sheets. Meals were served through both day and night shifts and there was no shortage of food. Films were screened once or twice a week and a dry canteen was provided. Recreational activities included fishing, pig-shooting and motorbike riding along the sweeping beaches; the prevalence of sharks, however, totally prohibited swimming.

Life was particularly hard for family men as they were expected to work every day for up to five months, and had no opportunity of returning home to see their families until the season finished. The only relief was provided by the 'Norman R. Wright', which was able to bring wives and children to Tangalooma for a day trip on weekends.

On the other hand, there was never any shortage of labour, despite the station being geared for efficient production and demanding very high standards. The attraction and compensation was good money. For example, a tradesman who was normally under an award salary of £19 per week could, by working twelve-hour shifts for seven days, earn in the vicinity of £70. Additionally, employees were entitled to a 'barrel bonus' at the conclusion of the season, based on the amount of oil produced.

Mishaps at Tangalooma were fortunately few. The station did have a scare one night, when two crewmen from a chaser failed to return to their vessel after seeing a film show ashore. A large-scale search was mounted, but the following morning a telephone call was received from Bribie Island saying that they were safe. Their dinghy had been carried away by wind and strong currents, and after spending a terrifying night drifting across the shipping lanes they managed to clamber ashore on the opposite side of the bay.

This incident occurred when whaling was still in full swing. The first hint of real trouble for the station came in 1959 when world oil prices began to fall, and the Tangalooma quota was increased to 660 in an attempt to overcome this setback. Around the same time there were indications that Antarctic whaling was having a detrimental impact on whale numbers. Yet, despite the problems, the full quota was taken in just sixty-five days.

The statistics for the 1960 season provide no evidence of any decline; the full quota was taken in seventy days, and the average length was above that recorded in previous seasons. Another cloud, however, was already forming on the horizon. The chasers certainly did have to travel further afield for their quarry, and often a full day was spent in effecting captures.

The 1961 season came as a shock to the whalers at Tangalooma. After effortlessly filling their quotas for nine years, they found that their quarry had suddenly become very scarce. After spending more than double the time they had the previous year, Tangalooma's quota had not been filled when the season terminated on 31 October.

The area of search had expanded until the chasers were travelling as far afield as the shoals, thirty-five kilometres from Maroochydore, south to Southport and well out to sea eastwards. A towing chaser became an absolute necessity. Indeed, as searching time extended, it became more economical to employ a light aircraft for spotting. On sighting a whale, the nearest chaser could be called in to effect the kill.

Due to the scarcity, chaser captains shot every allowable whale that came within reach and little selectivity was possible. Many of those taken were on their southern migration to the Antarctic and were thus in poor condition. The average yield of oil was some two tonnes down on the previous year. By the close of the 1961 season 591 whales had been taken – 69 short of the quota.

Whale Products Pty Ltd had suffered a serious setback, and efforts were made to improve the company's chances for the 1962 season. While aircraft were again utilised, two new chasers were also purchased. These were larger and faster than the old KOS vessels, and fitted with modern equipment. In view of the previous year's difficulties, the quota was also reduced to 600 whales.

The two new chasers arrived on 31 May, and the season commenced on 18 June 1962. Unfortunately the pattern of the previous season was not only confirmed, but also reinforced. By 5 August only 68 whales had been taken. In the previous season 253 had been captured in an equal period of time and it was obviously not an economic proposition to continue at the current rate; the whales were simply not there and the station closed down on that date. Not long afterwards both Byron Bay and Norfolk Island whaling stations also closed after experiencing similar scarcities.

The casual visitor to Tangalooma today would find it hard to imagine it as an efficient whaling station, for now it is the site of a luxury tourist resort. Former employees would nevertheless recognise many of the buildings. The flensing deck has been converted into a tennis court and the factory below replaced by guest facilities, but the water supply and electrical generator, along with a number of houses and sheds remain in use. The oil wharf stands derelict, and the landing ramp has been demolished.

About a kilometre up the beach a few obsolete dredges and hopper barges have been beached to form an artificial harbour for the boating fraternity. As a result, Tangalooma is now noted as a holiday and camping area rather than an industrial site. Yet, apart from the change in purpose, the island is otherwise little altered from the days when the whalers lived and worked there. Moreover, on a crisp winter's day the spout and rolling black backs of humpback whales is now becoming increasingly common, giving hope that the population is again returning to its pre-hunting levels.

*Chapter 11*

# Layers on the landscape: Dunwich Benevolent Asylum

## *Nonie Malone*

Dunwich now stands as the gateway to Stradbroke Island. While its character is an obvious hybrid of tourist and mining dependence, there is a hint of maturity beneath the surface suggesting greater experience. On approach from Moreton Bay, the first impression is mixed: modern mineral-loading facilities project into the bay; tall spreading trees dot the landscape; and warmth and charm emanate from timber and iron buildings in the vista across the sportsfield. Dunwich has been performing its mining and tourist functions since the Second World War, and while these, particularly sand-mining, strongly imprint upon its character, they do not explain all.

To account for the mixed impression, Dunwich needs to be examined as a sequence of layers, with particular reference to the penultimate layer – the benevolent asylum – which served the poor, needy, aged and infirm people of Queensland from 1865 to 1946. The built and vegetative landscapes of present-day Dunwich incorporate remnants from this earlier identity. These may be treated in two contexts: those elements which remain in their original locations; and those which have been relocated elsewhere in the township. To give meaning to the remnants, reference will be made to the physical lay-out of the benevolent asylum immediately prior to its closure in 1946, and to the process by which Dunwich changed from total government control to private residential status. An assessment will be made of the extent to which Dunwich has remained true to this earlier period, and how the period itself influenced the character of the township as it existed in 1995.

Dunwich is a layered place, with the location having been used for different human purposes at different periods. Moreover each period and purpose has been distinct, and yet has influenced the transition into the next phase. The site of the township has passed from hosting an Aboriginal settlement, to being occupied by a convict station, Passionist missionary post, quarantine station, and then for almost eighty years the Queensland government's benevolent asylum.

The choice of the site by Passionist missionaries in 1843 was determined by the existence of vacant buildings remaining from the convict settlement between 1827 and 1831.[1] Its adoption for use as a benevolent asylum was determined by the existence of vacant buildings and infrastructure from the quarantine station. The jetty, part of which is the earliest convict-built structure of Moreton Bay,[2] undoubtedly influenced the selection of the site as a quarantine station. The abundant fresh water supply in the area had originally influenced Aboriginal settlement and also the selection of the locality as a convict station.[3] In turn, the infrastructure which developed to support the inmates of the benevolent asylum became important in the transition to a residential township.[4]

The importance of the benevolent asylum to the historical development of Dunwich is reflected in the establishment and purpose of that charitable institution.[5] Between 1867 and 1947 the whole of the present township site was gazetted as a reserve for the benevolent asylum. This reserve, which encompassed the six buildings of the earlier quarantine station, had been adapted

*11.1 Dunwich Benevolent Asylum c.1891 (JOL)*

for use during a time of crisis in the colony.[6] The relocation of the state-supported aged and infirm from Brisbane to Dunwich in 1864 was intended to be temporary. By 1866 it had become institutionalised and permanent.[7]

Indeed, the number of buildings on the site expanded to accommodate increasing numbers of needy people and staff. By 1913 there were nearly seventy buildings within the boundary of the reserve.[8] Laid out on an area radiating from the jetty to the cemetery were twenty-three ward buildings for male inmates; a series of interconnected ward buildings for female inmates; staff quarters and housing; mess rooms; administrative buildings; stores and warehouses; recreational buildings, including a hall and library; a church, a school, a mortuary and artisans' workshops. Separate tent accommodation, mess and recreational facilities were provided for consumptive inmates on Polka Point, to the northeast.

The institution's imprint on the landscape was intensified by the development of infrastructure to service the asylum population. The entire area was fenced to confine the cattle used for food by the resident population.[9] This was supplemented by a dairy farm, piggery and vegetable garden, although it was still necessary to bring additional supplies from the mainland. The asylum had its own sawmill to aid expansion and maintenance, and its own quarry to provide gravel for road construction.[10] A small powerhouse generated electricity, and a pumping station on Yerrol Creek supplied water; these utilities enabled operation of a large steam laundry. The convict-built causeway was extended with a timber jetty to suit the needs of the institution.[11] In effect, Dunwich *was* the benevolent asylum and the benevolent asylum *was* Dunwich.

When the asylum closed in 1946 the site contained roughly the same number of buildings as it had in 1913, but the pattern of the landscape had changed. Some ward buildings had been demolished and the inmates relocated to tents erected in the Mitchell Park area.[12] Some staff housing had been erected near Polka Point after removal from St Helena.[13] Other staff housing had been built along Finnegan Street.[14] The school was housed in a different building elsewhere within the reserve. The vegetable gardens had also been shifted.[15] The Aboriginal population, previously accommodated at Myora Mission had moved to rudimentary housing on the One Mile, between the cemetery and Myora; Aborigines were under the supervision of the benevolent asylum's medical superintendent.[16]

Despite this patterning of buildings, the natural features of the landscape were reasonably undisturbed during the period of the benevolent asylum. Certainly roads and trolley tracks impacted on the terrain, but the buildings were environmentally sympathetic. Most were constructed with timber walls and frames on wooden stumps rather than concrete slabs. The location of buildings was further influenced by the topography, and a number were aligned to take advantage of the outlook over Moreton Bay.

Much of the area was swampy, and several small creeks drained into the bay; and the limits of the reserve were defined by natural features, including a ti-tree swamp, Yerrol Creek, the hills and coastline.The limits of Dunwich are no longer determined by the natural features. The swamp and creeks no longer remain, as they were considered incompatible with residential and tourist development.[17] The township's postwar purposes dominate the streetscape, but isolated areas nevertheless remain and speak of another time and a different purpose. These derive from the benevolent asylum era. Some of them are concentrated, others scattered. They determine the visibility of the benevolent asylum layer within the current form of Dunwich.

At the corner of Fraser Street and Flinders Avenue near Polka Point a cluster of relocated timber buildings remained until 1999, when the University of Queensland upgraded its Moreton Bay research station. One of those buildings was moved yet again to the local school.

Other isolated and scattered remnants within the Dunwich landscape include staff housing along Welsby Street, between Parsons and Pamphlet streets; St Marks Church on Ballow Road; the brick mess hall built in 1913 and currently used as the public hall; half of Ward Thirteen, which is one of Consolidated Rutile's administration buildings; concrete draught boards in Ballow Park and on the esplanade between Hospital Point and Polka Point; the swimming enclosure between the jetty and Hospital Point; the dairyman's shed on the local government reserve situated on the corner of Mitchell Crescent and Welsby Street; a few headstones and unmarked graves of deceased asylum inmates in the cemetery; part of the extended main school building fronting Bingle Road and the trees within the school yard; and the old pumping station and equipment on Yerrol Creek.

Remains of the tennis court can also be found on the ground beside the eastern wall of the new visitors' centre. Concrete slabs remain from a portion of Victoria Hall in Ballow Park, and from the recreation and mess building in the consumptive camp at Polka Point. Evidence of the lazaret, which closed in 1901, can be found on a mining lease off Ballow Road, where it has been partly preserved by Redland Shire Council.[18]

The buildings and facilities remaining from the asylum period are not the only features from that time which have been integrated with the present landscape. Large camphor laurels, Moreton Bay figs and palm trees, planted when the asylum occupied the site, were often an aide memoire to people who provided oral information for this research. The trees assisted with visual placement of buildings long since removed, and thus served as markers to determine alignments and the positions of buildings such as the post office, Victoria Hall, the female division of the benevolent asylum and the doctor's residence.

The preservation of trees has been both deliberate and coincidental. Particular trees were considered worthy of preservation by the surveyor charged with town planning, and by road workers involved in the process of conversion from asylum to township.[19] Trees intentionally preserved in this way include those which line both sides of Junner Street, between the jetty and the main business area, and also those which formed part of the Visitors' Cottage gardens and now shade the playground adjacent to the jetty. As well as the large palm tree in the former grounds of the doctor's residence, and a similar specimen on the esplanade at Hospital Point, which once graced the entrance to the asylum's female division, the various trees surrounding the main school building also have historical importance. Each year the children of staff members planted trees here to celebrate Arbor Day.[20]

*11.2 Dunwich Benevolent Asylum 1906 (JOL)*

While a number of buildings have been relocated, other structures within the existing Dunwich landscape stand as evidence of another time and purpose. The present pharmacy in Ballow Street, for instance, was once Ward Twenty of the benevolent asylum. The former asylum manager's residence (later school principal's residence), remains as a private dwelling on Dickson Way at One Mile.[21] Moreover, a number of houses on Oxley Parade can be identified as belonging to the asylum period by their pyramidal iron roofs.

The main determinant of building relocation on the historical landscape was the decision made by the Queensland government to dispose of most of the benevolent asylum buildings.[22] Initially it was expected that the Housing Commission would utilise the materials and buildings due to post-war shortages.[23] That department declined the offer for three specific reasons: the material was in extremely poor condition; labour was in short supply; and, importantly, the exorbitant cost of transportation to the mainland.[24] The few buildings that remained were therefore incorporated into the town plan.

Many dilapidated buildings were disposed of in various ways. Much of the remaining material was taken by the Department of Native Affairs for use at Cherbourg, Woorabinda and Foleyvale.[25] Some were used by the Department of Harbours & Marine in the Fisheries Research Station building at Dunwich, while the remainder was offered at public auction in March 1949.[26]

It is those buildings taken by the Department of Harbours & Marine and by members of the public which contribute so significantly to the integration of benevolent asylum features with the present landscape. The Fisheries Research Station, which was a joint venture with the CSIRO, impacted for some years on the cultural landscape of Dunwich. It was its decline and disuse contemporaneously with the expansion of mining activities, that created the currently enduring mining dominance of the township's character. The buildings afterwards formed the university premises.

Without doubt, however, the most significant factor which determined the patterning of the benevolent asylum on the present landscape was the work of the government planner.[27] Work commenced at the end of 1946 and continued until the first sale of land under perpetual town leasehold in December 1948. It involved adapting the charitable institution for civic purposes, with a number of features deliberately being left in their original location.[28] As a consequence, many roads overlay the original trolley and gravel tracks. These include Junner Street, running from the jetty; Ballow Road, heading eastwards to the old lazaret; Cunningham Street and Oxley Parade, which led to the female division of the asylum; and Bingle Road, which was earlier known as Cemetery Road. The continued use of existing access ways, built features and the endurance of vegetative landmarks have given the township the physical form of its previous layer. Other streets and buildings have subsequently been superimposed on this form.

These features, especially those which have remained in their original locations, create a discernible imprint. Those which have been re-arranged on the landscape contribute a certain enigma to the multi-faceted character of Dunwich. Despite these strong influences, it can no longer be said that Dunwich *is* the benevolent asylum or that the benevolent asylum *is* Dunwich. The township is characterised by recent mining activities and tourism, though the underlying form contributes a warmth and charm which effectively counter-balances the cold and commercial.

*11.3 Dunwich Benevolent Asylum c. 1935 (JOL)*

*Chapter 12*

# The history of Moreton Bay: A saga of lost dreams

**Rod Fisher**

Over 20,000 years of Aboriginal occupation had little impact on Moreton Bay; yet less than two centuries of Australian settlement blighted the land, the sea and the original inhabitants. Historical accounts are peppered with high hopes, noble deeds and admirable pioneers in an island paradise. When pieced together, they constitute a saga of lost dreams.

After touching upon the geographical configuration and Aboriginal dreamtime, this overview identifies patterns concerning the impact and outcome of white history. Seven overlapping *modes* or emphases are distinguished, and various major *themes*, from 1770 until 1993:

| | |
|---|---|
| **Mode 1:** | **Discovery 1700s to 1840s** |
| Themes: | exploration, survey |
| **Mode 2:** | **Incarceration 1820s to1840s** |
| Themes: | institutionalism, exploitation |
| **Mode 3:** | **Experimentation 1840s to 1870s** |
| Themes: | recreation, exploitation, plantation, institutionalism |
| **Mode 4:** | **Occupation 1870s to 1940s** |
| Themes: | institutionalism, fishing, farming, recreation, war |
| **Mode 5:** | **Development 1940s to 1980s** |
| Themes: | exploitation, suburbanism, recreation |
| **Mode 6:** | **Conservation 1970s to 1980s** |
| Themes: | communication, conflict |
| **Mode 7:** | **Management early 1990s** |

While placing the bay in context of developments on the mainland, this overview concentrates on the islands: especially Bishop, Bribie, Coochiemudlo, Karragarra, Lamb, Macleay, Moreton, Peel, Russell, St Helena and Stradbroke.

### Configuration 6000BP to 1800s

School children were taught that Moreton Bay comprised no less than one island for each day of the year. Bordered on the Pacific Ocean by Bribie, Moreton and Stradbroke islands and along the mainland by numerous inlets and promontories, the expansive bay of some 1500 square kilometres is entered by four passages from the ocean, seven rivers and several creeks from the land.

The shape of Moreton Bay was determined primarily by the natural elements. As the climate warmed after the last Ice Age, the sea rose to its current level about 6000 years ago. This flooded the river basin, bringing the shoreline in from about twenty-five kilometres east of Moreton Island and turning various eminences of rock, soil and sand into islands. The subsequent movement of sand and sediment by water and wind, the growth of coral and vegetation, and a slight drop in the sea level continued to change the shape of the bay – a natural process which goes on today.[1]

**Dreamtime 2000BP-1800s**

In this maritime environment the Aborigines developed two distinct economies or lifeways by some 2000 years ago: the inland-terrestrial and the coastal-littoral. The sub-coastal or mainland groups were hunter-gatherers who ventured out into the bay for island resources; those who lived on various islands were primarily fishing people with spear, line and net.[2]

Both economies relied on abundant food resources of the bay which supported a population of over 5000.[3] One of the earliest British visitors in 1836, the Quaker missionary George W. Walker, wrote of the 'immense shoals' of mullet which were 'crowding into the bay, darkening the waters by the ripple they produced when pursued by sharks, porpoises, &c'. At Amity on Stradbroke Island he also observed the flocks of pelicans, and at the southern end of Moreton Island the numerous crabs and a party of Aborigines gathering berries.[4]

Other commentators recorded the native custom of using porpoises to herd mullet towards nets along the shore;[5] also the mammals, reptiles, honey, grubs and plant food which supplemented the plentiful marine life.[6] Consequently Thomas Welsby, the later authority on Moreton Bay matters, spoke of this 'paradise' where 'lazy life for man could be lived with but little work'.[7]

For this reason the island Aborigines formed long-term settlements of substantial huts rather than the flimsier inland variety. These were depicted by Captain Owen Stanley in his watercolour on Moreton Island in 1848. They were also described by others, especially the botanist Allan Cunningham who observed 'a deserted village' on Stradbroke Island in 1824:

> These huts were formed on a frame work of large sapling trees, and thatched in parts with tufts of grass and the thin bark of Melaleucae, like those observed on the low shores in the vicinity of the Brisbane River. One of these habitations within which I had entered by a low doorway, presented a capacious area, nearly 50 feet across, amply sufficient to afford shelter and accommodation to forty persons – the roof, which rose gradually from the low sides to the centre of the hut exceeding a height of six feet.[8]

Smaller more temporary abodes and short-term dinner camps were located near marine and terrestrial sources, especially fish, shellfish and crabs on various islands and flying foxes on St Helena. On Coochiemudlo in 1799, Matthew Flinders found some boughs arranged to shelter fireplaces from the southerly winds, but no regularly constructed huts.[9]

The ensuing contact history of Moreton Bay is rather fragmentary. It is clear, however, that settlement, commencing at Redcliffe in 1824, undermined this way of life by the 1860s. The Aborigines were almost annihilated by a deadly cultural cocktail: disease, especially smallpox, alcoholism and venereal disease; conflict, including armed confrontation on Stradbroke Island between 1831 and 1833, and native police action in the Bribie area around 1860; prostitution and intermarriage, possibly involving infanticide; usurpation of land, prime sites and resources; relocation, willingly or otherwise, to an alien environment; and assimilation, including the attraction of European commodities and employment as dugong fishermen, oystermen, boatmen, servants and rouseabouts.[10]

Remnants of the Moreton Island clans were moved to Stradbroke in 1847, where the Aboriginal population totalled about 65 by 1887. In 1891 they were placed on Bribie Island as a reserve but moved back to Myora Mission at Moongalba in 1892.[11] Monuments were erected at Moongalba to Sydney Rowlands (d.1917) and near the Bribie Island bridge to Alma Turner (Kalmakuta, d.1897) as the last of their respective Moreton and Bribie Island clans.[12] However, Lizzie Bulsey, reportedly the last of the Noonuccal of North Stradbroke, died in 1935, and Gurri of the Nooghie tribe of Moreton Island in 1940. Moreover descendants of the Noonuccal continued to utilise traditional pathways across North Stradbroke to collect shellfish as late as the 1950s.[13] They also laid legal claim to ownership of the island in 1988.[14]

Consequently most of the physical evidence of Aboriginal occupation is archaeological. This includes bora-rings, stone scatters, quarries, fish-traps and scarred trees, but especially middens of shell and bone on the islands including Coochiemudlo, Lamb, Moreton, Peel, Russell, St Helena and Stradbroke. Many of these sites have suffered from human interference and natural erosion:

> Moreton Island is therefore significant because it contains a pattern of archaeological evidence relating to a system of Aboriginal settlement and subsistence over at least the last 2000 years. Furthermore, the evidence can be used to produce models about past Aboriginal lifeways applicable to wallum areas of southeast Queensland of which only a small fraction of the archaeological evidence or its context remain.[15]

**Discovery 1700s to 1840s**

In the early decades of European contact, the main historical mode was discovery of the dimensions of the land and sea, and of the original inhabitants. Therefore exploration and survey were two of the earliest *themes*.

During the preliminary stage of *exploration*, Lieutenant James Cook named Point Lookout and Cape Morton (without an 'e') in 1770, as well as calling the bight in-between Morton Bay. It was not Cook but Lieutenant Matthew Flinders who appreciated that Moreton was an island with passages into a larger bay. He entered through the north passage and partially mapped and named the bay in 1799, including various islands. He also experienced the first known clash with Aborigines at Point Skirmish (now South Point on Bribie Island).

While searching for a large river in 1822, John Bingle noticed another opening to the south. He guessed that Pumicestone in the north was also a passage rather than a river, and first referred to the whole expanse as 'Morton Bay'. It remained for the surveyor-general of NSW, John Oxley, in 1823 to explore the river, which he called the Brisbane, and to advertise that the land south of Point Lookout was an island. In 1824 Oxley also named Peel Island, but not until 1827, following the survey of the bay by Captain Rous, did Stradbroke and other localities receive their titles. Various places were named by later surveyors and officials, especially between 1839 and 1842. Nevertheless the outline of Moreton Bay was known by the late 1820s.[16]

*Survey* of the bay for navigational purposes also proceeded apace. The South Passage between Moreton and Stradbroke islands, which was sounded by surveyor Robert Hoddle with sailing master Charles Penson and traversed by Oxley in 1824, was charted and buoyed by pilot John Gray in 1825. This tricky channel served as the main entrance until the steamer 'Sovereign' foundered in 1847 with the loss of forty-six lives. Consequently the survey and buoying of the entrance to the north of Moreton Island was accelerated by Captain John C. Wickham, Lieutenant C.B. Yule and Captain Owen Stanley, and became the main shipping route into Moreton Bay.[17] Another well-used passage was marked inside the bay between Stradbroke and the other islands for coastal and island shipping from Brisbane to the Southport bar and beyond.[18]

Over the succeeding years many navigational aids were provided on islands and promontories, including lighthouses, pile lights, beacons, markers and buoys. The prominent lighthouse at

Cape Moreton, constructed from local stone in 1856-57, was but the first of seven on Moreton Island. Many of these aids have vanished, including the Pile Light which was demolished by a tanker in 1949.[19]

Despite the additional provision of charts, pilots, dredges and other items, countless ships have foundered in Moreton Bay. In addition many hulks have been scuttled for protective reefs, particularly around Moreton and Bishop islands. The most celebrated of these was the 'Lucinda', the Queensland government steam yacht on which the Australian constitution was drafted in 1891. As a result the bay is littered with wrecks.[20]

Until recent times, countless immigrants and travellers have approached Brisbane via Moreton Bay. Many were quarantined on the islands until given a clean bill of health. Their voyage of discovery, which merits full-scale study, is recorded in diaries, letters, logs and other accounts.

**Incarceration 1820s to 1840s**

The next historical mode may be termed incarceration, with institutionalism and exploitation as major *themes*. Oxley's task in 1823 was to evaluate Moreton Bay for a possible convict settlement. At Point Skirmish he found John Finnegan and Thomas Pamphlet, who with Richard Parsons, a fellow ticket-of-leave convict and timber-getter, had been shipwrecked on Moreton Island over seven months earlier. In trying to find Sydney, they traversed much of the bay, assisted by Aborigines. Finnegan was responsible for informing Oxley about the existence of the elusive Brisbane River.[21]

Following Oxley's recommendations, the convict settlement was sited at Redcliffe in 1824 and shifted upstream to Brisbane in the following year. Thus began the first stage of *institutionalism* which lasted for almost eighteen years until 1842. Outstations were not only established at Eagle Farm, Limestone (later Ipswich) and Cowpers (Coopers) Plains, but also on the bay itself.[22]

To assist the passage of ships and maintain navigational aids, pilots were provided with a hut at Amity on North Stradbroke in 1825. More permanent buildings were erected two years later for pilots, guards, crew and their families, boats and stores. Erosion was so bad by the 1840s that the station needed to be moved.[23]

Since the bar across the mouth of the Brisbane River necessitated the transhipment of goods, these were off-loaded at Amity until 1827, when military and convict barracks and a storehouse were erected at Dunwich. Though Commandant Patrick Logan proposed making Dunwich the principal convict settlement, the depot was vacated in the 1830s. Little remains visible today except the stone base of the convict-built causeway and a privy pit.[24]

There were individuals who found themselves isolated from white society: escapees such as 'Bribie the basket-maker' whose name was eventually given to the northernmost island; the convict Tim Shea whose island was later renamed Macleay; and the Aboriginal offender 'Napoleon' who was placed on the island which thus became known as St Helena.[25]

Apart from social deviants, outstations and shipping, the other main impact resulted from the *exploitation* of resources which began in this era. Lime was produced by burning shells along the river and bay; and timber, especially cypress, was taken from the islands.[26] Otherwise Moreton Bay itself remained largely untouched by convictism.

**Experimentation 1840s to 1870s**

Following the land surveys, which commenced in 1839, the northern district of NSW was opened to free settlement in 1842. The major economic thrust was pastoralism of the Darling Downs and Brisbane Valley. Cleveland and Sandgate developed into bayside resorts. As Brisbane grew from a port town into the capital city of Queensland, much more was required of the bay than mere access. A large degree of trial and error accompanied this growth, often resulting in limited returns if not failure. While experimentation was the principal historical mode, the major *themes* were recreation, exploitation, plantation and institutionalism.

During these decades Moreton Bay was a favourite haunt for boating, picnicking and fishing. Small parties also hunted and camped on the islands, while larger groups went on schnapper parties and excursion steamers. In his diary and account of early Brisbane life, the auctioneer Tom Dowse exemplified his view that in a confined settlement, where indoor activities were few, the bay was a major source of *recreation*.

At the same time there was commercial gain to be had. The growing populace demanded resources, particularly fish and oysters, turtles for soup, dugong for oil and soap, shells and coral for lime, and timber for building. Enterprising settlers worked to supply such needs, such as Dr William Hobbs who produced dugong oil for medicinal purposes in the 1850s.[27]

Some of the suppliers dropped out of Brisbane society to spend their time roaming the bay in association with Aborigines. Two of the early fishermen who employed native boatcrew during the 1850s were Timothy Duffy and Eugene Lucette alias Doucette, the latter being a former convict from Mauritius.[28] However, Charles Gray, skipper of the 'Aurora', was killed by Bribie Islanders for beating one of the Aboriginal boys he employed in gathering oysters.[29]

Others preferred to make a life for themselves by settling on the bay. Fernandez Gonzales, a Filipino fisherman and hunter of dugong and turtle, married an Aborigine and settled at Amity by the 1850s, where he raised a large extended family.[30] Later in the decade John Cassim, an Indian/Mauritian, and his Irish wife left their Kangaroo Point lodging-house and established a unique bayside resort called Cleveland House, which was staffed by Aboriginal servants.[31] The former squatter and industrialist John 'Tinker' Campbell and his sons occupied Macleay Island by the mid 1860s – hence the so-called Kanaka Wharf at Thompson Point.[32]

Due to these pursuits the dugong were depleted by the 1860s and fears for the oyster beds led to an act for preventing undue lime-burning in 1863.[33] During those decades and the next, trees were cut on various islands, by campers and settlers as well as timber-getters, including Bribie, Coochie, King, St Helena, Russell, Stradbroke and Tabby Tabby.[34] Though generally unsuitable for hard-hooved stock due to the difficult access and terrain, Bribie, Coochiemudlo, Russell and Stradbroke islands were also used spasmodically for grazing cattle which could be

*12.1 Ruins of St Helena sugar mill 1989 (AHC)*

walked or swum from mainland stations; yet the benefit seems to have been minimal. Between 1868 and 1870 the newly-formed Queensland Acclimatisation Society negotiated with the government to run imported species of stock on Coochiemudlo, then called Innis Island, but the approach was unsuccessful.[35] In 1865 the navy released pigs, horses and goats on Moreton Island to provide rations in case of shipwreck, though these later became a nuisance.[36] Thus began the spasmodic *exploitation* of natural resources which quickened thereafter, with little replenishment of resources by users themselves.

Of greater impact on the land itself were speculative efforts to establish plantations in the 1860s to 1870s. Encouraged by the Queensland government and overseas conditions, settlers acquired and cleared large areas of land along the mainland waterways for growing cash crops, especially cotton and then sugar, worked by indented Pacific Islanders.[37] Sugarmills were built to process the local cane including the lone survivor at Little Rocky Point, established in 1879.[38]

This *plantation* phase also affected the red soil islands off Redland Bay. In 1866 the Campbells obtained 640 acres (256 hectares) on Macleay Island and grew cotton, sugar and castor oil, as well as breeding goats and collecting sponges. By the late 1860s they also operated a saltworks (perhaps a distillery) at the southern end of the island, as did the Brisbane firm of Alexander & Armour at Canaipa Point on Russell Island.[39] The prominent Brisbane merchants John & George Harris owned the 'Sugar Estate' at the southern end of Macleay Island in 1871, when over 40 acres (16 hectares) were under cultivation by Pacific Islanders. Improvements consisted of a verandahed residence, huts and stockyard, as well as the saltworks and sugarmill.[40] According to the census of that year, Macleay Island had three sugarmills, a castor oil plantation and a mill.[41] John Harris also purchased land on Lamb Island in 1866, though Colonial Secretary Robert Herbert had previously applied for all of this island plus Karragarra Island.[42]

Most of these private ventures were so speculative that they soon crashed. Cotton lapsed after the American Civil War, as did salt when the import duty was lowered. Sugar remained profitable, but small-scale farming became dominant rather than large plantations. The known remains of this activity are some stone walling and a boiler shell on Macleay Island. Called the 'saltworks' to this day, these remnants more likely belonged to the sugar mill.[43]

During these decades a greater imprint was made on the northern islands by *institutionalism*. For practical purposes, government authorities saw fit to establish scattered settlements on Moreton, Stradbroke, Peel and St Helena. These were viewed by some persons as paradise and others as exile or worse.

To service the North Passage, the harbourmaster took up residence at Bulwer on Moreton Island in 1847, followed by the pilot station from 1848 to 1909 and land sales in 1863. Where lighthouses were built at Cape Moreton, Bulwer and Cowan Cowan, these became small settlements of domestic, community and institutional buildings. As depicted by a visitor in the late 1860s: 'The pilot-station consists of some eight or nine buildings, used as a boat-house, church, and school-house, and the dwellings of the pilots and a school-master. Here is a telegraph station communicating with the lighthouse at the Cape and the head office at Brisbane'.[44]

Though Amity on Stradbroke Island was officially vacated, Dunwich was declared a quarantine station in 1850, just in time to receive the typhus-ridden ship 'Emigrant'. Tents and makeshift shelters supplemented the meagre accommodation provided by decrepit convict buildings, which had been used last as a catholic mission to the Aborigines in 1843 to 1844.

This immigrant drama of the day is starkly conveyed by twenty-six identical crosses in Dunwich cemetery by the sea, and adjacent monuments to the unfortunate Dr George Mitchell, the ship's doctor, and Dr David Ballow, Brisbane's resident surgeon. More permanent quarters were provided for quarantine by 1863; but the station was transferred to the eastern end of Peel Island in 1874, where ships had also been sent periodically since 1865.[45]

*12.2 Pilot Station, Bulwer 1856 (ML Frederick Korff collection)*

In the meantime the benevolent asylum was transferred from Brisbane to Dunwich in 1865-66. Until relocated to Sandgate in 1946 it provided for elderly indigents, and during varying periods any inebriate, consumptive or leper who had nowhere else to go or was placed there by authority. On first sighting the asylum in 1882, Scottish immigrant Mrs Mary McConachie was quite impressed:

> They are not confined in a large building here like the poorhouses at home but every one has their own little cottage on a beautiful island. When we were Quarintined on Peel Island we could look across the bay to Dunwich, and indeed it looked like a little paradise with the cottages and garden.

This leisurely atmosphere changed as institutionalism progressed. To accommodate an average of 1000 inmates plus staff, the asylum became a government-regulated town. Though most of the buildings have been removed, much of the streetscape owes its origin to the institution, including the public hall, St Marks Anglican Church, historical museum, sandminers' board room, draughtboards, cemeteries, planting and various houses.[46]

As Moreton, Peel and Stradbroke were quite large, much of their terrain remained untouched. In the case of St Helena, which was intended as the quarantine station in 1866, the island was rapidly denuded of native vegetation and replanted, except for its broad mangrove fringe. Proclaimed a male prison in 1867, St Helena ran successfully as a sugar plantation until 1889, supplemented by quarrying of beachrock, lime-burning of shells, cattle-raising, farming, manufacturing and building. In the 1870s, Brisbane's memorialist Tom Dowse called this 'a remarkable transformation':

> The pretty looking island of St. Helena with its belt of dense scrub, the breeding place of thousands of flying foxes, and the rendervoux of the Men carrying on the "Dugong" and Turtle fishery, has had its features improved, by the locating thereon of a Penal establishment, the denizens of which, grow sugar cane and manufacture the same into a state fit for consumption; they, the prisoners, do a little in the growth of other Agriculture Productions, and make themselves useful, and it is to be hoped profitable in the manufacture of other productions.

By 1900 the settlement accommodated over 300 of the toughest prisoners and their warders, whose garden, complete with peacocks and fountains, was quite a showpiece. Though continuing as a prison until 1921 and a prison farm until 1932, the complex is more depleted today than any medieval ruin.[47]

**Occupation 1870s to 1940s**

Compared with the preceding decades of trial and error, scattered settlements with a more stable way of life became an important feature of Moreton Bay by the interwar years. This increasing mode of occupation of the bay had a greater impact on natural resources since land was more extensively cleared and settled, and produce shipped to urban markets. The feeling also grew that the bay had great potential for recreation as well as cultivation. Thus the main *themes* are institutionalism, fishing, farming and recreation, as well as war.

*Institutionalism* became more entrenched, as the St Helena prison and Dunwich Benevolent Asylum expanded until their decline and demise by 1932 and 1946 respectively. Between 1873 and 1906 and 1910 to 1912 the eastern end of Peel Island was used as a quarantine station, which was transferred to the Lytton riverside in 1917. By 1906 large areas of the island had been cleared of timber for grazing and crops to help supply Dunwich, which also sent its inebriates there from 1910 to 1916. Most buildings were cannibalised and the cemetery destroyed by fire, so that the main relics are a brick cell block, a well and the old stone causeway.[48]

The jetty at the eastern end of Peel Island was also important since it served the lazaret. This institution was located on the far western side of the island in 1907, comprising 57 lepers from Dunwich and Friday Island and rising to a peak of 85 plus staff in 1911. Living arrangements reflected social attitudes at large, since the huts of Aborigines and other 'coloureds' were separated from the main dwellings, and women's cottages with cooking facilities from the men's quarters. Nevertheless Rose Harris managed to circumvent this arrangement by trading her favours for grog.

As at Dunwich and St Helena, expansion was accommodated largely by timber-and-tin buildings. Many were removed or overgrown with vegetation after the last patients were transferred to South Brisbane (Princess Alexandra) Hospital in 1959. All the same the remaining structures, cemetery and planting provide the most complete impression of institutionalism on an island paradise.[49]

*12.3 Peel Island jetty 1989 (AHC)*

After the failure of the Bribie Island mission, the Aborigines were shifted back to Stradbroke Island via Peel in 1892. Buildings were erected for the Myora Mission at Moongalba, a traditional site for the long-standing settlement and cemetery.[50]

Navigational centres proliferated, including lighthouse settlements on Moreton Island and the house on the Pile Light of 1883. Little of these structures remain today, except the Cape Moreton lighthouse.

This era was also characterised by the increased exploitation of natural resources, including the continuation of timber-getting and cattle-grazing. However, it was *fishing* of all kinds which attracted locals, amateurs and professionals alike, despite complaints about declining yields.[51] There was a greater degree of commercialism, as larger groups and companies entered the field. Two mullet factories operated on Bribie Island between 1898 and 1914 and a cannery around 1908.[52] Most apparent was the growth of the oyster industry throughout the islands. After legislation in 1874, areas of Moreton Bay were divided into leases for auction, resulting in the widespread operation of the Moreton Bay Oyster Company from 1876 to 1955 before its demise in 1963.

Currigee on Stradbroke Island became a company settlement of some 200 workers with families, many being European or Aboriginal rather than British in origin. When the school was built for twenty-four children in 1890, the settlement included two weatherboard cottages and various huts of bark and slab.

From the late 1890s the oyster settlements declined, as did the catch. This was due to Stradbroke being separated into two islands in 1896, the subsequent siltation and mudworm infestation, increasing competition from northern New South Wales and over-harvesting. In 1909 the main centre was described 'as nothing to the Curriggee of years ago':

> In that time long past, when the oyster beds gave up their toll to the hardy seamen, Southport often resounded with their mirth. They were stalwart men. They made money quickly, and they spent it as freely. Though oyster beds are there still, yet the old days are past. Huts can be noticed scattered in all directions on the island, while a schooner and a few boats, moored a distance from the shore, remind the stranger of what has been.

Nevertheless local dances were still being held at Currigee in the 1930s, and one of the oystermen's cottages survived until the 1980s.[53]

More significant in terms of impact on the environment was the alienation and occupation of land by settlers, particularly on the southern islands. Large portions of crown land, which had been planted, grazed or left vacant during the speculative boom of the early 1860s, were further surveyed and auctioned in the later 1860s to 1870s, including Coochie, Lamb, Garden, Russell, Karragarra, Tabby Tabby, Woogoompah, Kangaroo and parts of Stradbroke Island.[54]

Land speculation peaked again during the economic boom of the 1880s. Multiple lots were surveyed and offered for auction including the town of Moondarewa on Stradbroke south (1880-82) and Amity to the north (1886), Potts/Patts Point on Macleay (1885), the western half of Coochiemudlo (1888), the town of Bribie (1887) and the north shore of Karragarra (1889).[55]

Contrary to government expectation, these sales were generally disappointing and produced some very sparse occupation based mainly on recreation, as at Amity, Bribie and Moondarewa, or grazing such as Stradbroke, Tabby Tabby and Woogoompah. The effort by Norm Wright and son to eke out a farm-living on Coochie in 1897 failed by the turn of the century. Moondarewa was shifted twice due to sea erosion, as was Amity over the years. The site of Booloong, a holiday village surveyed on the southeast tip of Moreton Island in 1906, was also submerged. One fortunate survival of subdivision and plundering was the remnant rainforest in the centre of South Stradbroke. Known as Thompsons Scrub, Welsby described it in 1921 as surpassing many Queensland 'scrublands' for its 'continuous beauty, and everlasting greenness'.[56]

Despite drawbacks, the greater availability of land facilitated *farming* on the red soil islands of Russell, Karragarra, Lamb, Macleay and Coochie. As fertile offshoots of the mainland, these islands specialised in growing fruit and vegetables, including bananas, pineapples, pawpaws, custard apples and avocados, which were shipped to the Brisbane market. By the interwar years they were acclaimed for the quality of their produce.[57]

Consequently the RKLM islands formed a local network centred on Russell Island. John Willes arrived by 1868 and farmed at Canaipa with his wife Elizabeth, followed by their son Fred who also became the postmaster. In the early 1900s, Mark Jackson opened a pineapple cannery and a sawmill at Jacksonville, followed by a picture theatre in 1950. The school, which served the islands, was opened in 1916, and the sports club about 1920. The telephone was connected in 1923.[58]

By this time Garden Island comprised two share-farms, and mixed farming was conducted on Tabby Tabby and Woogoompah. Couran, an oyster centre on South Stradbroke, was subdivided in the 1920s and farmed until devastated by high tides in 1948. Coochiemudlo also came into its own, with red soil farms and orchards on the western side, pioneered by returned soldier Doug Morton from 1919 onwards.[59]

The main exception was Bribie Island, which was not fertile enough for successful farming. In 1891 the irrepressible Archibald Meston derided the island as 'the meanest piece of country in Australia .... There is not an acre of useful soil on the whole island .... It is inhabited principally by snakes and kangaroos; this howling desert of ti-tree swamps, rank aquatic vegetation and unimaginable cussedness'.[60]

Nevertheless Bongaree in the south developed as a small community of shacks for retirees, holiday-makers and fishing-folk after being declared a township in 1912. This was stimulated by the provision of a jetty and shop in that year followed by land sales in 1915. Further signs of development were the telephone in 1923, a school two years later and a church in 1928, as well as shops, boarding houses, a dance hall, a bowling green and a couple of dairies. In 1923 a gravel road was formed for visitors to cross the island to Woorim on the Ocean Beach, where land was sold and a kiosk provided in 1924. That settlement expanded in 1927, when the government transferred fifteen small houses from the Beerburrum Soldiers Settlement. By the

12.4 *SS 'Koopa' (AHC)*

1930s the island had become a popular resort for residents and holiday-makers alike. Contrary to Meston's condemnation, Bribie appealed to people because of its bountiful beaches, fishing, scenery and tranquility along both the Pumicestone and ocean sides of the island.[61]

The main impetus was the urban demand for *recreation*, combined with entrepreneurs who grasped the opportunity. On Stradbroke south in 1885, Reginald Heber Roe, the innovative headmaster of Brisbane Boys Grammar School, and his family friends established what became known as Roes Kamp where they holidayed for many years and accommodated parties of students. Regular boat trips also ran excursions from Southport to the island, including a new steam launch in 1897. A jetty was built at Moondarewa, followed by a shelter-shed and kiosk, which serviced the ferry until severe storm damage in 1938.[62] During the early 1900s the tugs 'Beaver' and 'Greyhound' ran weekend and holiday excursion trips to Bribie, followed by the more regular services of the steamship 'Koopa' and then 'Doomba', from 1911 until the Second World War. During holiday periods, thousands of campers pitched their tents on the foreshore behind the jetty.[63]

By interwar years the demand for recreation from an increasingly mobile population affected much of the bay, as well as the growth of resorts on what became known as the Gold and Sunshine coasts. Though Bribie via Redcliffe was the best patronised run, many excursions were offered, including Hayles' cruises to the Dunwich Benevolent Asylum and the fruit islands further south.[64] Nevertheless there was plenty of room for everyone, as conveyed by one keen yachtsman in 1925:

> There are no Coney Islands, no regular steamer excursions anywhere, except to Redcliffe and Bribie, no settlement except on one or two of the islands. A trip down the bay is a complete change and rest from the bustling city life. The bay is ideal from the cruising yachtman's point of view, and at holiday times up to 250 craft of various sizes, carrying altogether about 1500 persons, are scattered about its waters. So large is the bay, and so many the places in which to go, that, with the exception of Southport, an average of not more than a dozen boats will be found anchored in any particular place.

The favourite boating haunts were: King Island off Wellington Point, which had been proclaimed a recreation reserve in 1887 but denuded of timber by campers; Amity Point, One Mile and particularly Myora on North Stradbroke; Coochiemudlo off Victoria Point; and around Jumpinpin on South Stradbroke.[65] Bishop Island also became a popular spot for boating, picnicking and camping. Seemingly well vegetated, it had been formed from dredging the Brisbane River bar between 1909 to 1912 and sinking defunct ships on the eastern side.[66]

Amity, where Tom Welsby had his shack on Stradbroke, was a popular holiday encampment, with roads to Dunwich and the Blue Lake by the 1930s. Hayles built the Cabarita kiosk there in 1935 and commenced running the everlasting 'Mirimar' across the bay. In the preceding year the enterprising Bill Clayton built his first guesthouse at Point Lookout and provided motor transport along the beach. Part of the point was occupied by the lighthouse and government reserve in 1932, but further land was sold in 1938.[67]

The first 'week-enders' on Coochiemudlo were built during the 1930s. Doug and Mary Morton also encouraged day-trippers and visitors from 'Hayles Fruit Cruises' to call at their produce shop and tearooms. In 1941 Amity Resorts & Cruises Pty Ltd promoted the island as a tropical-fruit farm attraction. Tourists from Brisbane were landed at Mortons' new jetty and transported by a horse-drawn trolley on wooden rails to disport themselves at the farm. There 'Acres of vegetables, fruits and flowers of almost every kind greet the eye in colourful pattern against a green-background'.[68]

Not content with these increasing opportunities, the Moreton Bay League, spearheaded by Welsby, was formed in January 1910 to gain 'the freedom of the beauty spots of Moreton Bay for sojourn and health-giving recreation'. In particular the league wanted to turn the government islands of Peel and St. Helena into public parks. Little could be done about the former because

*12.5 SS 'Emerald' at Redcliffe jetty (AHC)*

of the stigma of leprosy, and the government was reluctant to relinquish St Helena at that stage. Nevertheless this activity heightened public awareness and raised the possibility of Green Island as a camping-ground for boating men.[69]

Agitation was resumed after interruption by the First World War. In 1925 the decision was made to close the prison and offer it to the Brisbane City Council as a recreation resort or to the Brisbane General Hospital as a convalescent home. The fate of St Helena was still uncertain when the prison closed in December 1932, as a kiosk and dance floor were deemed requisite. A year later the council opened the recreational reserve to the public, with the inducement of buildings, electricity, camping and transport. Nevertheless the venture failed by 1934, due partly to the Great Depression, and the site reverted to the government in 1939 for leasing as a cattle run.[70]

The final theme of the 1940s was *war*, which interrupted the preceding development since the bay was needed to protect the sea approaches to Brisbane. During the Great War a jetty, signal station and gun had been located at Cowan Cowan on Moreton Island.[71] Much more extensive were defences against the Japanese in the Second World War. These included: batteries at Cowan and on the ocean side at Toompani Beach, manned by some 900 troops; naval mine control buildings at Cowan and Tangalooma, where a jetty was built and a track across the island; a radar station at Point Lookout on Stradbroke, operated by the US Army and later the RAAF; heavy gun emplacements along the ocean beach of Bribie Island, the evacuation of civilians to the west, requisition of the 'Koopa' and 'Doomba' and transformation of the island into a military camp, plus a strategic road from Caboolture to the major port at Toorbul Point. An Australian Water Transport Small Ships Training School was established at Victoria Point to complement a similar unit at Toorbul Point, and Coochiemudlo was used as the training ground for the amphibious Third Australian Water Transport Group.

Three of the most dramatic wartime incidents were the shot fired accidentally at HMAS 'Tambar' by Cowan Cowan battery in 1941, the wreck of the American liberty ship 'Rufus King' at the South Passage in 1942 and the sinking of the hospital ship 'Centaur' thirty-nine kilometres east of Point Lookout in 1943. There is now little obvious evidence of this momentous era when Brisbane was a garrison town, other than Fort Bribie and concrete emplacements at Cowan and Toompani.[72]

Altogether the outcome by the 1940s was a mosaic of island communities with differing economies, based on varying degrees of institutionalism, fishing, farming, recreation and war, but linked to each other and the mainland by external concerns. As settlement tended to be patchy and episodic, much of the environment remained untouched. Yet it was hardly true that Moreton Bay was 'still in the same primeval state as when Flinders explored it more than one hundred years ago'.[73]

**Development 1940s to 1980s**

Following the war, development of the bay became the dominant historical mode, with exploitation, suburbanism and recreation as principal *themes.* The concentration of a more urban, mobile and affluent population in the southeast corner of Queensland produced a greater degree of *exploitation* than ever before. This was facilitated by the government of Queensland which adopted a developmental stance.

After the benevolent asylum was transferred from Dunwich to mainland Sandgate in 1946 to become Eventide, the future of Stradbroke was allied with sandmining due to leases over much of the island. Exploration of mineral sands began in 1942, followed by prospecting rights in 1947. With rutile prices booming by the 1950s, minerals were removed from South Stradbroke Island between 1951 and 1970 and from North Stradbroke after 1950.[74]

On Moreton Island, prospecting began in 1947, followed by extensive leases in the next year and further exploration in 1955. But mining at Eagers Swamp in 1956 to 1958 was very limited and hardly profitable compared with Stradbroke where the water supply and access were superior. Nevertheless leases were held over much of the island, including Yellow Patch where some mining was underway in 1969. The island remained largely undisturbed until 1979, when mining was resumed.[75]

Apart from the mineral sands and some silica extraction, another form of exploitation was the dredging of dead coral. In 1937 the Queensland Cement & Lime Company (QCL) began operations at Mud Island. Having also held leases at Green Island, St Helena, Wellington

*12.6 First private store at Dunwich (AHC)*

Point, Cleveland Point and Empire Point north of Cleveland since 1956, QCL moved to St Helena in 1983 until work was suspended five years later. In 1991 the company sought to renew operations, despite claims of major damage to Mud Island.[76]

As with dugong before the war and oysters shortly after, the supply of whales which passed along the ocean side of the islands was exhausted by the early 1960s. It is possible that prawns will suffer a similar fate from trawling, which began in 1950.[77] Queensland's only whaling station opened at Tangalooma on Moreton Island in 1952. During the season the factory worked to capacity, employing about 120 men of various nationalities in two twelve-hour shifts per day for seven days a week. Wives, families and girlfriends were shipped in for two hours on each Saturday afternoon. Watching a chaser bring in the kill inspired a Brisbane music-teacher in 1953 to compose a sea shanty called 'Tangalooma', with the following start and refrain:

*I've got a wife in Brisbane Town*
*Aye Tangalooma.*
*She pipes up and I pipe down*
*Aye, Aye, Aye.*

*Sing Tangalooma!*
*You roaming, roving sailor:*
*You never dreamt you'd serve aboard*
*A Tangalooma whaler.*

Can anyone supply the full text and tune of such a priceless Moreton Bay ditty? The whole quota of 600 whales was filled in two months of the first season and the company increased its dividends to 20 percent. But the quota could not be filled in 1961, and the station closed in the following year. Inflated estimates of the number of whales and over-fishing from the Antarctic upwards was evidently responsible for reducing their population from 10,000 to less than 500. Yet not until 1977 was field research on the humpback whale resumed, by the University of Queensland. Of the purpose-built whaling complex at Tangalooma, only the concrete skeleton of the flensing deck, renovated huts and some relics are left.[78]

After the 1912 pile light was wrecked in 1949, the signal station was set up on Bishop Island. This well-vegetated man-made island, with its huts, kiosk, tavern and pool, was also a popular leisure spot until the late 1980s when it was earmarked for Port of Brisbane extensions. Commencing in 1976, the development of the port at Fisherman Islands reshaped the area opposite the mouth of the Brisbane River, though significant mud banks and mangroves remained on the bayside.[79]

At the same time, the island communities and farming areas of the pre-war years were affected by developing *suburbanism*. These settlements continued to cater for tourists, holiday-makers, boaties and retirees, as well as genuine islanders; but the previous trickle became a horde by the 1980s. Large areas were progressively subdivided and sold, the new dwellings built in town style and their inhabitants gradually provided with utilities little different from bayside suburbs. At the same time the authorities tightened their grip on the more casual island way of life, without necessarily achieving a stranglehold.

In 1947 the public domain on Stradbroke Island was placed under the control of Redland Shire Council. The former asylum site at Dunwich was surveyed in the same year and sold as building blocks in 1948. Sandmining and further subdivision benefited the place materially, without enhancing its appearance as a gauche little town.

Amity to the north retained its reputation as a fishing base despite a substantial number of new suburban-style dwellings contrasting with the shacks which littered the road grid and eroded beachfront. Bypassed by the road which volunteers put through to the surf, Amity was outstripped by Point Lookout which sprouted haphazardly along the end of the Dickson Way and on government subdivisions. With superior scenery and better access by barge and road, holiday-makers packed accommodation at the point, including its guesthouses and famed Hotel Stradbroke (est. 1962).

In comparison, settlement lapsed on South Stradbroke Island with the decline of oystering and farming. Land continued to be offered periodically at Moondarewa between the 1930s and 1960s, and then in the early 1970s for those relocating from the oyster reserve at Currigee. But occupation declined, despite speculative development proposals. At Couran between 1967 and 1972 the attempt to turn farmland into a canal estate also failed. South Stradbroke remained a natural backwater for boaties, except for Tipplers' hotel which was refashioned as a resort in 1982.[80]

More affected by suburbanism were Russell, Karragarra, Lamb, Macleay and Coochiemudlo islands, as was Redland Shire as a whole. Most of the farms were subdivided by developers, commencing in 1961 on Coochiemudlo and the late 1960s elsewhere. Though ostensibly residential, these estates generally lacked basic amenities and public space. About 10 percent of those on Russell Island had what was euphemistically called a 'drainage problem'; hence the great Russell Island scandal and abortive fraud conspiracy case of 1981 to 1983 which became the longest criminal trial in Queensland.

Over 17,000 blocks were subdivided on RKLM, for a potential population of at least 40,000 persons, plus 700 blocks on Coochiemudlo. The municipal problem, which the shire inherited when it gained control of the islands in 1972, remained to be resolved, as did their destiny as either suburbs or resorts.[81]

Due to the changing character of these islands, the demand increased from owners, investors and developers for a bridge from the mainland to Stradbroke, preferably via Russell Island. Such a bridge was suggested as early as 1932 and its impact investigated in the 1970s. During the expansive 1980s, the scheme received such government favour that land sales boomed again. Nevertheless the project lapsed in 1988 after the new National Party cabinet decided against a bridge as far as Stradbroke, while supporting a Russell Island step in principle.[82]

The likely impact of a bridge is exemplified by Bribie Island which lost much of its individuality after 1963. Not only crowded with day-trippers, cars and boats, Bribie Island acquired many of the accoutrements of a nondescript seaside suburb, complete with canal estates of the 1980s and diminishing vegetation including mangroves.[83]

Since the southern islands are close to the burgeoning urban corridor, a bridge would turn them into dormitory suburbs. While the required capital was lacking during the early 1990s recession, the vehicular ferries and fast water-taxis filled the breach. But city-dwellers continued to demand their suburban place in the sun.[84]

In comparison Moreton Island remained relatively uncivilised, with only a few creeping traces of suburbanism – due some would say to its distant location, lack of sheltered moorings and exposure to westerly winds. The shacks and holiday houses among the sandtracks and trees at Kooringal, Cowan and Bulwer were mostly collected together from the 1960s onwards, long after the earlier settlements lapsed or were eroded by the elements. The only other signs of habitation were the lighthouse settlement at Cape Moreton, the squatters' camp nearby, the compound of the National Parks & Wildlife Service at Cowan, the tourist resort which took over at Tangalooma in 1963 and the inveterate campers with their four-wheel drives.

If Moreton Island is not deserted enough for anyone, there are still possibilities amongst the other 330 islands which are hardly mentioned in this roundup, such as pretty little Bird Island where the casuarinas have been replanted.

While urban centres expanded on the mainland and suburbanism spread its influence across the bay, the demand for *recreation* grew apace. Marinas and breakwaters were constructed along the mainland which, in conjunction with a rash of foreshore improvements, canal estates and apartment blocks, have depleted the mangroves, polluted the waters and turned more of the bayside into a built environment.

In the new age of tourism, island shacks and tents, as well as bayside holiday houses, were no longer adequate. Modern resorts with motel-style accommodation, restaurants, bars, entertainments and sports became the flavour of the 1970s to 1980s.

Some proposals turned out to be more speculative than real, including: the staged development from a permanent tent-town with restaurant facilities and amenities blocks to a motel and marina on St Helena in 1973; a high-rise casino and hotel at Tangalooma in 1981; a cable-car skyway to Coochiemudlo Island from Victoria Point in 1988; the eighty million dollar Perulpa Bay Resort Village on Macleay in 1986-90; a further tourist resort on Russell Island at the same time; and similar developments on North Stradbroke, evidently stimulated by the expectation of a bridge. The outcome of plans for multi-million dollar resorts for South Stradbroke at Couran remained to be seen in the 1990s.[85] Some of those which reached fruition were: the development of Tangalooma Moreton Island Resort, from an upgrading of the old whaling station in 1963 to the more modern complex, complete with coconut palms, which was commenced in 1981 and turned into time-share in 1984; the $3 million facelift which converted the Tippler Passage pub on South Stradbroke into Tipplers Resort and reportedly attracted 1500 daily tourists in 1982; and on North Stradbroke the $3.7 million Anchorage Village Beach Resort, nestled amongst the vegetation of the foreshore near Point Lookout in 1984.[86]

Despite efforts to tap the tourist market, none of these resorts belonged to the international league such as those in northern Queensland and New South Wales. Tangalooma and Tipplers remained family-oriented; and both Tangalooma and Anchorage Village found themselves in financial difficulty by the late 1980s recession.

The recreational urge also affected St Helena and Peel Island, which remained in government hands; but developments there, as elsewhere, were affected by the growing demand for conservation.

### Conservation 1970s to early 1990s

From the mid-1970s onwards, increasing concern about the state of the environment caused a reaction against the development of Moreton Bay. Consequently the historical mode of conservation became significant during these years, characterised by the major *themes* of communication of information and conflict with development, resulting in recognition of the need for coordinated management.

Various areas had been set aside in the past, including King Island as a recreation reserve in 1887, Stradbroke Island as a fauna reserve in 1920 and Point Lookout as a government reserve in 1932.[87] The public had campaigned for national parks before, especially the Moreton Bay Protection League. Various individuals stand out like prophets in the wilderness, as well as groups including the Moreton Bay Protection Society and Stradbroke Island Management Organisation. Yet conservation as a conscious, growing and influential movement may be dated from the 1970s.

In conservation terms, the years between 1974 and 1976 stand out from the ruck, not for what was achieved then, but in *communication* of information and drafting policies. This included: a government working committee report on future planning needs of southern Moreton Bay which opposed canal estates infringing on mangrove swamps or fronting seagrass beds (1974); a coastal management investigation report recommending the protection of almost all tidal wetlands remaining in Moreton Bay (1974); the Royal Society of Queensland symposium on North Stradbroke (1974); the Moreton region growth strategy investigation (1974); the Moreton region non-urban land suitability study (1975); the report of the Coordinator-General's Department on the use of coastal land for South Stradbroke (1975); the Redland Shire Council's strategic plan for North Stradbroke (1975); the Queensland Archaeological Branch survey of Moreton Island (1975); Brisbane City Council town plan including Moreton and other islands (1976); the Moreton Island impact study and strategic plan (1976); the Moreton Island committee of inquiry into sandmining (1976-77).[88] That the *Sunday-mail* published a special colour magazine on Moreton Bay in 1974 reflected more than an academic or administrative interest in the future.[89]

The second significant peak was reached in 1989, the Brisbane City Council's 'Year of the Bay'. The year's activities included two Moreton Bay search seminars conducted by the council, an Australian Littoral Society information kit, and the state government's Moreton Bay strategic plan for 'sustainable development'.[90] As well as increasing general awareness, this activity focused attention on how conflicting interests and issues might be reconciled by coordinated management. What was made public was the division between the Liberal Party-controlled Brisbane City Council and the National Party State Government. What was concealed, however, was the fact that during the intervening years, when conflict was rife, conservation as opposed to development had won a recognised place in the minds of the public, the corridors of power and the confines of Moreton Bay. This change of awareness through *conflict* may be illustrated by the following cases.

Regarding St Helena, Charles Carroll bought the grazing lease from a previous owner in 1971, including the ruined prison, and a special tourist licence in 1973. Carroll was unable to build a resort, but conducted guided tours. After two years of negotiations between the lessee and the government, which was keen to purchase the lease, the island was gazetted as a national park in 1979. However, Carroll succeeded in gaining thirty-year licences for both grazing and tourism.

*12.7 Grave of 'Rosie', Peel Island 1989 (AHC)*

The following year the park was gazetted as an historic area under the Forestry Act, the first in Queensland, followed by the preparation of a management plan. Under pressure from various groups, including the National Trust, Australian Heritage Commission and National Parks & Wildlife Service, the government resumed the lease in 1985, unveiled the park to the public in 1986 and continued the conservation work with a 1988 bicentennial grant. Thus recreation and conservation together, after some conflict with private interest, sealed the fate of St Helena Island.[91]

Plans for Peel Island developed along similar but belated lines. In 1948 a jetty was built at the western end for a proposed motel-style lazaret, but the government decided on a mainland base by 1950. However, the success of sulphone drugs made isolation redundant by 1959, when the remaining patients were transferred to the mainland. Calls for tourist tenders in 1960 and 1962 resulted in only one American proposal, for a 'Disneyland by the sea'.

Though claiming in 1963 to abandon its intention of a tourist resort and deciding to preserve the island in its natural state, the government called for applications for the development of 13½ acres (5.4 hectares) at The Bluff or eastern end in 1966. This was also unsuccessful as control of Horseshoe Bay, the boaties' haven and only beach, would be in the hands of Redland Shire and not the prospective developers, who included Keith Williams of Seaworld fame.

Consequently buildings were sold for removal in 1968 and the remainder, on 2_ acres (1 hectare) leased to the Church of England Grammar School as a field study centre. The rest of Peel Island was designated an environmental park.In 1980 the government proposed a kiosk and other facilities at Horseshoe Bay. Such development was opposed by the boat clubs.

Eventually, in 1991, negotiations commenced between the state government and Redland Shire Council, accompanied by some refurbishment with a federal government grant and a conservation study in 1992 to 1993. As a result the island was gazetted as a national park under state government management in 1993, thereby resolving the uncertainty regarding its future. Since excursion boats began landing tourists on Peel Island in 1989 and about 200 craft anchored off the beach on any weekend, the demands of recreation and conservation still had to be reconciled in practice.[92]

At Bribie Island, where pine plantations replaced large areas of the native vegetation and suburbanism took root after the war, there was less pressure to conserve the land than the sea. Pumicestone Passage was declared a marine park in 1986 and a national park two years later. An ocean beachfront strip running south from the Caloundra bar, including lagoons and islands, was declared an environmental park in 1989, while the bulk of the island remained a flora and fauna reserve.[93]

On the subdivided southern islands, the provision of residential amenities became the main concern. Redland Shire Council began buying back freehold land in the 1980s to ensure the provision of public open space. Local concern was also expressed about the future of remaining mangroves and rainforest. Nevertheless tree protection regulations to preserve the remnant flora were not introduced on Coochiemudlo until 1993.[94]

*12.8 Peel Island Quarantine Station beach 1989 (AHC)*

In the case of Stradbroke, the impact of sandmining was a controversial issue. Between 1981 and 1982 there was negative publicity regarding damage to Aboriginal middens. The beneficial outcome was that the Archaeological Branch set about surveying mining leases on Stradbroke and Moreton islands in 1982-83.

In 1984 the Mining Wardens Court granted a mining lease, subject only to the salvage of middens, despite archaeological objections. However, further applications for prospecting on the southern part of the bay near North Stradbroke Island were rejected by the Mines Department in 1987.

Though much of North Stradbroke Island remained under lease, a trade-off between the government and the sandminers resulted in 50 percent being declared a national park in 1991. Most of South Stradbroke came under environmental control by the following year when the Gold Coast City Council prevented commercial development on vacant crown land.[95]

On Moreton, which remained relatively unscathed, the main issue was whether to sandmine the island at all. In 1974 the state government transferred control to Brisbane City Council, which re-zoned the island as open space or parkland despite the existing mining leases. To circumvent the Brisbane town plan, the government passed a Mining Act amendment in 1979 which overrode these provisions and labelled Moreton 'uncommitted'. This was despite the Cook (committee of inquiry) report in 1976-77 which endorsed limited mining on 6.4 percent of the land but recommended that leases should be revoked and 90 percent of the island become a national park by 1990.

The issue peaked in 1982-83, when the Queensland Mining Wardens Court heard objections to the renewal of mining leases. These were not granted as tourism was considered to be a viable alternative and the federal government was unlikely to allow the necessary export licences for processing the minerals outside of Australia. That ban, which was tantamount to halting mining on Moreton, was implemented in 1984. A National Parks headquarters with permanent staff was established on Moreton in the preceding year.

Nevertheless the Queensland government decided in 1986 to allow further exploration in the northeast of the island, which happened to be the most popular holiday area adjacent to the Blue Lagoon. This decision was opposed by conservationists, the labour movement and Brisbane City Council, as well as being publicly unpalatable. The conflict was defused in 1987 when the new National Party cabinet announced that mining leases would be relinquished. The national park, which comprised ninety percent of the island by the mid 1980s, was subsequently put under the jurisdiction of Queensland National Parks & Wildlife Service in 1991 and enlarged to 96 percent by 1993. In this case, conservation allied with recreation won the day.[96]

On environmental issues in Queensland a shift took place in political ethos, from a National Party regime favouring development to a Labor government encouraging conservation, on balance at least. This change was reflected in government policies from 1989 onwards, especially the expansion of national parks for the sake of the populace and the environment. However, this contrast should not be drawn too starkly, since the social ethos was swinging towards conservation as early as 1974 and quickening by 1989, when the new government rolled in on the wave of conservation.

### Management early 1990s

Though conservation might have caught up with development, subsequent events indicated that the new mode for Moreton Bay was one of more coordinated and comprehensive management in accordance with an agreed masterplan. The thrust was not to develop or to conserve exclusively, but to reconcile the two. According to the official jargon, the goal was 'ecologically sustainable development'.This concept was defined in a Queensland conservation strategy discussion paper as 'development which meets the needs of the present without compromising the ability of future generations to meet their needs':

> Human health and welfare depend on the continued functioning of those ecological processes that maintain the fertility of the soil, purify the air and water, renew living resources, and conserve biological diversity. Development must be compatible with the continued functioning of these ecological processes.[97]

To these might be added those elements of cultural heritage which fulfil present and future needs for personal and social identity within the continuum of time.

On this conceptual basis the government drafted its management proposals for Moreton Bay in 1991, followed by the Moreton Bay Strategic Plan in February 1993 with the simultaneous declaration of the Moreton Bay Marine Park. The plan stated succinctly that the overall goal was 'To provide for ecologically sustainable use of Moreton Bay and for protection of its natural, recreational, cultural heritage and amenity values'.

Aims and objectives were provided for each policy area of nature conservation, landscape character, cultural heritage, water quality, recreation and tourism, and education and research, as well as the major planning decision areas of transport, development, fishing, industry and management. These were embodied in primary and secondary intents for each of the management categories of protection, habitat conservation, general use, port and industrial, marinas and harbours, island village and special management as shown on the map of Moreton Bay.[98]

The underlying values, issues and needs had been identified in the draft plan which emphasised the need to balance conflicting uses of the bay by appropriate management strategies. It dealt with the future as well as the present, particularly the population pressures which appeared as 'demands for additional coastal development including residential, recreational and tourism projects and expansion of port, commercial and industrial activities'. But what of the past?

This saga of Moreton Bay from 1770 to 1993 might make us pessimistic. The Aboriginal writer Oodgeroo Nunukul (formerly Kath Walker), wrote of the despoliation of Stradbroke

*12.9 Victoria Point Jetty (AHC)*

Island by 1972, whereby 'Greedy, thoughtless, stupid, ignorant man continues the assault on nature. But he too will suffer. His ruthless bulldozers are digging his own grave'.[99]This history might also make us think idealistically that none of the islands or foreshore should ever have been alienated or developed in the first place.

Unfortunately we cannot re-create paradise on earth. The next best thing is to understand what happened and how the remnants might be pieced together, protected and promoted for lasting benefit – a vision, not just a plan. What might be heartening is the realisation that so many misguided dreams have faltered, as if the bay had a life of its own. After all, 'Nature's beauty resists all mankind's attempt, deliberate or otherwise, to denigrate it'.[100]

# *Measures*

See manuals for more exact conversion tables, especially for larger multiples

## *Area*

perch (p): 30.25 square yards = 25.3 square metres ($m^2$)
rod (rd): 40 perches = 1012 square metres
acre (ac): 4 rods = 0.405 hectare (ha)
square mile: 640 acres = 259 hectares

## *Distance*

inch (") = 25.4 millimetres (mm)
foot ('): 12 inches (in) = 30.5 centimetres (cm)
yard: 3 feet (ft) = 0.914 metre (m)
Chain (ch): 22 yards = 20.1 metres
furlong: 10 chains = 201 metres
mile (m): 1760 yards = 1.61 kilometres (km)
fathom: 6 feet depth = 1.83 metres

## *Liquid*

pint (pt) = 568 millilitres (mL)
gallon (gal): 8 pints = 4.55 litres (L)

## *Money*

penny (d): 4 farthings (¼) or 2 halfpennies (½)
1d in 1890s = 31c in 1920s-30s, 42c in 1999
shilling (/-) = 12 pence
1s in 1890s = $3.76 in 1920s-30s, $5 in 1999
pound (£): 20 shillings
£1 in 1890s = $75 in 1920s-30s, $100 in 1999
florin: 2 shillings
sovereign: 20 shillings
guinea (gn): 21 shillings

## *Temperature*

Degrees (°): 32 fahrenheit = 0 celsius
$c = (f - 32) x5 \div 9$

## *Weight*

ounce (oz) = 28.3 grams (g)
pound (lb): 16 ounces = 0.454 kilogram (kg)
stone (st): 14 pounds = 6.35 kilograms
ton = 1.02 tonnes (t)

# *Abbreviations*

Note the following abbreviations in notes, references and captions.

| | |
|---|---|
| AHC | Applied History Centre |
| AMG | Australasian Medical Gazette |
| AJCP | Australian Joint Copying Project |
| AUS | Australian |
| BC | Brisbane Courier |
| BCC | Brisbane City Council |
| BHG | Brisbane History Group |
| BS | Bribie Star |
| CM | Courier Mail |
| DM | Daily Mail |
| EO | Evening Observer |
| FL | Fryer Library, University of Queensland |
| JQLC | Journals of the Queensland Legislative Council |
| JOL | John Oxley Library |
| MBC | Moreton Bay Courier |
| MJA | Medical Journal of Australia |
| MLS | Mitchell Library, Sydney |
| MMSKA | Mackay Mercury and South Kennedy Advertiser |
| MS | Moreton Star |
| MSS | Manuscripts |
| NAM | North Australian Monthly |
| NLA | National Library of Australia |
| NSWVP | New South Wales Votes and Proceedings |
| QDEH | Queensland Department of Environment and Heritage |
| QDR | Queenslander |
| QG | Queensland Guardian |
| QGG | Queensland Government Gazette |
| QNPWS | Queensland National Parks & Wildlife Service |
| QPD | Queensland Parliamentary Debates |
| QPP | Queensland Parliamentary Papers |
| QSA | Queensland State Archives |
| QVP | Queensland Votes and Proceedings |
| RHSQ | Royal Historical Society of Queensland |
| SG | Sydney Gazette |
| SM | Sunday Mail |
| SMH | Sydney Morning Herald |
| TEL | Telegraph |
| TR | Truth |
| UQP | University of Queensland Press |
| WK | Week |

# Notes

Note the format below for volume or series number/issue number: page number.

**Chapter 1:** ***John Mackenzie-Smith*****, Dunwich: Convicts, Passionists and shattered hopes**

1 Steele 1975, 5.
2 SG 21 Oct. 1824.
3 Aus 9 Dec. 1824.
4 Evans 1992, 25.
5 Steele 1975, 27.
6 Evans 1992, 226-27.
7 Steele 1975, 48-49.
8 Ibid. 74-81.
9 Ibid. 78-9.
10 Bateson 1966, 112.
11 Evans 1992, 27.
12 Bateson 1966, 114-15.
13 Ibid. 90-1.
14 Evans 1992, 27.
15 Ibid. 28.
16 Steele 1975, 175-76.
17 Ibid. 174-75.
18 OM68-18, James Porter papers, JOL.
19 OM78-72, McConnel papers, JOL.
20 NSWVP, J.B. Polding evidence.
21 Thorpe 1950, 25-29.
22 Ibid. 26.
23 Ibid. 24.
24 Ibid. 90.
25 Ibid. 5.
26 NSWVP, J.B. Polding evidence.
27 Harris 1990, n.p.
28 Martin 1988, 30.
29 Moran 1894, 411.
30 Martin 1988, 30.
31 Ibid. 33.
32 Ibid. 37.
33 Ibid. 28.
34 Ibid.
35 Moran 1894, 417.
36 Ibid. 414.
37 Martin 1988, 30.
38 Ibid. 34.
39 Ibid. 41-51.
40 Ibid. 39.
41 Ibid. 44.
42 O'Farrell 1977, 121.
43 Moran 1894, 419.
44 O'Donoghue 1982, 72.

**Chapter 2:** ***Murray Johnson*****, 'Whose guilt? What reward?': The loss of the 'Sovereign', 1847**

1 Reynolds 1920, 14.
2 Welsby 1967, 2:83.
3 MBC 20 Mar. 1847, 2; Whitmore 1987, 119.
4 Davies 1937, 7.
5 Knight 1898, 162.
6 MBC 20 Mar. 1847, 2.
7 Leichhardt 1847, xiv.
8 MBC 7 Aug. 1847, 3.
9 MBC 20 Mar. 1847, 2.
10 MBC 7 Aug. 1847, 3.
11 MBC 20 Mar. 1847, 2.
12 Steele 1972, 11.
13 Ibid. 179.
14 Evans 1992, 26-27.

15 Pixley 1969-70, 160.
16 MBC 7 Aug. 1847, 3.
17 MBC 13 Mar. 1847, 2.
18 Ibid.
19 MBC 6 Mar. 1847, 2.
20 BC 6 Sep. 1871, 3.
21 BC 28 Jul. 1923, 19.
22 MBC 17 Mar. 1847, in Welsby 1967, 2:297; Knight 1898, 201.
23 Welsby 1967, 1:284.
24 MBC 13 Mar. 1847, 2.
25 Welsby 1967, 1:297-8; Knight 1898, 201-02.
26 Knight 1898, 202.
27 MBC 20 Mar. 1847, 2.
28 Welsby 1967, 1:298; Knight 1898, 202.
29 BC 6 Sep. 1871, 3.
30 Knight 1898, 204-5.
31 BC 6 Sep. 1871, 3.
32 Welsby 1967, 2:113.
33 Ibid. 85.
34 Welsby 1967, 1:302.
35 MBC 20 Mar. 1847, 2.
36 MBC 27 Mar. 1847, 2.
37 MBC 3 Apr. 1847, 3.
38 Ibid.
39 MBC 14 Aug. 1847, 3.
40 MBC 17 Apr. 1847, 3.
41 MBC 5 Jun. 1847, 3.
42 Russell 1888, 378-9.
43 Knight 1898, 206.
44 MBC 14 Aug. 1847, 3.
45 MBC 26 Jun. 1847, 3.
46 Welsby 1967, 2:85.
47 BC 6 Sep. 1871, 3.
48 Welsby 1967, 2:114-15.
49 MBC 7 Aug. 1847, 3.
50 Knight 1898, 205.
51 BC 6 Sep. 1871, 3.
52 MBC 20 Mar. 1847, 2.
53 Knight 1898, 357.
54 Welsby 1977, 33.
55 Welsby 1967, 2:114-15.
56 Ibid. 89-90.
57 Ibid. 88.
58 BC 6 Sep. 1871, 3.
59 MBC 13 Mar. 1847, 2.
60 Fisher 1992, 32.

**Chapter 3: *Yvonne Reynolds*, 'Sweet surrender': Sugar production at St Helena Penal Establishment 1867-89**

1 COL/A98, William Thornton to Colonial Secretary, 3 Dec. 1867, QSA.
2 Wood 1965, 5-6.
3 Ibid. 6-9; Wood 1964-65, 567.
4 Johnston 1982, 57.
5 Nilsson 1963-64, 358.
6 Courtenay 1978, 31-3; Schlomowitz 1982, 340.
7 Laverty 1970, 33
8 Schlomowitz 1982, 337.
9 Laverty 1970, 28.
10 COL/A100, Batch 68/17, William Thornton to Colonial Secretary, 2 Jan. 1868, QSA.
11 Ibid.
12 Ibid. Batch 68/64, John McDonald to Colonial Secretary, 31 Dec. 1867, QSA.
13 COL/A102, Batch 68/611, William Thornton to Colonial Secretary, 2 Mar. 1868, QSA.
14 Ibid. John McDonald to Colonial Secretary, 1 Mar. 1868, QSA.
15 Ibid. Batch 68/613, John McDonald to Colonial Secretary, 1 Sept. 1868, QSA.
16 COL/A112, Batch 68/3132, John McDonald to Colonial Secretary, 1 Oct. 1868, QSA.
17 COL/A113, Batch 68/3536, John McDonald to Colonial Secretary, 1 Nov. 1868, QSA.
18 COL/A117, Batch 69/395, John McDonald to Colonial Secretary, 1 Feb. 1869, QSA.

19 COL/A119, Batch 69/819, John McDonald to Colonial Secretary, 1 Mar. 1869, QSA.
20 COL/A124, Batch 69/1749, T.H. Barron to Colonial Secretary, 13 May 1869, QSA.
21 Ibid.
22 Ibid. Batch 69/1861, John McDonald to Colonial Secretary, 18 May 1869, QSA.
23 Ibid. 69/1926, T.H. Barron to Colonial Secretary, 26 May 1869, QSA.
24 Ibid.
25 QVP 1869, 1:884-5.
26 QDR 30 Oct. 1869, 6.
27 Ibid; Easterby 1932, 67-9.
28 Lund 1955, 1106.
29 Ibid. 67.
30 Wood 1965, 34.
31 Ibid.
32 Ibid. 10.
33 COL/A133, Batch 69/3985, John McDonald to Colonial Secretary, 1 Nov. 1869, QSA.
34 Ibid. Batch 69/3753, John McDonald to Colonial Secretary, 1 Oct. 1869, QSA.
35 Ibid.
36 COL/A137, Batch 70/346, John McDonald to Colonial Secretary, 25 Jan. 1870, QSA.
37 COL/A141, Batch 70/1333, John McDonald to Colonial Secretary, 6 May 1870.
38 COL/A145, Batch 70/1915, John McDonald to Colonial Secretary, 1 Jul. 1870, QSA.

**Chapter 4: *Murray Johnson*, 'A modified form of whaling': The Moreton Bay dugong fishery 1846-1920**

1 Montgomery 1997, 3.
2 Maher 1997, 84.
3 Senior 1890, 211.
4 Thorne 1876, 251.
5 Jefferson, Leatherwood & Weber 1993, 207-11.
6 Heinsohn 1977, 134.
7 Nishiwaki & Marsh 1989, 9-11.
8 Ibid. 9.
9 McCrindle 1960, 175.
10 Troughton 1928, 222.
11 Page & Ingpen 1989, 23.
12 Nishiwaki & Marsh 1989, 23.
13 Marsh 1997, 52.
14 Heinsohn 1977, 138.
15 Anderson 1981, 640.
16 Saville-Kent 1893, 328.
17 Thomson 1934, 246.
18 Ibid. 242-3.
19 Backhouse 1967, 369.
20 Petrie 1904, 67.
21 Steele 1972, 19.
22 Lee 1925, 520.
23 Steele 1972, 27.
24 Petrie 1904, 68; Thorne 1876, 263.
25 Petrie 1904, 66.
26 Backhouse 1967, 369.
27 Welsby 1931, 81-2.
28 Cilento 1959, 220.
29 SMH 19 Aug. 1846, 3.
30 SMH 25 Jan. 1847, 2.
31 Ibid.
32 Welsby 1905, 108.
33 SMH 8 Feb. 1847, 3.
34 Brasch 1987, 162.
35 Pers. Comm. from Althea Vickers, Dunwich, 2 Feb. 1998.
36 MBC 25 Oct. 1851, 3.
37 MBC 5 Feb. 1853, 3.
38 BC 8 Oct. 1869, 2.
39 Senior 1890, 207.
40 MBC 13 Aug. 1853, 3.
41 BC 4 Sep. 1862, 2; Cilento 1959, 220.
42 Lack 1968, 5.
43 Cilento 1961-62, 894-5.
44 Thorne 1876, 248.

45 SMH 19 Oct. 1857, 6.
46 MBC 16 Jan. 1858, 2.
47 SMH 18 Sep. 1858, 6.
48 Ibid.
49 SMH 6 Dec. 1858, 5.
50 SMH 22 Jan. 1859, 5; MBC 9 Feb. 1859, 3.
51 SMH 11 Mar. 1859, 8.
52 MBC 30 Jul. 1859, 2.
53 MBC 9 Feb. 1859, 3.
54 MBC 30 Apr. 1859, 4.
55 SMH 6 Dec. 1858, 5.
56 MBC 29 Jan. 1859, 2.
57 SMH 7 Feb. 1859, 8.
58 Petrie 1904, 8-10.
59 Jones 1970, 121.
60 Cilento 1959, 220.
61 Lack 1968, 5.
62 Saville-Kent 1893, 328.
63 QGG 60/8, Sep. 1893, 79.
64 Welsby 1905, 103.
65 Welsby in BC 9 Aug. 1924, 18.
66 Thorne 1876, 251.
67 Ibid.
68 MBC 15 Oct. 1859, 2.
69 MBC 19 Mar. 1859, 2.
70 MBC 30 Apr. 1859, 4.
71 QG 15 Dec. 1859, 8.
72 QG 4 Sep. 1862, 3.
73 MBC 30 Jul. 1859, 2.
74 Loyau 1897, 365.
75 Senior 1890, 207.
76 BC 18 Sep. 1862, 2.
77 Bertram & Bertram 1971, 146.
78 Thorne 1876, 252.
79 BC 16 Sep. 1862, 2.
80 Welsby 1931, 82-3.
81 Welsby in BC 30 Aug. 1924, 18.
82 Thorne 1876, 252.
83 Wight 1862, 139.
84 Singe 1989, 130.
85 Senior 1890, 205.
86 Welsby 1931, 84.
87 BC 18 Sep. 1862, 2.
88 Welsby 1931, 76.
89 Jones 1970, 121.
90 BC 8 Oct. 1869, 2; Thorne 1876, 258.
91 Harris 1912, 227.
92 Marsh, Channells & Morissey 1979, 6.
93 Welsby 1905, 101.
94 Senior 1890, 206.
95 Welsby 1931, 77.
96 Walker 1972, 73-4.
97 Petrie 1904, 66.
98 Troughton 1954, 247; Marsh 1997, 53.
99 Senior 1890, 206.
100 MBC 19 Mar. 1859, 2.
101 Welsby 1931, 85.
102 NAM 4/2, Sep. 1957, 44.
103 Easterby 1932, 76.
104 BC 8 Oct. 1869, 2.
105 Senior 1890, 206.
106 BC 8 Oct. 1869, 2.
107 Cannon & Goyen 1989, 126.
108 BC 8 Aug. 1862, 3.
109 BC 4 Sep. 1862, 2.
110 Lang 1861, 72-3.

111 BC 8 Oct. 1869, 3.
112 MBC 14 Jul. 1860, 3.
113 BC 8 Oct. 1869, 3.
114 Bertram & Bertram 1971, 146-7.
115 BC 5 Aug. 1871, 6.
116 BC 6 Sep. 1871, 3.
117 Welsby 1905, 104; Welsby 1931, 69.
118 BC 27 Nov. 1871, 2.
119 Petrie 1904, 214.
120 Welsby 1931, 87.
121 QDR 1 Oct. 1892, 631.
122 Ibid.
123 QGG 44/95, Aug. 1888, 1244-5.
124 QDR 1 Oct. 1892, 631.
125 QDR 2 Jan. 1892, 29.
126 QDR 1 Oct. 1869, 630-1.
127 Bartley 1892, 86.
128 QGG 56/116, Aug. 1892, 1203.
129 QGG 59/38, Jun. 1893, 269; Welsby 1905, 100.
130 QGG 60/8, Sep. 1893, 79.
131 Welsby 1905, 104; Welsby 1931, 69.
132 Thorne 1876, 251.
133 Cannon & Goyen 1989, 126.
134 Collins 1975, 343.
135 Troughton 1928, 224.
136 Evans 1959, 49.
137 Marsh 1997, 55.
138 Ibid. 55-6.
139 Welsby 1905, 100.
140 Weedon 1898, 262.
141 Queensland year book 1901, 299.
142 Cilento 1959, 220.
143 Marsh, Channells & Morissey 1979, 44-5.
144 Beitz 197-, 16.
145 Cilento 1959, 220.
146 Lack 1968, 5.
147 Harris 1912, 227.
148 Cilento 1959, 221.
149 Lack 1968, 5.
150 Commonwealth Advisory Council of Science & Industry 1917, 28.
151 BC 26 Jul. 1920, 9.
152 WK 17 Aug. 1923, 33.
153 BC 23 Feb. 1929, 23.
154 A/59643, File 9T/69, QSA.
155 QGG 230/42, Mar. 1969, 929-30.
156 Heinsohn 1977, 137.
157 Cantley 1973, 35; Paterson 1979, 18.
158 Colwell 1969, 2-3.
159 Montgomery 1997, 3.

**Chapter 5: *Joseph Goodall*, 'Nothing beyond myself and Mr Watkins': James Hamilton and the Dunwich Benevolent Asylum**

1 QPD 1884, 9-10.
2 Ibid. 89.
3 Ibid. 453.
4 JQLC 1884.
5 Ibid.
6 Fitzgerald 1982, 195.
7 BC 8 Jul. 1891, 2.
8 COL/A19, In-letter 2085 of 1861, QSA.
9 COL/A35, In-letter 3037 of 1862, QSA.
10 HOS/IG2, Secretary Brisbane Hospital Committee to Colonial Secretary 19 Nov. 1862, QSA.
11 COL/A37, In-letter 390 of 1863, QSA.
12 COL/A64, In-letter 311 of 1865, QSA.
13 COL/A66, In-letter 1039 of 1866, QSA.
14 COL/A72, In-letter 2943 of 1865, QSA.

15 BC 12 May 1868, 3.
16 BC 22 May 1865, 2.
17 COL/A67, In-letter 1303 of 1865, QSA.
18 Ibid. In-letter 1284 of 1865, QSA.
19 HOS/ID7, Minute Book of Brisbane Hospital Committee, Jan. 1863-Jan. 1867, QSA.
20 COL/A68, In-letter 1676 of 1865; Ibid. In-letter 1711 of 1865, QSA.
21 HOS/ID7, Minute Book of Brisbane Hospital Committee, Jan. 1863-Jan. 1867, QSA.
22 COL/A78, In-letter 1136 of 1866; QVP 1866, 1617.
23 QVP 1866, 1617.
24 Hurd Cuttings Book, 'Death of an Identity', JOL.
25 QVP 1871, 986.
26 COL/A90, In-letter 1046 of 1867; COL/A92, In-letter 1727 of 1867, QSA.
27 A/100, In-letter 120 of 1868, QSA.
28 QGG 15/60, 30 May 1874, 1027.
29 QVP 1872, 584, 1879, 513, 1881, 415, 1886, 1191.
30 JQLC 1884, 1.
31 COL/A19, In-letter 2085 of 1861, QSA.
32 COL/A89, In-letter 529 of 1867, QSA.
33 QVP 1871, 986.
34 COL/A209, In-letter 1487 of 1875, QSA.
35 COL/A235, In-letter 1015 of 1877, QSA.
36 COL/A88, In-letter 452 of 1867, QSA.
37 COL/A100, In-letter 198 of 1868; BEN2/1, 45, QSA.
38 COL/A323, In-letter 4265 of 1882, QSA.
39 JQLC 1884, 37-8.
40 COL/A261, In-letter 2518 of 1878, QSA.
41 JQLC 1884, 25.
42 QPD 1889, 1616.
43 QPD 1893, 843.
44 JQLC 1884, 53.
45 BEN2/1-6, Dunwich Benevolent Asylum registers 1859-1906, QSA.
46 COL/A414, In-letter 627 of 1885, QSA.
47 COL/A186, In-letter 1712 of 1872, QSA.
48 COL/A411, In-letter 039 of 1885, QSA.
49 COL/A414, In-letter 898 of 1885, QSA.
50 COL/A444, In-letter 8521 of 1885, QSA.
51 QVP 1895, 2:141.
52 QPD 1885, 193-224.
53 QPD 1887, 672.
54 JQLC 1884, 37.
55 Ibid. 9-10.
56 Ibid. 49.
57 Ibid. 50.
58 Ibid. 34-5.
59 Ibid. 39.
60 Ibid. 17-19.
61 COL/A414, In-letter 752 of 1885; COL/A419, In-letter 2415 of 1885, QSA.
62 COL/A428, In-letter 4672 of 1885, QSA.
63 COL/A472, In-letter 5486 of 1886, QSA.
64 COL/A420, In-letter 2469 of 1886; 2619 of 1885, QSA.
65 COL/A471, In-letter 2668 of 1886, QSA.
66 COL/A472, In-letter 5486 of 1886, QSA.
67 Ibid.
68 COL/A400, In-letter 6395 of 1884, QSA.
69 COL/A472, In-letter 5486 of 1886, QSA.
70 COL/A436, In-letter 6719 of 1885, QSA.
71 COL/A447, In-letter 8222 of 1885; COL/A443, In-letter 8488 of 1885, QSA.

**Chapter 6: *Shirleene Robinson*, 'Keep them as much as possible away from Brisbane': Bribie Island Aboriginal reserves 1877-79 and 1891-92**

1 Petrie 1904, 214.
2 COL/A287a, In-letter 4428 of 1879, QSA.
3 EO 17 Nov. 1892, 3.
4 BC 14 Jul. 1923, 18.
5 Ford & Blake 1998, 59.
6 Ibid.

7 Kamminga 1981, 31-5.
8 McArthur 1979, 35.
9 QDR 26 Sep. 1891, 607.
10 BC 20 Oct. 1923, 18.
11 Ibid.
12 Welsby 1937, 1.
13 MBC 14 Jul. 1849, 3, 6 Sep. 1851, 3, 7 Feb. 1852, 3, 28 Oct. 1854, 2.
14 Meston 1895, 80.
15 Ibid. 81.
16 Ibid.
17 LAN/A55, In-letter 4890 of 1877, QSA.
18 BC 31 Jan. 1877, 3.
19 WK 9 Jun. 1877, 3.
20 Evans 1971a, 26-38; Evans 1971b, 3-14.
21 MMSKA 18 Jan. 1873, 2.
22 QVP 1876, 3/1:161.
23 QVP 1877, 1:24.
24 Ibid.
25 Ibid.
26 LAN/A55, In-letter 4890 of 1877, QSA.
27 FL MSS 2/1748.
28 Ibid.
29 LAN/A55, In-letter 4890 of 1877, QSA.
30 QDR 25 May 1877, 1.
31 QVP 1878, 2:65.
32 Ibid.
33 Petrie 1904, 70.
34 Ibid. 214.
35 QVP 1878, 2:65.
36 Ibid. 66.
37 Petrie 1904, 216.
38 COL/A252a, In-letter 459 of 1878, QSA.
39 FL MSS 2/1748.
40 QDR 3 Feb. 1879, 184.
41 QDR 25 Jan. 1879, 120.
42 QDR 3 Feb. 1879, 184.
43 QDR 1 Mar. 1879, 184.
44 Evans 1971b, 8.
45 COL/A287a, In-letter 4428 of 1879, QSA.
46 Ibid.
47 Petrie 1904, 215.
48 BS 1963, 2/9:27.
49 Cowin 1950, 73.
50 QDR 14 Feb. 1891, 380.
51 QDR 16 Jun. 1932, 4.
52 QDR 21 Feb. 1891, 363; Walker 1998, 139-40.
53 Ibid.
54 QDR 15 Jun. 1879, 337.
55 QDR 21 Feb. 1891, 363.
56 Ibid.
57 QDR 16 May 1891, 954.
58 QDR 21 Feb. 1891, 363.
59 QDR 16 May 1891, 954.
60 Welsby 1937, 389.
61 QDR 21 Feb. 1891, 363.
62 WK 31 Dec. 1891, 20.
63 TEL 30 Sep. 1891, 2.
64 WK 31 Dec. 1891, 20.
65 TEL 30 Sep. 1891, 2.
66 TEL 1 Oct. 1891, 5.
67 QDR 16 Jun. 1932, 4.
68 WK 18 Nov. 1892, 6.
69 QPP 1906, 2:913.
70 McArthur 1979, 67.
71 BC 20 Oct. 1923, 18.
72 Lergessner 1993, 64.

**Chapter 7:** ***Rosemary Ahearn*****, 'Leading lights': The first Moreton Island lighthouse communities**

1 Davenport 1986, 130.
2 Dagg 1985, n.p.
3 M & T Ward collection, 24 Sep. 1983, RHSQ.
4 Davenport 1986, 60.
5 Ibid.
6 Ludlow 1992, 37.
7 Davenport 1986, 131.
8 Ibid. 132.
9 Ibid. 59.
10 Ibid. 130.
11 Ibid. 132.
12 M & T Ward collection, 24 Sep. 1983, RHSQ.
13 Jean Trundle MSS, OM85-7/C13, JOL.
14 EDU/Z379, In-letter 2435 of 1881, QSA.
15 Ibid. 8056 of 1884.
16 Ibid. 8193 of 1885.
17 Ibid. 01365 of 1891.
18 Ibid. 10603 of 1894.
19 Ibid. 03135 of 1895.
20 Ibid. 21635 of 1902.
21 Telephone interview with Eleanor Beck, Sydney, 1 Jun. 1995.
22 Interview with Kathleen Hurst, Brisbane, 11 Jun. 1995.
23 Telephone interview with Eleanor Beck, Sydney, 1 Jun. 1995.
24 EDU/Z379, In-letter 18498 of 1909, QSA.
25 Ibid.
26 Ibid.
27 Ibid. 16 Nov. 1911.
28 Ibid. In-letter 26956 of 1912.
29 Davenport 1986, 130.
30 EDU/Z512, In-letter 3298 of 1876.
31 Ibid.
32 Personal collection of Terry Ward.
33 Ibid.
34 Ludlow 1992, 6-7.
35 Bell 1991, 20.
36 Ibid.
37 Personal collection of M & T Ward.
38 EDU/Z512, 7 Mar. 1890.
39 Ibid. 14 May 1909.
40 Ibid. 21 Jun. 1912.
41 Ibid. 15 May 1913.
42 Ibid. 4 Dec. 1925.
43 Ibid. In-letter 26529 of 1926.
44 Personal collection of R & M Day.
45 SM 14 Oct. 1990.
46 Horton 1983, 115.

**Chapter 8:** ***Yvonne Reynolds*****, Patrick Roche and HM Prison Farm of St Helena 1926-31**

1 St Helena file MB, Fred Pedissen, 24 Dec. 1930, QNPWS.
2 QPP 1930.
3 QVP 1895.
4 PRI/044, QSA.
5 On Welsby, see Susan Martin 2000.
6 QPP 1923.
7 BC 1 Oct. 1926.
8 St Helena file MB, taped interview with Mary Bell, 30 Apr. 1987, QNPWS.
9 Ibid. Alec Whyte, 2 Jun. 1926.
10 Ibid. Friend Taylor, 3 Oct. 1930.
11 Ibid. Lewis Turner, 14 Jan. 1931.
12 Ibid. T. Purcell, 14 Jan. 1927.
13 Ibid. Annie Oelkers, 29 Dec. 1927.
14 Ibid. Fred Thompson, 26 Jan. 1928.
15 Ibid. Victor Wearne, 8 Feb. 1928.
16 Ibid. J. Martin, 21 Feb. 1928.
17 Ibid. M. Bateman, 24 Mar. 1928.

18 Ibid. B. Payne, n.d.
19 Ibid. Thomas Moran, 14 Jan. 1931.
20 DM 29 Apr. 1932.
21 TEL 21 Dec. 1928.
22 St Helena file MB, taped interview with Mary Bell, 30 Apr. 1987, QNPWS.
23 Ibid. John Williams, Jun. 1929.
24 Ibid. Friend Taylor, 3 Oct. 1930.
25 Ibid. V. Kelsey, 2 Sep. 1930.
26 Ibid. C. Martin, 16 May 1928.
27 Ibid. author unknown, 14 Sep. 1928.
28 Ibid. 'Bill', 30 Sep. 1930.
29 Ibid. Paul Werner, 18 Oct. 1928.
30 Ibid. Patrick Roche, 4 Aug. 1927.
31 Ibid. Patrick Roche, 23 Mar. 1934.
32 QGG, 129/9 1927, 1333-4.
33 TR 3 Feb. 1929.
34 St Helena file MB, Sidney Webb, 3 Dec. 1931, QNPWS.
35 Ibid. Thomas Scotney, 23 Jun. 1931.
36 Ibid. 'W.T.', 8 Dec. 1931.
37 TR 3 Feb. 1929.
38 St Helena file MB, W. Gordon Graham, 18 Aug. 1927, QNPWS.
39 Ibid. H. Doolan, 7 Oct. 1928.

**Chapter 9: *Thom Blake*, 'The leper shall dwell alone': A history of Peel Island lazaret**

1 Richards 1977, xv.
2 AMG 1892, 427-30.
3 Evans 1969, 302-8.
4 QPD 1892, 46:40-41.
5 Ibid. 36-40.
6 Evans 1969, 231-51.
7 DAS Batch 1, Peel Island lazaret, 6 Mar. 1906, QSA.
8 QGG 1906, 2:232.
9 Evans 1969, 238-41.
10 DAS Batch 1, Peel Island lazaret, 7 May 1907, QSA.
11 QDR 3 Aug. 1907.
12 Ibid.
13 DAS Batch 1, Peel Island lazaret, 16 Apr. 1907, QSA.
14 Ibid.
15 WOR/P11, QSA.
16 QPP 1907, 2:957.
17 DAS Batch 1, Peel Island lazaret, 10 May 1907, QSA.
18 QDR 3 Aug. 1907.
19 DAS Batch 1, Peel Island lazaret, 10 Sep. 1907, QSA.
20 Ibid. Batch 2, 27 Apr. 1909.
21 Ibid. 10 May 1909.
22 Ibid. 13 Feb. 1910.
23 Ibid. 25 Feb. 1910.
24 Ibid. 7 Mar. 1910.
25 Ibid. Batch 1, 13 Aug. 1907.
26 Ibid. 12 Feb. 1909.
27 Maguire 1991, 145-6.
28 DAS Batch F5D/99, 9 Jun. 1955, QSA.
29 HOM/J35 08/5110, QSA.
30 QPP 1937, 2:934; COL/278 36/9150, 29 Sep. 1936, QSA.
31 QPP 1937, 2:935.
32 Ibid.
33 QDR 3 Aug. 1907.
34 DAS Batch 2, Peel Island lazaret, 13 Mar. 1911, QSA.
35 Ibid. Batch 1, 26 Mar. 1908.
36 Ibid. Batch 2, 13 Feb. 1910.
37 Evans 1969, 251-52.
38 Ibid. 253.
39 COL/277, Donovan file 10/1612, QSA.
40 COL/322, 21/9463, 18 Nov. 1921, QSA.
41 Evans 1969, 258.
42 Ludlow 1991, 37.

43 CM 20 Sep. 1946.
44 Ibid. 17 Mar. 1950, 18 Mar. 1950, 20 Mar. 1950, 23 Mar. 1950.
45 QPP 1954, 2:805.
46 QPP 1914, 2:14.
47 QPP 1922, 1:1162.
48 QPP 1924, 1:733.
49 Rees 1985, 30-31.
50 QDR 3 Aug. 1907.
51 Evans 1969, 256.
52 Ibid. 255.
53 Gabriel 1961, 19-27.
54 DAS Batch 1, Peel Island lazaret, 13 Feb. 1910, QSA; Evans 1969, 256.
55 DAS Batch F5, Peel Island lazaret, 2 Jun. 1937, QSA.
56 QPP 1910, 2:859; Evans 1969, 257.
57 COL/322 11/7676, 4 Aug. 1911, QSA.
58 QPP 1927, 1:710.
59 QPP 1947-8, 2:923; Interview with Eric Reye, Brisbane, 24 Mar. 1993.
60 QPP 1953-4, 2:18.
61 Browne 1985, 10.
62 QPP 1948, 2:689; QPP 1952, 2:804.
63 Saunders 1990, 168-81.
64 MJA 1926, 2:372.
65 Ibid. 377; MJA 1927, 1:387-90.
66 MJA 1930, 2:525-7.
67 MJA 1926, 2:801-3; Cilento 1937, 45-52.
68 CM 29 Mar. 1939.
69 A/31760 49/10892, QSA.
70 PD/84.3, QSA.
71 MS Apr. 1951, 1.
72 QPP 1952, 2:805.
73 QPP 1959-60, 2:945.
74 CM 6 Aug. 1959.
75 DAS Batch E5, Peel Island lazaret, 1 Oct. 1959, QSA.
76 Ibid. Batch F5/594, 7 Jan. 1960.
77 Ibid. Batch F5/673, n.d.
78 TEL 3 Jul. 1962.
79 CM 26 Nov. 1964.
80 LAN Reserve File 06/180, 11 Apr. 1967, QSA.
81 Ibid.

**Chapter 10: *David Jones*, The Whalers of Tangalooma, 1952-62**

1 This paper has been extracted with permission from a publication by Tangalooma Island Resort. Some of the main sources are: Bateson 1972; Chittleborough 1961-2-3; 1965; Colwell 1969; Dakin 1963; Gates 1963; Jones 1980; Moncrieff 1969; Pix 29 Sept. 1962; CM; TEL; SM; SMH.

**Chapter 11: *Nonie Malone*, 'Layers on the landscape': Dunwich Benevolent Asylum**

1 Carter, Durbidge & Cooke-Bramley 1994, 1:44.
2 Ibid. 42, 164.
3 Steele 1975, 92.
4 Lands Department File RES/4987, QSA.
5 Goodall 1992, 24-36.
6 Johnston 1988, 402-04.
7 Goodall 1992, 24-36.
8 BEN2/6, QSA.
9 Lands Department File RES/4987, QSA.
10 BEN2/6, QSA.
11 Rahnsleben Manuscript, FL.
12 Lands Department File RES/4987, QSA.
13 Personal communication with G. Ferguson, Jul-Oct 1994.
14 Personal communication with Dawn Ferguson, Jul. 1994.
15 Ibid.
16 Lands Department File RES/4987, QSA.
17 Ibid.
18 Mines & Durbidge 1994, 62.
19 Lands Department File RES/4987, QSA.
20 Personal communication with Dawn Ferguson, Jul. 1994.

21 Personal communication with G. Kennedy, Oct. 1995.
22 Lands Department File RES/4987, QSA.
23 Ibid.
24 Ibid.
25 Ibid.
26 Rahnsleben Manuscript, FL.
27 Lands Department File RES/4987, QSA.
28 Ibid.

**Chapter 12: *Rod Fisher*, The history of Moreton Bay: A saga of lost dreams**

1 Horton 1983, 9-11; Hall 1987, 18.
2 Hall 1990, 175-82.
3 Ibid. 176.
4 Walker 1862, 240-41.
5 Hall 1984, 16.
6 Hall 1987, 17.
7 Welsby 1967, 2:427.
8 Steele 1984, 99; Evans 1992, 11.
9 Alfredson 1984, 1; Dagg 1985, 20; Pearn 1993, 15.
10 Durbidge & Covacevich 1981, 54, 65; Goodall 1992, 253-58; Salter 1983, 10-14.
11 Horton 1983, 19; Welsby 1967, 2:388-90; Colliver & Wolston 1975, 253-58; Salter 1983, 10-14.
12 Durbidge & Covacevich 1981, 64; Horton 1983, 18.
13 Richardson 1984, 31; Colliver & Wolston 1975, 92.
14 AUS 7 May 1988.
15 Robins 1984, 39-40.
16 Horton 1983, 1-3, 28-29; Jones 1993, 23-27.
17 McLeod 1984, 100-6.
18 Davenport 1986, 204, 286; Horton 1993, 94-95; Rowe 1991, 20, 32.
19 Horton 1983, 114-15; Ludlow 1992, 37-41; Welsby 1967, 2:143-47.
20 Coleman 1984; Davenport 1986.
21 Steele 1972, 51-101.
22 Steele 1975; Johnston 1988.
23 Durbidge & Covacevich 1981, 73-75; Steele 1975, 76-78.
24 Durbidge & Covacevich 1981, 75-76; Steele 1975, 44-46.
25 Steele 1975, 92, 232, 252; Welsby 1967, 2:353-60; Horton 1983, 18, 47, 86.
26 Steele 1975, 53-54, 73.
27 Horton 1983, 47.
28 Fisher 1987, 78; Welsby 1967, 2:101.
29 Horton 1983, 15-17; Welsby 1967, 2:374-76.
30 Durbidge & Covacevich 1981, 77-78; Welsby 1967, 1:276-81.
31 Fisher 1987, 84; Welsby 1967, 2:126.
32 Horton 1983, 86-7; Sanker 1984, 120.
33 Horton 1983, 47; Rowe 1991, 55; Salter 1984, 113.
34 Horton 1983, 25, 48-49, 69-70; Jones 1988, 205-06; Foley & Pearn 1993, 167.
35 Goodall 1992, 258-61; Horton 1983, 94; Jones 1988, 47-53; Thorne 1876, 12.
36 Dagg 1985, 13; Jones 1993, 25-28.
37 Jones 1988, 43-130.
38 Rowe 1991, 32-33.
39 Horton 1983, 86-87; Rowe 1991, 10; Sanker, 1984, 118-23.
40 Sanker 1984, 122; Horton 1983, 87.
41 Rowe 1991, 40.
42 Horton 1983, 89; Rowe 1991, 15.
43 Welsby 1967, 1:292; Sanker 1984, 120-22.
44 Thorne 1876, 9; Horton 1983, 114-15; Davenport 1986, 12, 130.
45 Durbidge & Covacevich 1981, 78; Goodall 1992, 27-28, 35.
46 Durbidge & Covacevich 1981, 80-83, 156; Goodall 1992, 236, 334-36.
47 MSS Tom Dowse reminiscences, JOL; Finger 1986.
48 Goodall 1992, 80-85, 306.
49 Ludlow 1988.
50 Durbidge & Covacevich 1981, 64-65; Goodall 1992, 279-85; Welsby 1967, 1:379-85.
51 Horton 1983, 8-9, 89.
52 Holthouse 1982, 51; Horton 1983, 26; Ludlow 1992, 8; Welsby 1967, 2:412.
53 Davenport 1986, 180-81, 329, 334, 476; Horton 1983, 84-100; Salter 1983, 4, 19-23.
54 Horton 1983, 75-87, 94; Rowe 1991, 44; Salter 1983, 17-18; CM 24 Aug. 1970.
55 Durbidge & Covacevich 1981, 155; Foley & Pearn 1993, 175; Goodall 1992, 100, 262.
56 Welsby 1967, 2:141-2; Jones 1993, 31-2; Salter 1983, 5-6.

57 Foley & Pearn 1993, 167-69; Goodall 1992, 259; Stewart 1993, 38-39; Rowe 1991, 11, 15-16.
58 BC 30 Oct. 1909; Branch 1966, 6-8, 16, 20; Horton 1983, 77-80; Rowe 1991, 7-9, 19, 38-39.
59 Horton 1983, 70-71, 75, 94; Salter 1983, 26-28; Salter 1984, 115; TEL 2 Oct. 1978.
60 CM 8 Jun. 1981.
61 Welsby 1967, 2:396-402; Holthouse 1982, 50-52; Horton 1983, 20-25; Ludlow 1992, 9-11.
62 Salter 1983, 31-3.
63 Welsby 1967, 2:403; Holthouse 1982, 51; Horton 1983, 20; Ludlow 1992, 9-11.
64 Rowe 1991, 11; Goodall, 1992, 276.
65 BC 15 Dec. 1925; Horton 1983, 54; Jones 1993, 32.
66 CM 17 Jun. 1950; CM 4 Jul. 1950; Horton 1983, 67.
67 Covacevich 1984, 98-9; Durbidge & Covacevich 1981, 93, 105-7, 158; Ludlow 1992, 86.
68 TEL 21 Nov. 1941; Bland 1993, 193; Foley & Pearn 1993, 169, 179.
69 Horton 1983, 50; Finger 1986, 41-43; Finger 1988, 39; SM 6 Oct. 1991.
70 Finger 1988, 45; Horton 1983, 50; Ludlow 1988, 16; Welsby 1967, 2:127.
71 Horton 1983, 114.
72 Durbidge & Covacevich 1981, 92-93, 107; Dagg 1985, 14; Holthouse 1982, 56-57.
73 BC 15 Dec. 1925.
74 TEL 6 Oct. 1947; Durbidge & Covacevich 1981, 101; Jones 1988, 232; Horton 1983, 114.
75 CM 5 Jul. 1969; Sun 18 Feb. 1987; Horton 1983, 107, 111.
76 Horton 1983, 64; CM 9 Aug. 1991; BCC 1989, 9.
77 Davenport 1986, 493.
78 Dagg 1985, 14-18; Davenport 1986, 493-96.
79 CM 17 Jun. 1950; CM 4 Jul. 1950; Horton 1983, 66-68; BCC 1989, 13.
80 Durbidge & Covacevich 1984, 109-11, 133; Goodall 1992, 335; Salter 1983, 24-48, 33, 35-57.
81 Foley & Pearn 1993, 168-82; Horton 1983, 72, 91; Ludlow 1992, 112-13; CM 22 Oct. 1978.
82 Durbidge & Covacevich 1981, 115; Ludlow 1992, 84-85; CM 25 Jan. 1983.
83 Horton 1983, 21; CM 7 Feb. 1989.
84 CM 3 Feb. 1993.
85 CM 29 Dec. 1973; CM 9 Jan. 1987; BCC 1989, 15; AUS 24 Feb. 1972.
86 CM 22 Jun. 1963; CM 22 Jan. 1983; CM 12 May 1984; Dagg 1985, 18, 46.
87 BC 26 Nov. 1932; Horton 1983, 44, 54.
88 BCC 1989, 32; Durbidge & Covacevich 1981, 7, 114-15; Robins 1984, 36; Horton 1983, 107.
89 SM 7 Jul. 1974.
90 CM 30 Jun. 1989.
91 CM 22 Jan. 1983; CM 14 Apr. 1984; CM 6 Sept. 1986; Horton 1983, 50.
92 Ludlow 1988, 63, 74-81; Ludlow 1992, 59-60; CM 13 Jan. 1960; SM 6 Oct. 1991.
93 BCC 1989, 24-26; CM 8 Nov. 1989; CM 25 Feb. 1993.
94 CM 11 Apr. 1989; CM 2 Jan. 1993; Foley & Pearn 1993, 167.
95 BCC 1989, 18; Durbidge 1984, 9-11; Ludlow 1992, 86-89; CM 5 Sept. 1991.
96 Minnery 1985, 137-38; Robins 1984, 39; CM 26 Nov. 1976; CM 19 Jan. 1993.
97 QDEH 1990, 8.
98 CM 22 Feb. 1993.
99 Walker 1972, 4.
100 CM 24 Nov. 1990.

# References

Note the format below for volume or series number/issue number: page number.


Ahearn, Rosemary, 1996, 'Moreton Island: Community and culture 1850-1995', UQ DipArts thesis, St Lucia, Qld.

Alfredson, Gillian 1984, 'The Aboriginal use of St Helena Island, Moreton Bay: The archaeological evidence', in Coleman, Covacevich & Davie 1984, 1-8.

Anderson, Paul 1981, 'The behaviour of the dugong (*Dugong dugon*) in relation to conservation and management', *Bulletin of marine science*, 3/3:640-47.

Backhouse, James 1967, *A narrative of a visit to the Australian colonies*, Johnson Reprint, New York.

Ba Pe, S, C. Ham & P. McDougall 1975, *St Helena: Moreton Bay*, Queensland Institute of Technology, Brisbane.

Bartley, Nehemiah 1892, *Opals and agates; or, Scenes under the Southern Cross and the Magelhans*, Gordon & Gotch, Brisbane.

Bateson, Charles 1966, *Patrick Logan: Tyrant of Brisbane Town*, Ure Smith, Sydney.

Beitz, M. 197-, *The Cleveland Log: History of South Moreton Bay area from 1770-1900s*, Redland Print, Cleveland.

Bell, Betty 1991, 'The way we were on Moreton', *SM*, 11 Oct., 20.

Bernays, Charles 1919, *Queensland politics during sixty years 1859-1919*, Government Printer, Brisbane.

Bertram, Kate & Colin Bertram 1971, 'The decline of the dugong', *Australian natural history*, 17/4:146-47.

Bland, Joan 1993, 'A pioneer island farm: A photo-archive', in Pearn 1993, 143-52.

Borey, Bernice 1984, *Myora Aboriginal Cemetery*, Friends of the Myora Aboriginal Cemetery, Brisbane.

Branch, W.J. 1966, *Russell Island souvenir*, The Author, Russell Island.

Brasch, Rudolph 1987, *Permanent addresses: Australians down under*, William Collins, Sydney.

Brisbane City Council 1989, *Moreton Bay seminar summary of papers*, Brisbane.

Brisbane City Council 1990, *Bay search seminar proceedings*, Brisbane.

Brisbane History Group 1987, *Brisbane: Aboriginal, alien, ethnic*, ed. Rod Fisher, BHG papers no.5.

Brisbane History Group 1992, *Brisbane: The Aboriginal presence 1824-60*, ed. Rod Fisher, BHG papers no.11.

Brisbane History Group 2000, *Brisbane: Squatters, settlers and surveyors*, ed. Rod Fisher & Jennifer Harrison, BHG papers no.16.

Browne, Stanley 1985, 'The history of leprosy', in *Leprosy*, ed. R. Hastings, Churchill Livingstone, Edinburgh, 1-14.

Cannon, Lester & Mark Goyen 1989, *Exploring Australia's Great Barrier Reef: A world heritage site*, Angus & Robertson, Sydney.

Cantley, Ronald 1973, 'A siren is dying', *Walkabout*, Jan., 34-35, 52.

Carter, Paddy, Ellie Durbidge & Jenny Cooke-Bramley, *Historic North Stradbroke Island*, North Stradbroke Island Historical Museum Association, Dunwich.

Cilento, Raphael 1937, 'Leprosy in Australia and its dependencies', *MJA*, 5:45-52.

Cilento, Raphael 1959, *Triumph in the tropics: An historical sketch of Queensland*, Smith & Paterson, Brisbane.

Cilento, Raphael 1961-62, 'Medicine in Queensland: Part 1 (1824-94)', *RHSQ journal*, 6/4:866-907.

Coleman, Roger, Jeanette Covacevich & Peter Davie 1984, *Focus of Stradbroke: New information on North Stradbroke Island and surrounding areas 1974-84*, Boolarong Publications, Brisbane.

Collins, David 1975, *An account of the English Colony in New South Wales*, A.H. & A.W. Reed, Sydney.

Colliver, F. Stanley & F.P. Woolston 1975, 'The Aborigines of Stradbroke Island', *Royal Society of Queensland proceedings*, 86:91-107.

Colwell, Max 1969, *Whaling around Australia*, Rigby, Adelaide.

Cowin, W. 1950, Aboriginal-European relations in early Queensland 1859-97, BA Hons thesis, UQ.

Courtenay, P.P. 1978, 'Agriculture in North Queensland', *Australian geographical studies*, 16:29-42.

Crimp, Olwyn N. ed. 1992, *Moreton Bay in the balance*, Australian Littoral Society, Brisbane.

Dagg, Annie 1985, *Tangalooma and Moreton Island* , Tangalooma Resort, Brisbane.

Davenport, Winifred 1986, *Harbours and Marine: Port and harbour development in Queensland from 1824 to 1985*, Queensland Department of Harbours & Marine, Brisbane.

Davie, Peter & others eds 1990, *The Brisbane River: A source-book for the future*, Australian Littoral Society & Queensland Museum, Brisbane.

Davies, A.G. 1937, 'Pioneer steamships in Queensland waters', *RHSQ journal*, 3/1:5-26.

Durbidge, Ellie & Jeanette Covacevich eds. 1981, *North Stradbroke Island*, Stradbroke Organisation, North Stradbroke Island.

Durbidge, Ellie 1984, 'Aboriginal middens, North Stradbroke Island', in Coleman, Covacevich & Davie 1984, 9-15.

Easterby, H.T. 1932, *The Queensland sugar industry: An historical review*, Frederick Phillips, Government Printer, Brisbane.

Evans, Raymond 1969, Charitable institutions of the Queensland government to 1919, MA thesis, UQ, Brisbane.

Evans, Raymond 1971a, 'Queensland's first Aboriginal reserve: Part 1—The promise of reform', *Queensland heritage*, 2/4:26-38.

Evans, Raymond 1971b, 'Queensland's first Aboriginal reserve: Part 2—The failure of reform', *Queensland heritage*, 2/5:3-14.

Evans, Raymond 1992a, 'Early racial contact and conflict on Stradbroke Island', in *Whose Island? The past and future of North Stradbroke Island*, ed. Regina Ganter, Queensland Studies Centre, Griffith University, Brisbane, 23-35.

Evans, Raymond 1992b, 'The mogwi take mi-an-jin: Race relations and the Moreton Bay penal settlement, 1824-42', *BHG papers*, 11:7-30.

Finger, Jarvis 1986, *True tales of old St Helena*, Boolarong Publications, Brisbane.

Finger, Jarvis 1988, *The St Helena Island prison*, Boolarong Publications, Brisbane.

Fisher, Rod 1987, 'The alien presence in early Brisbane 1840-60', *BHG papers*, 5:61-113.

Fisher, Rod 1992, 'From depredation to degradation: The Aboriginal experience at Moreton Bay 1842-60', *BHG papers*, 11:31-47.

Fitzgerald, Ross 1982, *A history of Queensland: From the dreaming to 1915*, UQP, Brisbane.

Foley, Denise & John Pearn 1993, 'The land and its uses', in Pearn 1993, 165-82.

Ford, Roger & Thom Blake, *Indigenous peoples in Southeast Queensland: An annotated guide to ethno-historical sources*, Foundation for Aboriginal and Islander Research Action, Woolloongabba.

Gabriel, M.H. 1961, 'A brief history of Peel Island', *Queensland health*, 1/3:19-27.

Ganter, Regina ed. 1992, *Whose Island: The past and future of North Stradbroke*, Qld Studies Centre, Griffith University, Nathan, Qld.

Gibbons, Denis S. 1974, *Russell Island: a real estate development rape*, D.S. & P.K.M. Gibbons, Randwick, NSW.

Goodall, Joseph 1992, Whom nobody owns: The Dunwich Benevolent Asylum: An institutional biography 1866-1946, PhD thesis, UQ, Brisbane.

Hall, H. Jay 1984, 'Fishing with dolphins: Affirming a traditional Aboriginal fishing story in Moreton Bay', in Coleman, Covacevich & Davie, 16-22.

Hall, H. Jay 1987, 'A short history of the Moreton Region', *BHG papers*, 5:15-22.

Hall, H. Jay 1990, '20,000 years of human impact on the Brisbane River and environs', in *The Brisbane River: A source book for the future*, ed. Peter Davie & others, Australian Littoral Society & Queensland Museum, Brisbane, 175-82.

Harris, John 1990, *One blood: 200 years of Aboriginal encounter with Christianity*, Albatross, Sydney.

Harris, Walt 1912, 'The Australian dugong', *Lone hand*, 1 Jul. 1912, 226-28.

Hastings, R.C. ed. 1985, *Leprosy*, Churchill Livingstone, Edinburgh.

Heinsohn, George 1977, 'Dugongs and turtles', *Wildlife in Australia*, 14/4:134-38.

Henry, Glenn 1998, Thompson Point, Macleay Island: Cultural heritage report, AHC paper.

Holthouse, Hector 1982, *Illustrated history of the Sunshine Coast*, Reed, Sydney.

Horton, Helen 1983, *Islands of Moreton Bay*, Boolarong Publications, Brisbane.

Jefferson, Thomas, Stephen Leatherwood & Marc Weber 1993, *Marine mammals of the world*, Food & Agriculture Organization of the United Nations, Rome.

Johnston, W. Ross 1982, *The call of the land*, Jacaranda Press, Brisbane.

Johnston, W. Ross 1988, *A documentary history of Queensland*, UQP, Brisbane.

Jones, Dorothy 1970, *Cardwell Shire story*, Jacaranda Press, Brisbane.

Jones, Edward 1993, 'Coochiemudlo in the nineteenth century', in Pearn 1993, 23-32.

Jones, M.R. 1992, 'Moreton Bay and the sand islands', in *Rocks and landscape of Brisbane and Ipswich*, ed. Warwick Wilmott & Neville Stevens, Geology Society of Australia, Queensland, Brisbane.

Jones, Michael 1988, *Country of five rivers: Albert Shire 1788-1988*, Allen & Unwin, Sydney.

Kamminga, J. 1981, 'The bevelled pounder: An Aboriginal stone type from Southeast Queensland', *Royal Society of Queensland proceedings*, 92:31-35.

Knight, J.J. 1898, *In the early days*, Sapsford & Co., Brisbane.

Lack, Clem 1968, 'Dugong fishing in early Queensland', *Newsletter of the Royal Australian Historical Society*, 75:4-6.

Lang, J.D. 1861, *Queensland, Australia: A highly eligible field for emigration*, Edward Stanford, London.

Laverty, John 1970, 'The Queensland economy 1860-1915', in *Prelude to power: The rise of the Labor Party in Queensland 1885-1915*, ed. Denis Murphy & others, Jacaranda Press, Brisbane, 28-44.

Lee, Ida 1925, *Early explorers in Australia*, Methuen, London.

Leichhardt, Ludwig 1847, *Journal of an overland expedition in Australia from Moreton Bay to Port Essington*, T & W Boone, London.

Lergessner, Jim 1993, *White specks on a dark shore: The Pumicestone Passage castaways*, Boolarong Publications, Brisbane.

Loyau, George 1897, *The history of Maryborough and Wide Bay and Burnett districts*, Pole, Outridge & Co, Brisbane.

Ludlow, Peter 1988, *Peel Island: Paradise or prison?*, The Author, Brisbane.

Ludlow, Peter 1991, *The Exiles of Peel Island*, The Author, Brisbane.

Ludlow, Peter 1992, *A Century of Moreton Bay people*, The Author, Brisbane.

Lund, H. 1955, 'The origin and development of cooperative sugar mills in Queensland', *RHSQ journal*, 5/3:1103-09.

Maher, Sid 1997, 'Davo's beast of burden', *SM*, 29 Jun., 04.

Maguire, John 1991, 'The Fantome Island leprosarium', in *Health and healing in tropical Australia and Papua New Guinea*, ed. R. Macleod & D. Denoon, James Cook University, Townsville, 142-48.

Marsh, H., P. Channells & J. Morissey 1979, *A Bibliography of the recent Sirenia*, James Cook University, Townsville.

Marsh, Helene 1997, 'Going, going, dugong', *Australia nature*, 25/9:50-57.

Martin, Denis 1968, *The foundation of the Catholic Church in Queensland*, Church Archivists Society, Brisbane.

Martin, Susan 2000, Recognition at last: Thomas Welsby, historian of Moreton Bay 1858-1941, PGDip thesis, UQ, Brisbane.

May, Louise B. 1958, 'Moreton ( A bay of islands', *Walkabout* 1 May, 29-33.

McArthur, Kathleen 1979, *Pumicestone Passage: A living waterway*, Inprint, Brisbane.

McCrindle, J.W. 1960, *Ancient India as described by Megasthenes and Arrian*, Chuckerverrty, Chatterjee & Co, Calcutta.

McLeod, G. Roderick 1984, 'The South Passage and Amity Point pilot station', in Coleman, Covacevich & Davie, 100-06.

Meston, Archibald 1895, *Geographic history of Queensland*, Government Printer, Brisbane.
Meston, Archibald 1923, 'Lost tribes of Moreton Bay', *BC*, 28 Jul., 19.
Mines, John & Ellie Durbidge 1994, 'The Dunwich lazaret cemetery', in Carter, Durbidge & Cooke-Bramley 1994, 62.
Minnery, John 1985, 'Queensland: Planning on the fringe', *Built environment*, 11/2:137-39.
Moore, Beryl 1993, *Island Eden: Point Lookout and its pioneers*, The Author, Point Lookout, Qld.
Moran, Patrick 1894, *History of the Catholic Church in Australasia from authentic sources*, Oceanic Publishing, Sydney.
Montgomery, Bruce 1997a, 'Hill plays world policeman on whales', *Weekend Australian*, 13-14 Sept., 3.
Montgomery, Bruce 1997b, 'More valuable alive than they are dead', *Weekend Australian*, 13-14 Sept., 3.
Nilsson, J.A. 1963-4, 'Mackay in the nineteenth century', *RHSQ journal*, 7/2:355-67.
Nishiwaki, Masaharu & Helene Marsh 1989, 'Dugong', in *Handbook of Marine Mammals: Vol.3*, ed. Sam Ridgway & Richard Harrison, Academic Press, London.
Nolan, Carolyn & Robert Longhurst 1996, *Brisbane's Moreton Bay: Our heritage in focus*, JOL, Brisbane (photographs).
North Stradbroke Island Historical Museum Association 1990, *North Stradbroke Island historical trail*, North Stradbroke Island.
O'Farrell, Francis 1982, *The bishop of Botany Bay: The life of John Bede Polding, Australia's first Catholic Archbishop*, Angus & Robertson, Sydney.
Page, Michael & Robert Ingpen 1989, *Out of this world: The complete book of fantasy*, Weldon Publishing, Sydney.
Paterson, Robert 1979, 'Shark meshing takes a heavy toll of harmless marine animals', *Australian fisheries*, 38/10:17-23.
Pearce, Chris 1993, *Through the eyes of Thomas Pamplett: Convict and castaway*, Boolarong Publications, Bowen Hills, Qld.
Pearn, John ed. 1993, *Chronicles of Coochiemudlo: Selected vignettes of a Moreton Bay island*, Amphion Press, Brisbane.
Pearn, John 1995, *Character, coves and cliffs: Vignettes of Coochiemudlo Island*, Amphion Press, Brisbane.
Pearn, John & Peggy Carter eds. 1995, *Islands of incarceration*, Amphion Press, Brisbane.
Petrie, Tom 1904, *Tom Petrie's reminiscences of early Queensland*, comp. Constance Campbell Petrie, Watson, Ferguson & Co, Brisbane.
Pixley, A.J. 1969-70, 'Shipwrecks in Queensland and adjacent waters', *RHSQ journal*, 9/1:151-61.
Prangnell, Jonathan M. 2000, Historical archaeology, paternalism and the Peel Island lazaret, UQ PhD thesis, St Lucia, Qld.
Queensland Coordinator-General's Department 1975, *The national estate in the Moreton and Wide Bay-Burnett regions*, ed. Patricia Mather, Brisbane.
Queensland Department of Environment & Heritage 1990, *Towards a Queensland conservation strategy: Facing the issues*, Brisbane.
Queensland Department of Environment & Heritage 1991, *Moreton Bay strategic plan: Proposals for management*, Brisbane.
Queensland Department of Environment & Heritage 1993, *Moreton Bay strategic plan*, Brisbane.
Queensland National Parks & Wildlife Service 1988, *St Helena National Park management plan*, Brisbane.
Rees, R.J. 1985, 'The microbiology of leprosy', in *Leprosy*, ed. R. Hastings, Churchill Livingstone, Edinburgh, 31-52.
Reynolds, Broda 1920, 'Woondu of Amity Point', *Sydney mail*, 3 Nov., 14.
Richards, Peter 1977, *The medieval leper and his northern heirs*, Brewer, London.
Richardson, N. 1984, 'An archaeological investigation of sandmining lease SML931 on North Stradbroke Island', in Coleman, Covacevich & Davie 1984, 23-32.
Riviere, Marc S. ed. 1996, 'Discovery of the Brisbane River', *RHSQ journal* 6/4:143-88.
Riviere, Marc S. ed. 1998, *Discovery of the Brisbane River, 1823: Oxley, Uniacke andPamplet*, RHSQ, Brisbane.
RKLM Islands Heritage Group 1998, *A boat to home: Historical recollections of boats around the southern Moreton Bay islands*, Russell Island, Qld.
RKLM Islands Heritage Group 1998, *The Campbell family of the Bay islands*, Russell Island, Qld.
RKLM Islands Heritage Group 1998, *Islands of freedom: Convicts of the southern Moreton Bay*, Russell Island, Qld.
RKLM Islands Heritage Group 1998, *The Qld Acclimatisation Society and the southern Moreton Bay islands*, Russell Island, Qld.
Robert Riddel Architect 1993, *The leper shall dwell alone: Peel Island lazaret conservation plan*, Fortitude Valley.
Robins, Richard 1984, 'Cultural resource management in practice: The Moreton Island example', in Coleman, Covacevich & Davie 1984, 33-43.
Rogers, Leonard 1930, 'When will Australia adopt modern prophylactic measures against leprosy?', *MJA*, 2:225-27.
Rowe, Enid 1991, *Bay islands: The living splendour of Moreton Bay*, Blue Bay Publications, Perulpa Island, Qld.
Royal Society of Queensland 1974, *Stradbroke symposium*, Brisbane. RSQ & ANZAAS, Brisbane.
Russell, Henry Stuart 1888, *The genesis of Queensland*, Turner & Henderson, Sydney.
Salter, Lindy 1983, *South Stradbroke Island*, The Author, Brisbane.
Salter, Lindy 1984, 'The early white history of South Stradbroke Island', in Coleman, Covacevich & Davie 1984, 33-43.
Sanker, Ian 1984, 'An early history in southern Moreton Bay', in Coleman, Covacevich & Davie, 112-18.
Saunders, Suzanne 1990, 'Isolation: The development of leprosy prophylaxis in Australia', *Aboriginal history*, 14:168-81.
Saville-Kent, W. 1893, *The Great Barrier Reef of Australia: Its products and potentialities*, W.H. Allen & Co, London.
Schlomowitz, R. 1982, 'Melanesian labour and the development of the Queensland sugar industry 1863-1906', *Research in economic history*, 7:327-61.
Senior, William 1876, *Near and far: An angler's sketches of home sport and colonial life*, Sampson Low, Marston, Searle & Rivington, London.

Singe, John 1989, *The Torres Strait: People and history*, UQP, Brisbane.

Smith, Glen S. 1982, 'Southern Queensland's oyster industry', *RHSQ journal* 11/3:45-58.

Southeast Qld 2001Regional Cultural Heritage Places Study 1996, *Aboriginal environment: an annotated bibliography*, comp. Karen Gillen, UQ Archaeological Services Unit, 1996.

Southeast Qld 2001 Regional Cultural Heritage Places Study 1996, *Historical Heritage bibliography*, ed. Rod Fisher, AHC, St Lucia Qld.

Steele, John ed. 1972, *The explorers of the Moreton Bay district 1770-1830*, UQP, Brisbane.

Steele, John ed. 1975, *Brisbane Town in convict days 1824-42*, UQP, Brisbane.

Steele, John 1984, *Aboriginal pathways in Southeast Queensland and the Richmond River*, UQP, Brisbane.

Stephens, E. 1953, 'Stephen Simpson, M.D., M.L.C.', *RHSQ journal*, 5/1:794-803.

Stewart, David 1993, 'Kids at Coochiemudlo: The pre-war years: A personal account', in Pearn 1993, 35-42.

St Helena Field Study Centre 1987-89, *St Helena island education kit*, Darling Point, Qld.

Thearle, John & others 1986, 'Roe's Kamp: A pioneer experiment in secondary education', *RHSQ journal*, 12/6:432-40.

Thomis, Malcolm I. 1979, 'Lone survivor', *Rocky Point and the Heck family: 100 years of sugar milling in Southeast Queensland*, n.p., pt.2.

Thomson, David 1934, 'The dugong hunters of Cape York', *Journal of the Royal Anthropological Institute of Great Britain and Ireland*, 64:237-62.

Thorne, Ebenezer 1876, *The queen of the colonies; or, Queensland as I knew it*, Sampson Low, Marston, Searle & Rivington, London.

Thorpe, Osmund 1950, *The first catholic mission to the Australian Aborigines*, Pelligrini, Sydney.

Troughton, Ellis 1928, 'Sea-cows: The story of the dugong', *Australian Museum magazine*, 3/7:220-8.

Troughton, Ellis 1954, *Furred animals of Australia*, Angus & Robertson, Sydney.

UQ School of Marine Science 1993, *The future of marine science in Moreton Bay*, ed. Jack Greenwood & Narelle Hall, UQ, St Lucia, Qld.

Walker, Faith 1998, 'Useful and profitable: History and race relations at the Myora Aboriginal Mission, Stradbroke Island, Australia, 1892-1940', *Memoirs of the Queensland Museum, cultural heritage series*, 1/1:137-75.

Walker, George 1862, *Life and labours of G.W.W.*, by James Backhouse & Charles Tylor, A.W. Bennett, London.

Walker, Kath 1972, *Stradbroke Dreamtime*, Angus & Robertson, Sydney.

Weedon, Thornhill 1898, *Queensland past and present: An epitome of its resources and development 1897*, E. Gregory, Government Printer, Brisbane.

Welsby, Thomas 1905, *Schnappering and fishing in the Brisbane River and Moreton Bay waters*, Outridge, Brisbane.

Welsby, Thomas 1931, *Sport and pastime in Moreton Bay*, Simpson, Halligan & Co, Brisbane.

Welsby, Thomas 1937, *Bribie – the basket maker*, Bakers Bookstores, Brisbane.

Welsby, Thomas 1967, *The collected works of Thomas Welsby*, 2 vols, ed. A.K. Thomson, Jacaranda Press, Brisbane.

Welsby, Thomas 1977, *Early Moreton Bay*, Rigby, Adelaide.

Wight, George 1862, *Queensland the field for British labour and enterprise, and the source of England's cotton supply*, G. Street, London.

Wood, C.T. 1964-5, 'The Queensland sugar industry as depicted in the Whish and Davidson diaries', *RHSQ journal*, 7/3:563-83.

Wood, C.T. 1965, *Sugar country: A short history of the raw sugar industry in Australia 1864-1964*, Queensland Cane Growers Council, Brisbane.

# *Index*

Note italics used for illustrations

**Brisbane History Group Papers**

# *Stylesheet for contributors*

This serial, which focuses on the history and heritage of the Brisbane region, commenced in 1981. Each volume comprises papers given orally at BHG sessions and additional articles related in subject matter.

Contributors may be invited to submit papers for publication or inquire themselves whether a particular article would be acceptable in a forthcoming volume. Drafts should be forwarded to the publication coordinator for consideration by the editorial committee and referees. Inclusion does not preclude publication elsewhere for a different audience; but contributors are asked to discuss this with the coordinator and to acknowledge publication in the BHG Papers. Contributors receive one free copy of the whole volume.

The new series of papers from Number 11 onwards is typeset on personal computer, desktop designed, offset or docutech printed and produced as a custom-sized paperback in perfect binding. The print run of several hundred copies is marketed widely to members, libraries, schools, societies, professionals and the general public.

Contributors are asked to forward drafts shortly after the related BHG session. If a paper is given orally, it may be amended or reshaped as necessary. There is no strict word limit, as long as everything is pertinent to the subject and succinctly expressed. Notes and references are kept to an essential minimum. The onus is on authors, not the editors, to provide a complete, accurate and presentable manuscript for publication.

Drafts should be submitted in crisp single-spaced typing on A4 sized paper and if possible on 3½ inch computer diskette in recent IBM-compatible format (e.g. WordPerfect, Word or ASCII text file). They need to be set out in accordance with the BHG style of publication in the latest volume. Otherwise they may be returned to contributors for amendment.

The required publication style is exemplified by the BHG Papers from Number 11 onwards. The basic format for the end-notes and reference list is set out in the *Style manual* of the Australian Government Publishing Service.

Notes are indicated in the text by superscript running numbers placed after and above the nearest appropriate punctuation mark, and not by author and date in brackets. The notes themselves and the accompanying list of references are set out at the end using the authordate format, but omitting the abbreviations 'vol.', 'no.' and 'pp.' (e.g. 4/1:1478 or 4:147-8).

The alphabetically arranged list of references includes all cited and other useful works, except newspapers, lesser manuscripts and obvious printed sources already in the notes (with author's family and given names (not initials), year plus small alpha-letter if more than one title that year by the author, titles of books with place and publisher, or titles of articles and serials with volume and page numbers).

Relevant illustrations of various kinds should be included with captions and sources stated, but these should be kept to an essential minimum. Good contrast, black and white prints are best, up to A4 in size (which may be reduced later). Letters of permission from the owners or repositories concerned are also needed for the BHG to reproduce (as a nonprofit, community and educational association).

A cover sheet should be added with the contributor's preferred title, given and family names (not initials), and a sentence or two of selfdescription (e.g. occupation, status, positions, research activity, publications) for the contributors' page.

Please contact the publication coordinator regarding these matters, including particular requirements and queries. The BHG looks forward to publishing papers by amateur, public and academic historians as professionally and beneficially as possible.

**Dr Barry Shaw**
**Publication Coordinator**
**(07) 3353 2210 (after hours)**

**Brisbane History Group**
**PO Box 12**
**Kelvin Grove DC, Q4059**

# Brisbane History Group Publications

Papers
1 *Brisbane: Public, practical, personal*, 1981
2 *Brisbane: Archives and approaches*, 1983
3 *Brisbane: Housing, health, the river and the arts*, 1985
4 *Brisbane at war*, 1986
5 *Brisbane: Aboriginal, alien, ethnic*, 1987
6 *Brisbane: People, places and pageantry*, 1987
7 *Brisbane: Archives and approaches II*, 1988
8 *Brisbane in 1888: The historical perspective*, 1988
9 *Brisbane: Local, oral and placename history*, 1990
10 *Brisbane: Mining, Building, Story Bridge, the Windmill*, 1991
11 *Brisbane: The Aboriginal presence 1824-60*, 1992
12 *Brisbane: The ethnic presence since the 1850s*, 1993
13 *Brisbane: Cemeteries as sources*, 1994
14 *Brisbane: People, places and progress*, 1994
15 *Brisbane: Corridors of power*, 1997
16 *Brisbane: Squatters, surveyors and settlers,* 2000
17 *Brisbane relaxation, recreation and rock'n'roll: Popular culture 1890-1990,* 2001
18 *Brisbane patriotism, passion and protest: Our Federation 1901,* 2001
19 *Brisbane: Moreton Bay matters,* 2002

Sources
1 *Brisbane by 1888: The public image*, 1987
2 *The Brisbane Courier in 1888: A select subject index*, 1987
3 *Brisbane Town news from the Sydney Morning Herald 1842-46*, 1989
4 *Brisbane butterflies and beetles*, 1989
5 *Brisbane River Valley 1841-50*, 1991
6 *Brisbane hotels and publicans index 1842-1900*, 1994
7 *Queensland architects of the 19th century: Index to the biographical dictionary*, 1999
8 *Brisbane timeline: From Captain Cook to CityCat*, 1999
9 *Moreton Bay in the news 1841-60: A select subject index,* 2000
10 *Brisbane in the news: Our Federation 1901,* 2002

Tours
1 *Petrie-Terrace walk/drive*, 1981 rev. 1989
2 *South Brisbane civic precinct walk*, 1985, 1986
3 *South Brisbane: Southbank suburbs drive*, 1986
4 *Caboolture to Kilcoy drive*, 1986
5 *Town to Toowong riverpath walk*, 1986
6 *Brisbane 1888 drive*, 1988
7 *Eastern suburbs placenames drive*, 1990
8 *Sandgate and Shorncliffe walks*, 1990
9 *Old Coorparoo Shire drive*, 1991
10 *Brisbane River Valley drive*, 1991
11 *Colonial George and William Street walk*, 1991
12 *Spring Hill walk: St Pauls to Gregory Terrace*, 1993
13 *Bald Hills drive*, 1993
14 *Northern suburbs Windsor to Kedron drive*, 1993
15 *Brisbane city churches walk/drive*, 1994
16 *Stafford and Wilston-Grange drive*, 1995
17 *Brisbane historical pub drive*, 1995
18 *Yeronga heritage walk/drive*, 1996
19 *Spring Hill walk: Wickham Terrace*, 1997
20 *St Lucia Campus walk*, 1998
21 *Stombuco heritage drive/walk,* 1999
22 *Brisbane heritage trail: Our Federation 1901,* 2001

Studies 1 *Brisbane's forgotten founder: Sir Evan Mackenzie of Kilcoy*, 1992
2 *Brisbane house styles 1880-1940: A guide to the affordable house*, 1998

Information about the BHG and its publications may be obtained by letter or phone or by visiting the BHG web page http://www.brisbanehistory.asn.au